The French Popular Front

Paul Warwick

The French Popular Front
A Legislative Analysis

The University of Chicago Press
Chicago and London

The University of Chicago Press, Chicago 60637
The University of Chicago Press, Ltd., London

82 81 80 79 78 77   987654321

Paul Warwick is assistant professor of political science
at the University of Washington.

Library of Congress Cataloging in Publication Data

Warwick, Paul.
  The French Popular Front.

  Revised version of the author's thesis, University of
Chicago, 1974.
  Bibliography: p.
  Includes index.
  1. France. Assemblée nationale, 1871–1942. Chambre
des députés—Voting.   2. France. Assemblée nationale,
1871–1942. Chambre des députés—Elections.   3. France—
Politics and government—1914–1940.   4. Front populaire.
I. Title.
JN2863.W37   1977   320.9′44′081   76–22952
ISBN 0–226–86914–8

To Ellen

Contents

vii

Acknowledgments

This study is a considerably revised version of a doctoral dissertation I wrote for the University of Chicago. Dissertations are generally tedious and solitary enterprises which require for their successful completion both personal and institutional sources of support. The personal influences that caused me to persevere are largely unspecifiable, but the equally indispensable institutional backing that I received deserves a note of acknowledgment. My livelihood during the research on this topic was chiefly provided by fellowships from the University of Chicago and the Canada Council. Additionally, much of the data collection was funded by the National Science Foundation through a dissertation fellowship (GS–39154). Lastly, the London School of Economics, the University of Chicago, and the University of Washington each supported the project at various stages through the provision of keypunching services and especially computer time, a resource that this study consumed in enormous proportions. My gratitude extends to all these institutions which, collectively, made this book possible.

The Radicals say they are attached to the principles of private property, individual freedom, and the idea of the nation. So they are. But they are unable to separate themselves from the Socialists of the SFIO who want to destroy property, individual freedom, and the idea of the nation. Does that make sense to anybody?

Maurice Le Corbeiller, right-wing deputy

Chapter One

Introduction

This study is concerned with one episode in the decline of a regime, the French Third Republic. That episode is the two-year tenure in power of a "Popular Front" coalition of Communists, Socialists, and center-left deputies, the most numerous of whom were the Radicals. It is generally held to have ended in a not unqualified failure. It is past history. Three regimes have since ruled France. Why study it?

The object of this chapter is to present a cogent response to this pointed question. The response will raise in turn considerations of the import of the Popular Front experiment for the understanding of French history and politics, and considerations of the unique availability of quantifiable data that allow us to address this matter in a statistical vein. Concerning the first aspect, we shall attempt to establish that the decline of the Third Republic in the years between the two world wars is an occurrence that requires systematic investigation and interpretation; and that the Popular Front experiment, which was not only a critical element in this decline but also an extraordinary attempt to reverse it, is central to this undertaking. Subsequently, we shall argue that the data sources from which this

1

study obtains its main thrust are exceptional in the opportunity they afford to study the Popular Front, especially with respect to the analysis of the beliefs and ideologies of the legislative participants in the coalition and the translation of these beliefs and ideologies into concrete behaviors of consequence for the coalition's fate.

The Context of the Popular Front: The Third Republic and Its Decline

The Third Republic (1875–1940), France's most durable regime since the monarchy was first overthrown in 1792, has not been looked upon with great favor by social scientists. The general view seems to be that the Republic epitomized a classic French (or perhaps "Latin") pattern of governmental instability and weakness, a stark contrast to the more successful Anglo-Saxon and Scandinavian models. The blame for this has been placed in many quarters, the political culture and the party system being the most popular, but the conclusion is typically the same: the Third Republic was one of the world's least adequate democratic creations.[1] Perhaps no more stinging diatribe against the Third Republic can be found than that of Luethy:

> In seventy years of republicanism France has not had a parlia-
> mentary working majority or a governmental coalition that could
> even agree on the foundations of a coherent policy, and it has
> never had a government which lived long enough to be able to
> work out and introduce such a policy. France is not ruled but ad-
> ministered and it is her apparent political instability which guaran-
> tees the stability and permanence of her administration. . . . The
> republic reigns but it does not rule.[2]

There is certainly much in the record of the Third Republic to commend this point of view: one hundred governments in sixty-five years; frequent paralysis in the face of pressing issues, crises, even challenges to the regime's right to rule; and so on. Yet there is an unfortunate tendency in this line of argumentation, however justified the argument is in itself, to imply the conclusion that the decline and eventual collapse of the Third Republic is not an occurrence that requires systematic explanation. After all, a regime whose democratic institutions functioned as poorly and whose political cultural base was as incompatible with stable democracy as has been suggested had to collapse sometime; do the idiosyncratic circumstances that finally brought the inevitable result to fruition have any real importance? Among social scientists who have commented on the Third Republic, Eckstein, with his remark that the longevity of the regime was due to "fortuitous circumstances," best exemplifies this negative view.[3]

The implications of such an approach for the study of the Popular Front are considerable. If the decline and collapse of the Third Republic was essentially idiosyncratic, it would imply that the Popular Front experiment, the regime's major attempt to halt this decline through the introduction of a legislative program of significant reform by a majority coalition of the Left, can be approached in the same terms. If, on the other hand, there was a noticeable and *systematic* shift for the worse in the regime's later years, an analysis of the failure of the Popular Front's mission of rescue might provide valuable clues to the determinants of the success or failure of the Third Republic. This perspective on the regime might in turn cast valuable light on the nature of French politics generally.

We intend, in this study, to adopt the second position. This position does not deny the validity of the weaknesses in French parliamentary regimes that much of the social science literature on France has pointed to; rather it interprets these accounts as descriptive of the broad constraints within which periods of relative success as well as periods of relative failure may be acknowledged. The decisive point for this position is, did the Third Republic, despite its shortcomings, enjoy enough "success" (enough stability to deal with the problems that it faced and enough effectiveness to bring about a conclusion to these problems consistent with the creation and maintenance of popular allegiance to it) to make its decline an event that requires explanation? As it turns out, this question has been answered in the affirmative by a second school of thought, more frequently followed by historians than social scientists, which tends to resort to the particulars of the regime and its history to build a case for a more favorable view of the regime's stability and effectiveness during its first fifty or so years. Let us consider some of the evidence that might be cited for this position.

Concerning the instability of the Third Republic, the indicator usually employed has been the frequency of governmental changes. It is true that the 1920–40 period, when the regime was in decline, did see by official count no less than forty-two governments. But if one refines the data somewhat by eliminating all the nonelectoral changes of government that were not forced by an adverse vote of the Chamber or Senate, or by the imminent prospect of one, or in which the outgoing and incoming premiers were one and the same, one finds the figure of forty-two changes of government reduced to eighteen. Of these eighteen real, forced, nonelectoral changes of government, eight involved merely a switch in roles between the premier and a cabinet minister with, on average, 65 percent of the ministers surviving the defeat and participating in the new government. The rate of turnover of cabinet ministers in all eighteen changes of government was 60 percent; including the other twenty-four official governmental changes, the figure drops to 47 percent.

This stability of ministers has led Ollé-Laprune to the conclusion that the more frequently espoused explanations for the instability of the regime—the subordination of the executive to the legislature, the failure of governments to use the power of dissolution when they fell into minority on important issues, and even the weak fights governments seemed to put up when challenged by the Chamber or the Senate—were not the causes but rather the consequences of the development of the ministerial crisis as a method of government. Occasionally such governmental changes marked major shifts in the orientation and management of the nation's politics. But much more frequently they arose over "disputes de ménage," in which a new government was formed, but largely, of course, with the same people. He concludes: "It is not one of the lesser paradoxes of the Third Republic to have transformed the [governmental] crisis into an element of conservation."[4]

Ollé-Laprune goes on to argue that this stability of ministers was the cause not only of the regime's relatively long life (sixty-five years) but also of its immobility. Redefining stability to refer to the rate of change of personnel rather than of governments, he sees the Third Republic as characterized not by instability but by excessive stability. His case seems to be overdrawn, however. The turnover of ministers, while low enough to readjust one's natural view of the regime's instability, is not extremely low (nor is the assumption necessarily valid that having the same men in office for extended periods of time would cause immobility). A more balanced view would be the one he presents earlier in his study: "Governmental instability, so often criticized, loses a large part of its importance."[5]

The concept of effectiveness is both intuitively easy to grasp and virtually impossible to operationalize. To establish without the aid of indicators of the concept that the effectiveness of the Third Republic was perhaps greater than it has sometimes been held to have been, one must therefore resort to a rather imprecise and impressionistic form of argumentation. Since the proponents of the interpretation of the Third Republic as ineffective have also been guilty of this deficiency, however, the three observations we shall make on this subject are not necessarily without value.

The first observation is that the ineffectiveness the regime has characteristically been charged with is probably exaggerated because of the failure to take into account the nature of the demands that were placed upon it. As Siegfried points out, in the political environment of the Third Republic, where for a considerable portion of its history the Right was not merely conservative but positively reactionary, to be in the Center or Left politically frequently meant to be moderate or conservative socially and economically. Reading the results of elections this way, one can more easily understand why the Republic seemed slow to respond to the need for social and economic reform:

> The regime in fact has to lean to the left in its ideology, but it can only organize itself and survive around the Center, not around the Right which as we have emphasized is reactionary, not conservative. Therefore it is necessary, with a majority from the Left, to follow a centrist policy, or more exactly a centrist economic policy.[6]

Eckstein has related the idea of effectiveness in democratic regimes to the concept of authenticity, the requirement that it actually be the democratic structures themselves that do the acting: "On the basis of this criterion the Third Republic comes out badly again, for it was a government carried on in normal times mainly by a nearly autonomous bureaucracy . . . and in times of crisis mainly by temporary dictators armed with *plein pouvoir*."[7] But this interpretation, too, can be questioned. Sharp, a contemporary student of the Third Republic, argued that the parliamentary committees were quite powerful in controlling the bureaucracy:

> Each committee . . . has a technical staff at its disposal for investigation purposes. Experienced committee members, and there are many of them, can put their fingers on the weak spots in the administrative armor. This is particularly true of the committees on finance, foreign affairs and the defence establishment.[8]

Moreover, the accepted doctrine, elaborated by the political philosopher Alain, deemed the protection from the bureaucracy which the deputy could provide for his constituents as of prime importance. The deputies' successful execution of this task has scarcely been disputed; in fact some have felt that the deputies succeeded too well for the purposes of national policy.[9] Whether this latter assertion can be sustained or not, it seems likely that the elected representatives were at least not as helpless before the bureaucracy as Eckstein has alleged.

Finally, the most important evidence used by the advocates of this position is the fact that the regime could and did act vigorously and effectively without "temporary dictators," and the fruit that such activity bore was by no means inconsequential:

Monarchism . . . had been routed and relegated to the camp of lost causes. Bonapartism and Caesarism of every kind had been fought and beaten in open combat and thrown into sullen acquiescence. The Church and the Army, acting in fatal alliance during the first generation of the Republic, had been rendered impotent to overthrow the Republic. The rights of organized labour had been recognized, and both CGT and Socialist parties had planted their feet firmly in French social life. The system of national education had been formally completed, and the State had asserted its power to determine the structure, substance, and spirit of training in which the great majority of its citizens were to be brought up. The new overseas empire had been acquired and consolidated, too, and the general shape of France as a great power in the modern world had become clear.[10]

In fact a major argument of this study will be that virtually every problem that could have threatened the regime, especially the challenges from antirepublican elements in French society, were successfully handled in the period up to the end of the First World War. The development of this argument will be more fully pursued in the concluding chapter; in the meantime we simply observe that Eckstein's puzzlement as to why the Third Republic is the only exception to his rule that effectiveness, authenticity, and longevity generally go together can be readily resolved by this interpretation: his view of the regime's ineffectiveness and lack of authenticity is overstated.

This readjustment of commonly held but sometimes overdrawn notions of the Third Republic's instability and ineffectiveness allows us to see more clearly what is meant by the decline of the regime in the interwar period. For one thing, although the stability of ministers did not noticeably deteriorate and the number of real, forced, nonelectoral changes of government averaged less than one per year, certain periods, such as 1925–26 and 1933, suffered acute governmental instability. For another, the effectiveness or competence of the regime in handling the great issues of the day seemed to dissolve with the new financial and economic problems of these years. To illustrate this failure, we shall refer to a frequently used index of the effect of the Depression, the industrial production levels. To give a comparative perspective, we have included in table 1 the figures for Britain, Germany, the United States, and the world, in addition to those for France, based on the 1928 level, which is set at 100. Clearly France stood well behind Britain, Germany, and the world in her ability to cope with the Depression by increasing industrial levels. The United States, while not as well off as Britain or Germany in 1937, had considerably improved from its low point in 1932. Although France did not fall as far behind at the outset, she managed to improve only slightly in the middle and late 1930s. As Goguel notes, the regime's failure in this area

> demonstrated the inability of the government to execute, or even conceive, an effective policy in fields remaining foreign to its pre-war concerns. The acute ministerial instability of the period 1925 to 1926, and then of 1933, so patently revealed this inability that . . . an entirely new procedure had to be set up: special powers were granted the government to regulate by decree certain problems which parliament proved incapable of handling. . . . The failure of the social and economic policies successively put into operation by this procedure made it unpopular with public opinion which, for the most part, did not seem to understand that it had become in-dispensable on account of the progressive degradation of the political regime instituted in 1875.[11]

Here, then is the resort to *pleins pouvoirs* that Eckstein regards as indicative of a lack of democratic authenticity.

Table 1   Industrial Production Levels

	United States	Britain	Germany	France	World
1931	73.2	88.5	68.5	94	87.3
1932	58.4	88.1	54.0	78	74.3
1933	69.4	93.2	61.5	88	83.5
1934	72.0	105.1	80.9	82	91.7
1935	81.7	109.4	95.3	79	103.2
1936	95.0	123.6	107.8	85	117.8
1937	99.1	131.2	118.8	89	126.6

Source: A. Sauvy, *Histoire Économique de la France Entre les Deux Guerres*, 2 vols. (Paris: Fayard, 1967), 2:536.

This somewhat pessimistic concluding note is far from being the whole story, however. Apart from the fact that after 1933 ministerial instability returned to normal levels, it must be noted that the Right (1934–35) and especially the Left (the Popular Front governments of 1936–38) had their chances to solve the Depression. Both in fact were given clear majorities in the Chamber that were willing to follow their lead, and time in which to formulate and execute policy. In short, it was not the instability of the governments that caused the ineffectiveness on this key issue. Yet, as we shall show, it was this particular issue, of all the issues the Republic had to face, that proved insoluble. Discovering why this was the case, why the economic crisis of the 1930s virtually alone was found to be beyond the regime's resources to handle, thus seems central to the explanation of the decline of the Third Republic. The Popular Front experiment, the most valiant effort to try to cope with the economic crisis and the social ills it generated, becomes critical to this explanation.

Thus we come back to the original question that launched this discussion: why study the Popular Front? Because the failure of the regime to handle the Depression successfully was a fundamental cause of the loss of allegiance and trust in the regime on the part of much of its citizenry that marked its decline; and the Popular Front was both the most notable and the final attempt to salvage this situation. As we shall see, the Popular Front experiment was an extraordinary effort to overcome the basic institutional and attitudinal deficiencies of the Third Republic through the formation of a majority coalition of all the Left under the leadership of a Socialist and with an agreed-upon program of serious reform. It failed, and sealed the fate of the regime, but why? Was it that the deficiencies in French political culture and the resulting organizational weaknesses undermined the ability of the left-wing political elite to remain united in the face of serious challenges and setbacks? Or was it that the newer economic problems of the interwar period were incompatible with the structure of party politics as it had been erected in the pre-1914 period to reflect and cope with the conflict between the republican and antirepublican elements in society? Could it be that a different ideological cleavage, a wide and ultimately unbridgeable rift between the Marxist and non-Marxist parties, became dominant in this era and condemned to failure any attempt at Marxist participation in bourgeois government? Or was it simply that certain policies, agreed upon by the Popular Front coalition, were not equal to the catastrophic situation of the economy? Apart from its considerable historical significance, the Popular Front experiment becomes a very valuable test of several interpretations of French politics, an episode in recent French history which may prove highly revealing for the entire drift of French politics in the last hundred years.

The Data Base

Up to this point we have outlined what we regard as sound theoretical and historical reasons for studying the Popular Front experiment. Yet the Third Republic and the Popular Front have already been extensively studied, and publications in the field abound. Why, then, another addition to an already substantial bibliography?

Let us approach the matter from the viewpoint of the sources of evidence available to the researcher who wants to understand the fate of the Popular Front. The most obvious source would be official statistics on the consequences of the actions of the Popular Front governments. Since the Popular Front came into office on the promise of a new economic strategy to pull the nation out of a depression, it would be relevant to examine statistics on the effect of Popular Front policies on the economy and to infer failure and discontent from these. This sort of economic history has in fact been done with considerable success by Sauvy[12] and others, and much of the discussion in the next chapter will draw heavily on this type of analysis. But the inference from economic failure, assuming the figures unequivocally show this to be the case, to dissension and discontent among members of the coalition on these very grounds is indirect and difficult to establish convincingly.

Another tack would be to utilize direct evidence of the deputies' political beliefs and opinions and of their actions in the Chamber. Since one cannot now ask the deputies of the Popular Front era what they thought and why they acted as they did, systematic evidence of this sort has never been an integral part of the scholarly debate on the Popular Front. Yet it is quite untrue that this evidence does not exist, for it does—in the public record. Concerning the deputies' actions, we have a very powerful indicator: a complete record of how every deputy voted on the roll-call votes in the Chamber of Deputies during the 1936–38 period. Analysis of these votes, which until now has been attempted only in the most superficial fashion,[13] should provide considerable information on what happened to the Popular Front in the Chamber. However, this source can only be a partial aid, for it suffers from two glaring faults: any pressures and dissension within the Popular Front coalition could have been more frequently evidenced in the hidden "corridors of power" than in the overt act of roll-call voting; roll-call analysis may not be able to determine if such dissension arose because of ideological differences within the Popular Front or more simply because of disillusionment with the results of the Popular Front's attempts to restore the nation's economy to prosperity. We have already noted the theoretical import of the determination of the latter distinction, but in one very crucial instance historians have uniformly emphasized that the first possibility has a significant role to play as well. The instance in question was the fall of the first Blum government. In June 1937, with the economy in trouble and the foreign exchange markets in crisis, the Socialist prime minister Léon Blum asked the Chamber of Deputies to give his government full powers to rule by decree in financial and economic matters so that it might institute drastic remedial actions and reforms. The measure was passed in the Chamber, defeated in the Senate, repassed in the Chamber, and redefeated in the Senate, amid considerable drama and tension, needless to say. Since the Senate was not controlled by a Popular Front majority (the Senate had not been elected in 1936), this turn of events was not in itself particularly surprising. Yet it did raise the difficult and controversial constitutional point of whether the Senate could by an adverse vote defeat a government supported by the Chamber. Blum wavered between resigning and fighting the Senate on this issue but finally chose the former alternative because, it is said, the Radicals indicated privately that, although they had voted in favor of the emergency-measures bill in the Chamber to maintain a public front of solidarity, they would not support Blum in such a fight with the Senate. It is even said that many Radicals had supported the Blum government as solidly as they did only because they could count on their more conservative colleagues in the Senate to oppose it.[14] If this is how the first and most important Popular Front government was defeated, how can roll-call votes provide any evidence that is relevant to it?

As we shall attempt to show in chapters 3 and 4, the roll-call votes do reveal a good deal of valuable evidence because the Popular Front coalition, while it never fell into minority in the Chamber of Deputies, nevertheless did suffer defections of various sorts. However the basic point, which is that these defections are likely to be only the tip of the iceberg with respect to what larger numbers of moderate deputies actually felt but would not express in votes, is nonetheless valid. To broach this matter, data of a different type are needed. Here, too, the data are part of the public record, although they have been utilized probably less frequently and certainly less systematically than even the roll-call votes. The source of data is the official compilation of electoral platforms ("professions de foi") of the winning candidates in the 1936 general elections.[15] These statements, whose content will be statistically analyzed in chapter 5, will allow us to fill in two gaps in our understanding of the Popular Front legislature. The first gap concerns the nature of the belief or "ideological" spectrum of this legislature. Was the Chamber characterized ideologically by a left-right continuum such as one might expect in most French legislatures, or did the special circumstances of the 1936 elections—a left wing united on a common program—cause the Chamber to be divided into two internally cohesive blocs ideologically distant from each other? Second, what are the implications of the ideological makeup of the Chamber? For instance, if there were ideological divisions in the

Popular Front coalition, were they independent of the voting defections that marked the Popular Front's decline, or can the seeds of future defections in roll-call voting be discovered in ideological differences that were expressed in these statements which were written before the Popular Front took office? If the latter, what were the bases of these differences and do they provide a credible explanation of the legislative loss of allegiance to the Popular Front that is consistent with the types of ideological division—republican vs. antirepublican, Marxist vs. non-Marxist—that have been hypothesized to be the main driving forces of political conflict in France? Finally, can we establish in a more reliable way the full extent of the dissension within the coalition—the rest of the iceberg, so to speak? It is the belief that the exploitation in a systematic manner of these untapped sources of data will throw new light upon the Popular Front and its place in French political history that provides the motivation for this undertaking.

Chapter Two

The Popular Front
A Historical Outline and Review
of the Evaluative Literature

A few general observations have been presented concerning the stability of governments in the Third Republic and their effectiveness in coping with the numerous problems and crises that the regime faced during its sixty-five year history. This is a large topic to which we shall return in the concluding chapter, where the aim will be to place the Popular Front experiment into the context of the political regime that both bred it and suffered from its demise. For the present, however, we have a more immediate concern, the history of the Popular Front itself.

The Prelude: French Politics in the Interwar Years

The dynamics of left-wing politics in France in the post–World War I period were characterized in a most fundamental sense by the divisions and mutual antagonism of the three main parties: the Communists (PCF), the Socialists (SFIO), and the Radicals. The intense Communist-Socialist hostility is generally held to have derived from the fact that both parties were fragments of a larger Socialist party that had split in 1920 over the question of adoption of the Leninist line, which entailed alignment with Moscow and membership in the Comintern. Although the Communist (pro-Moscow) faction gained control of the party newspaper and won over the majority of the party membership, the Socialists emerged from the schism electorally in a far stronger position and carried much more parliamentary weight throughout this period.

While rejecting Leninism, the Socialists were nevertheless very distant ideologically from the Radicals, a moderate party of the center-left. Here the division resembled more a classic working-class-middle-class distinction, with the Socialists devoutly Marxist and the Radicals just as devoutly petty bourgeois. Curiously, the Radicals before 1914 had represented a strong left-wing position on all the key issues of the time: they were anticlerical and antimilitarist at a time when the church and the army were strongholds of authoritarianism, vigorous defenders of the republican regime against those who would have a monarchist or bonapartist restoration, keen supporters of individual rights and liberties during the Dreyfus affair, main architects of the separation of church and state and the creation of a secular school system, and representatives of the little man against the big corporations and financial interests. Yet they represented, more than anything else, a rural and small-town concern for individualism, distrust for authority and privilege, and abhorrence of large-scale state interference in social and economic life; and because of this they never made an impact on the urban working classes that were emerging as an important political force in the twentieth century. Although the Radicals sported a somewhat flamboyant ideology about profit-sharing and nationalization of monopolistic industries, they showed little real enthusiasm for social and economic change and, indeed, were profoundly tied to middle-class values. For them, as Larmour notes, "two fundamental conditions for the Republic were private property and public order."[1] Thus the ideological bases for chronic disunity within the Left were solidly laid.

There were, however, points of contact, at least between the Radicals and the Socialists. The Radicals had emerged as a political party at a time when the most important tenet of left-wing ideology was republicanism, of which they were wholehearted supporters; this, plus their moderately reformist ideology (as distinct from practice), had allowed them to consider themselves leftist long after their basic social and economic conservatism was fully apparent to all and long after the Right had ceased to be antirepublican. This leftist inclination on the part of the Radicals was one factor that justified their participation with the Socialists and other smaller left-wing parties in electoral alliances which were generally presented to the voters every four years and which, if victorious, were supposed to form the basis for the governments of that legislature. But an even stronger inducement for these alliances came from the electoral laws themselves. The electoral mechanics of the era usually provided for two rounds of voting: if no candidate won an absolute majority in the first round, a second round would be held later; then a plurality would do. To maximize the likelihood that the Left would win this plurality, it was necessary for just one candidate from the Left, usually the one who had received the most votes in the first round, to enter the second round; in this way, since the Left was in the majority in the country, it would most likely win enough seats to control the Chamber of Deputies. If, however, the Socialists and the Radicals both entered candidates in the second round, the left-wing vote would be divided, and a single candidate representing the Right could conceivably win even in a left-wing constituency. Hence what was termed "republican discipline" usually functioned at election time, and only the best-placed candidate from the (non-Communist) Left in the first round of voting would stand for the second round.[2]

Where this republican discipline failed to work was in the Chamber. On the two occasions in the 1919–36 period when an electoral alliance of the Left won a majority in the Chamber—in 1924 and again in 1932—the formula of a basically Radical government supported in the Chamber by the Socialists fell through by mid-term, leaving the Radicals to look to the Right for governmental allies. In both cases, economics or finance constituted the rationale for the split between the Socialists and the Radicals. In 1926 the issue centered on what to do about a treasury bankrupt from the debts of the war and the reconstruction, a rampant inflation resulting from a massive increase in the stock of money in circulation to pay those debts, and panicky short-selling of the franc on the currency exchanges. The solution to the crisis ultimately lay in the conferral of *pleins pouvoirs* (full powers) on a prestigious wartime leader and man of the Right, Raymond Poincaré, who represented a financial orthodoxy that both the Right and the Radicals found comforting and that reassured the conservative circles of high finance that alone could stop the currency crisis. But before this was achieved, an event occurred which demonstrated to the Left the tremendous influence of big money in politics and nurtured an important left-wing article of faith.

The assumption of power by Poincaré had been preceded fifteen months earlier, in 1925, by the fall of the left-wing Herriot government. This was the direct result of the refusal of the privately owned

Bank of France to provide further advances to the bankrupt treasury of the sort that it had willingly given previous Poincaré governments. This event, correctly interpreted by many as a deliberate attack on the ruling left-wing alliance by the Bank, reinforced a belief in the sinister control over the nation's economics and politics by the "Two Hundred Families,"—the two hundred largest stockholders who had voting rights in the Bank—a belief that the flight from the franc had made popular. The fact that Herriot was a Radical made the Radicals almost as sympathetic to the theory as the Communists and the Socialists, even though the Radicals went on to support the Poincaré government. Thus was provided a common element of belief that, reinforced by a similar sequence of events in 1933, was to help bring together these three parties in the Popular Front coalition.

Apart from the salutary psychological effect of the mere presence of the solidly conservative Poincaré, the financial crisis of the mid-1920s was resolved by a badly needed devaluation of the franc. This action, too, had repercussions for the Popular Front experiment. Because the state had financed so much of its wartime expenses and postwar reconstruction efforts through massive bond issues, the devaluation meant that millions of small bondholders who had paid in old francs were now to be repaid in new francs that were worth considerably less. Since the devaluation had been necessitated by inflation, the patriotic savings of a considerable portion of the population had been effectively slashed. This, together with an almost universal belief in stable parities (a belief that is quite understandable in that the Poincaré devaluation had marked the first occasion the franc had significantly changed value since the time of Napoleon), created a psychological climate severely inimical to further tampering with the currency. This climate survived into the 1930s and made further devaluation politically unthinkable at a time when it had once again become economically necessary.

The second reversal of a left-wing majority came in 1934 when the crisis in question was the Depression. In this France had been caught completely unawares and unprepared. The Poincaré devaluation had created a situation where the franc was in reality an undervalued currency. The result was that foreign trade boomed in the late 1920s and for a brief interlude France's economic performance improved dramatically.[3] This boom, which provided a cushion of perhaps two years before the Depression started seriously to take its toll, created for Frenchmen an illusion of immunity from disaster that was freely attributed to all sorts of admirable qualities inherent in the French economy and its management.

When the Depression did hit, the French political and economic elite was no more able to arrive at a remedy than were most of its counterparts in other Western countries. The necessity of balanced budgets and reduced governmental expenditures was virtually unanimously agreed upon. Where the Socialists and the Radicals fell out was over the question of whether this goal was to be achieved by the cutting of civil service salaries and pensions and by reducing benefits to needy segments of society. In this dilemma the fundamental conservatism of the Radicals shone through, and they gradually became aligned with the right wing.

The dominance in the 1934–36 period of center-right cabinets supported by Radicals meant that economic orthodoxy ruled the day. At first this response to the Depression represented little more than blind faith in the balanced budget as an economic cure-all. But by the time of the right-wing Laval government in 1935, when it was most rigorously applied, this policy had been elaborated into the theory of "deflation." Reflecting the popular reluctance to have the franc devalued once more (it had already lost four-fifths of its prewar value), the overriding concern of the deflationists was to right the overvaluation of the time, and the consequent noncompetitiveness of French goods, by driving wages and prices, rather than the franc, down. A balanced budget achieved by drastically reducing government expenditures was believed to be the correct means. The reasons given were that (a) the uses to which the state put tax money were sterile, and hence the more money left in private hands the better; and (b) a balanced budget would restore business confidence, which in turn would lower interest rates and thereby stimulate the economy. But with a 21 percent drop in production between 1928 and 1935 and the resultant losses in tax revenue, a huge public debt, and public needs that were greater than ever (especially for defense), economies of the scale needed to do any real good were impossible to realize.[4] Few seemed to sense this at the time.

Three considerations must be kept in mind in questioning why the Radicals and the Right could persist in this policy in the face of economic disaster at home and the example of some economic successes through innovation abroad. The first is the unique conjuncture of events in the 1920s that we mentioned earlier:

Understanding the deflationary policies of the government requires that we recognize the power of the belief in France that there were special features of the economy and of the country's "safe and sane" economic management that would see her through the turmoil without the need for new and upsetting policies. There were three main reasons for this belief: the splendid achievement of the 1920's; the almost neurotic rejection of arguments for further devaluation of the franc; and the high and mighty fact that for about eighteen months after the New York crash France did not show many signs of economic distress.[5]

The second consideration is the marked lack of interest or training in economics among the political leaders of the period. As Larmour notes of the Radicals:

With regard to economic and financial matters, the Radicals had little experience. All but five of the deputies had grown up before the First World War. Their education had been humanistic and the content of their formative years had been Boulangism, the Dreyfus Affair, and the anti-clericalism of Combes—all purely political issues.[6]

Finally, the business and financial circles to which the various governments turned for advice consistently and persistently backed deflation. Wolfe expressed the attraction of this policy in these terms:

This immense and perverse effort was accepted by ruling government and business circles . . . because it seemed to promise to make French products competitive in world markets without devaluation and so to preserve for the *rentiers* the full gold value of their investments.[7]

Thus the lack of any influential economic opinion to the contrary, plus the extraordinary recovery and performance of the French economy in the previous half-decade, combined to cause moderate French leaders not only to adopt the wrong policies but to do so with little opposition from any qualified sectors of the public.

While the various governments of the era were attempting without success to cope with the Depression by means of deflationary policies, a failure that eventually disenchanted even the Radicals and contributed to their adherence to the Popular Front, a crucial event occurred which in a more immediate sense triggered the Popular Front movement. This event was the right-wing antiparliamentary riots of February 6, 1934. The stimuli that provoked these riots were complex, but the immediate events were as follows. The extreme right-wing press discovered that a certain financial swindler, Stavisky, had avoided imprisonment and managed to keep in business for some years through the protection of a few important political figures of the Radical party, including a cabinet minister of the then-ruling Chautemps government. This scandal, raised to a fever pitch by the right-wing press, reached its height when Stavisky himself was found dead by the authorities; suicide was the official verdict, but the circumstances were such as to suggest the complicity of the police and perhaps even of the prime minister, Chautemps. The Chautemps government was obliged to resign, and another Radical leader, Édouard Daladier, was chosen to form a new government.

Daladier initially attempted to form a center-right majority, but failing in this he offered the necessary sop to gain the Socialists' support—the dismissal of the right-wing prefect of police, Chiappe, who was notorious for treating the then-frequent right-wing demonstrations in an entirely different manner from left-wing ones. (Chiappe consequently found himself named resident-general of Morocco, a post he readily declined.) The extreme Right took the removal of Chiappe, not without reason, as a blow directed against their side, and several extreme right-wing organizations arranged a mass demonstration in front of the Chamber of Deputies on the day the Daladier government was to be invested with power. The result was a police-mob confrontation on a massive scale, resulting in twenty-seven deaths and over two thousand wounded. At the height of the siege it looked as if the Chamber of Deputies, then sitting, would actually be invaded, and Daladier, never as strong-willed as he was held to be (he was to represent France at Munich in 1938), resigned the next day despite repeated votes of confidence from the Chamber. The whole sequence of events was a shock to the Left, in part because it provoked the resignation of a left-wing government and occasioned the actual switch-over of control of government to the Right, but even more because it was commonly taken (in all likelihood wrongly) as an attempted fascist coup d'etat that just missed succeeding.

Almost immediately, large-scale Communist and Socialist demonstrations were organized in support of the Republic, and the Communists began to "extend the open hand" to the Socialist rank-and-file, while continuing attacks on the Socialist leadership. The Communist insistence on the right to criticize the Socialist leadership made any steps towards formal cooperation between the parties impossible for the moment, but very quickly this obstacle was eliminated. In May 1934, two *Pravda* articles (one written by the secretary-general of the PCF, Maurice Thorez, who had been hastily summoned to Moscow) announced a fundamental change in Communist strategy; united left-wing action to combat fascism was to replace the Communist-Socialist hostility of previous years. The continuing pressure on the PCF leadership from Moscow, matched on the Socialist side by pressures exerted by the left-wing of the SFIO, proved to be an irresistible combination. In July 1934, a Unity of Action Pact between the PCF and the SFIO was signed in which the parties agreed on a campaign to mobilize opposition to the right-wing paramilitary ("fascist") leagues and declared their common rejection of war, the government's deflationary decrees, and their support for democratic liberties.

The example of the defection of the lower-middle classes to fascism in Germany functioned for the Communists as a prime motivating force for the extension of the pact into a broad coalition of the working- and lower-middle classes against fascism and for the Republic. But the Socialists instinctively distrusted the proposal for a mass movement that the Communists might attempt to manipulate and control. In addition, they argued that a program of mere superficial social and economic reforms that would be acceptable to the middle classes would not suffice to remedy the economic situation and thereby assure a future for the regime. Instead what was needed, in their view, was "structural reforms," such as nationalization of key industries and monopolies, measures middle-class parties were hardly likely to welcome.

The movement towards a broad alliance of the Left therefore languished, but events were beginning to weaken the mutual suspicions and disagreements. First, the PCF, at the behest of a Soviet government increasingly fearful of Germany, became more and more "patriotic," accepting the need for France to be prepared to defend itself against Germany if it should some day come to that. After the signing of the Franco-Soviet Pact in 1935, the pressure on the PCF to work for a strong antifascist France increased, and its immediate objective shifted away from a mass movement of proletarians and petty bourgeois against fascism in favor of a political coalition of Communists, Socialists, and Radicals.[8] Also, apart from the fact that the economy did not seem to be responding to deflation in the hoped-for-manner, the Radicals' fear of disorder was continually being aroused by the violence of the extreme Right. As Larmour notes, "The Leagues really passed all bounds when they began beating up Radical deputies."[9] By July of 1935, a *Rassemblement populaire* of Radicals, Socialists, and Communists, plus a smattering of splinter parties and left-wing organizations of all sorts, had been created.

Still, problems persisted. The Rassemblement populaire could agree on certain generalities, such as opposition to fascism and war and support for civil liberties, peace, and the Republic. But what specific kinds of actions and policy positions did its formation entail? The Radical party seemed little disposed to take account of the fact that many of its deputies persisted in supporting the right-wing governments of the time. The Communists, for their part, rejected any suggestion that the Rassemblement populaire might become a *governmental* coalition. The critical weakness, however, was the inability of the parties to agree on a coherent policy statement. The stumbling block continued to be Socialist insistence that structural reforms were necessary if any real change were to be effected in the worsening domestic situation. The Communists, however, were not particularly concerned with domestic affairs, as Brower points out.[10] Instead, their attention was concentrated on foreign affairs, and this meant support of the Radical party, the principal architect of the Soviet alliance. The result was that, when the parties finally attempted to draw up a definite program, "The Communist delegates to the Committee made a point of supporting the Radicals virtually every time there was difficulty with the Socialists."[11] Eventually the Socialists were obliged to give in. Structural reforms were abandoned, and in return the Communists agreed that the Rassemblement populaire would remain a coordinating organization of member parties in which each party participated "without abdicating anything of its doctrine, its principles and its special goals."[12] The Communist goal of a mass-based *Front populaire* independent of the existing parties was never to be.

In January 1936, at long last, the programme of the Rassemblement populaire, or Front populaire as the Communists still preferred to call it, was ready. In brief summary it stated the following proposals. Under the rubric of the defense of liberty, the coalition declared itself in favor of a general amnesty for all political offenses, dissolution of the right-wing parliamentary leagues, controls over "unwholesome" influences in the press, enforcement of respect for the rights of organized labor, protection of the public school system against church interference, and extension of the school-leaving age to fourteen. Concerning the "defence of peace," the signatories favored collective security through the League of Nations, including the use of sanctions against aggressors, multilateral disarmament (which somewhat contradicted the collective security principle), and nationalization of all private war and munitions industries. In the economic sphere, the basic policy to overcome the Depression was to be the restoration of the purchasing power of the masses. This was to be achieved by the repeal of the deflationary measures (particularly the most recent and severe, the Laval decrees), a reduction in the length of the work week without corresponding loss in salary, adequate old-age pensions so that older men could retire and relinquish their jobs to the unemployed young, a national unemployment insurance scheme, and extensive rural and urban public works. In the area of agriculture, the aim was to restore farm prices to their previous levels; this was to be achieved principally through the creation of a wheat board, which would control pricing and marketing of a variety of farm products and eliminate exploitation by middlemen. Finally, in the field of credit and finance, there was to be stricter regulation of all banks, a reorganization of the largest credit bank—the Bank of France—to eliminate its control by an economic oligarchy (the "Two Hundred Families"), and a stricter control over flights of capital abroad such as had caused so much havoc in the mid-1920s and in 1933.

The Popular Front program was an admirable effort to arrive at a policy position that could unite the working-class and lower-middle-class parties and bring into effect reforms that the Depression had shown to be desperately needed. It must be observed, however, that there were certain limitations. First, the Socialists had failed to secure Radical, and consequently Communist, consent to make the program binding on the signatories either as an electoral platform or as a governmental program.[13] This meant that Radical candidates, for example, were free to campaign on platforms contrary to the Popular Front program and would not be subject to enforced voting discipline in the Chamber. Second, there were problems in the program itself. Consider the matter of the rejection of structural reforms. What if the Popular Front was to fail to revive the economy because the owners of industry would not respond to the coalition's moderate reforms by making efforts to rationalize and modernize their plants to cover the higher labor costs? The Popular Front, possessing no threat of sanctions in the form of nationalization, could be left in a very difficult position. Similarly, while the Popular Front committed itself to checking flights of capital abroad, the use of exchange controls, should they become necessary, had not been explicitly provided for. The parties of the Left had reason from past experience to fear speculation and short selling of the franc during their tenure in power, yet it must have been evident that any action not included in the program could only with great difficulty be instituted, given the problems of getting the parties to agree. The same may be said of the absence of any mention of the possibility of a currency devaluation, a step which other nations like Britain and the United States had found necessary to improve their economic situations. Finally, the need to be prepared to resist fascism internationally had not been translated into any mention of a possible need to rearm should the international situation continue to deteriorate. In short, several contingencies that might have been anticipated were not covered by the program, most likely because of differences between the parties on these matters, yet

because of these very differences there could not be left to any Popular
Front government a great deal of discretionary latitude of action. The
extent to which the failure to cover contingencies like these were to
handicap the Popular Front experiment will be examined next as we
turn our attention to the experience of the Popular Front in power.

The Blum Experiment

The principal outcome of the 1936 legislative elections for the Popular
Front, apart from the fact of its resounding victory, was the Radicals'
loss of a sizeable number of seats to the benefit of the Socialists and
Communists, who greatly increased their representation in the Chamber. As a result, for the first time in their history, the Socialists
emerged as the largest single party in the Chamber, and it fell upon
Léon Blum, the Socialist leader, to head the first Popular Front
government.[14] Unfortunately, in the month-long gap between the
Popular Front electoral victory and the date when the Blum government was officially to assume power, the first unanticipated contingency hit the Popular Front: the impatience of large segments of the
working classes expressed itself in a steadily growing wave of strikes.
The strikes, totally unorganized and spontaneous, generally took the
form of nonviolent factory occupations. Despite their concern over
the very obvious negative impression these "sit-down" strikes could
have for the middle classes and those of their parties who had aligned
with the Popular Front, neither the Marxist parties nor the unions
were able to check the spread of the strikes, which by the time of the
assumption of power on June 4, 1936, had affected every major
industry and involved approximately two million workers. Blum,
presumably, could have assumed power earlier than was strictly
speaking proper, and attempted to appease the workers' impatience
for the promised reforms; but characteristically he refused, out of
deference to the electoral promise given the middle classes that the
Popular Front, despite the presence in it of Marxist elements, would
respect "bourgeois legality." Blum's devotion to legality was to be
exhibited at other critical points in the Popular Front experience, and,
as in this instance, it is debatable whether the interests of the nation or
the Popular Front were best served by his stance. But the result was
clear: the Popular Front government, when it finally did assume
power, faced a crisis of immense proportions.

Two aspects of the situation, however, led the employers to seek
terms. The first was Blum's refusal to evacuate the factories by force,
despite his admission that the occupations constituted infringements

of the rights of private property. The second was even more disturbing to the owners. Not only did the workers not damage the machinery, they meticulously saw to its upkeep and maintenance; this suggested that the workers, although never making claims to that effect, were treating the factories and machinery as if they owned them. Fearing a revolutionary mentality, the employers' organization, the CGPF, called for and obtained a summit conference attended by the leaders of the General Confederation of Labor (CGT), with Blum presiding. At this conference, when it became clear to the CGPF representatives that the union leaders were not in control of their members, they agreed that, given the critical situation, large concessions would have to be offered if the CGT were to regain control and terminate the strikes. The result was the Matignon Agreement, in which the CGPF recognized the right of collective bargaining, the right of workers to join unions without being sanctioned for it, and the right of workers to elect delegates to negotiate wages and grievances with management. Blum arbitrated on the question of immediate wage claims, setting the range of increases at 7 to 15 percent (12 percent average); and the principles of paid vacations and the forty-hour workweek were acknowledged by the employers' representatives.

The forty-hour week was a particularly important reform because of the effect it was to have on the Popular Front attempts to revive the economy. Interestingly, its origins lay outside the Front. The Popular Front program had mentioned only the desirability of a shorter work week, but no exact figure had been indicated. From the early moments of the strike movement, however, the forty-hour week became a rallying cry of the strikers. Under intense pressure from labor leaders, Blum soon found it necessary to commit the government to immediate legislation for this particular reform. Blum himself had hoped that a reduced workweek could be instituted very gradually under the auspices of the International Labor Organization (ILO) so that the effect on production, both absolutely and relative to that of other nations, could be minimized; but his hand had been forced. The effects of this reform have generated considerable literature which we shall assess in due course.

One of the consequences of the spontaneity of the sit-down strikes was the fact that few general nationwide grievances were articulated. In fact, in many factories no demands were formulated at all, and the factory occupations took on more the character of a holiday or a *fête* than that of a purposeful form of industrial action. Even where demands were made, they had usually been decided upon after the sit-down strikes had begun, and they tended to be factory-specific.[15] As a consequence, the Matignon Agreement did not put an immediate end to the strikes, and a few tense weeks passed before the Socialist and Communist leaders, principally the latter, were able to coax the workers to evacuate the factories.

In the meantime Blum began the process of introducing the necessary legislation to bring into effect the terms of the Matignon Agreement and other promised reforms. Speed was essential. As Colton notes:

> The timetable of reform had to be accelerated immediately . . . .
> Certainly neither the opposition in the Chamber and Senate nor the nation's employers would have sanctioned these sweeping changes had it not been for the sense of panic and the acute need to restore industrial peace. As Blum later said, it was "the ransom that had to be paid to avoid civil war."[16]

The result was an amount of legislation unsurpassed in French history; according to one count, 133 laws were passed in 73 days. The key measures provided for the forty-hour week (to be introduced one industry at a time by the government), paid vacations, collective bargaining rights, the extension of the school-leaving age to fourteen, the institution of the wheat board, a massive public works program, controls on unjustifiable price rises, loans to small and middle-sized businesses, revisions in the statutes of the Bank of France, steps towards nationalization of war industries, and the dissolution of the right-wing paramilitary leagues. It was an admirable feat, yet it was to be blemished in one crucial respect: not all the reforms produced the results in practice that they were meant to achieve in theory.

An important case in point is the collective bargaining act and its follow-up, the conciliation and arbitration law. The idea was that these laws, plus the benefits the workers had derived from the other reforms, would serve to lessen the traditional industrial hostility and pave the way for an orderly process of industrial relations. Instead, the reaction on both sides was negative. For instance, the CGPF and the CGT were to collaborate in setting up conciliation and arbitration machinery, but in the fall of 1936 the employers abruptly broke off the negotiations with the CGT, leaving it to the government to follow through (which it did with laws in December 1936 and March 1938). This was but one manifestation of the sharp rebound that the CGPF took from its concessions of June 1936, a reaction that also caused it to stage a major internal reorganization that included the firing of its president, who had negotiated the Matignon Agreement, and the launching of "a belligerent counter-offensive against the

Matignon Diktat, the forty hour week and all Popular Front reforms." "The result," Colton concludes, "was a vigorous reaction on the part of the unions and an embittering of industrial relations."[17]

As for the workers, the concessions wrung from the employers and enacted into law did not have the morale-boosting effect that Blum claimed. Instead of productivity increasing to compensate for benefits, higher wages, and shorter hours, it more frequently declined.[18] Moreover, labor did not cooperate with management to help get industry back on its feet; the habitual mistrust of management and aversion to capitalism by labor prevailed in the form of rigid and belligerent insistence on its own interpretations of laws, interpretations that seldom reflected the needs of the industries involved. The industrial peace that Blum hoped for and needed never became reality; instead, industrial strife persisted throughout the Popular Front experiment, confounding the economic hopes of the government and alienating the lower middle class and its Popular Front representatives, the Radicals.

Just as the Popular Front was going through the turmoil of the sit-down strikes and the massive legislative effort deemed necessary to satisfy the workers, a second unanticipated contingency arose. In July 1936 the Spanish Civil War broke out. Not only was there cause for the French government to want to help a neighboring legally constituted democratic regime defend itself against a military revolt, but in this case the government involved was also a Popular Front government. The temptation for Blum was tremendous, therefore, to come to the aid of the Spanish Republic or at least not to interfere with those who were supplying Spain from France via the Pyrenees. A critical consideration was the position of Britain, on whom France would necessarily depend in the event of a confrontation with the fascist powers. The response from London to the French overtures was unequivocal, however; the British government did not favor aid to Spain in any form. Moreover, there were other problems. The Popular Front had campaigned on a platform of peace internationally and social unity at home. Intervention or assistance to Spain would compromise the pacifist stance of the Popular Front and might bitterly divide Frenchmen, even to the extent of civil war. Consequently, with great regret, Blum had to settle for second best, and a very poor second best it turned out to be: the policy of nonintervention.

Unfortunately, nonintervention was not at all acceptable to the Communists, who were relatively free to take independent policy positions because they had refused to participate in the Blum cabinet (a refusal that was in itself a blow to the Popular Front experiment). Although the PCF was careful to abstain rather than oppose the government in the Chamber of Deputies on this issue, its attitude was more harmfully reflected in an increase in political strikes protesting noninterventionism that served to compound the already high level of labor unrest. The politically motivated labor troubles in turn further disturbed the Radicals, who were largely in favor of nonintervention and resolutely against disorder.

On top of all these tensions and difficulties, the economy took a downward turn. The war in Spain and the German announcement in August 1936 of the extension of military service to two years had naturally shaken business and investment confidence. Domestically, the same effect had been achieved by the electoral victory of a left-wing coalition led by a Marxist, as well as by its immediate consequence, the sit-down strikes. The deleterious effect of the strikes on production was marked, moreover, and the fact that many industries were obliged for the first time to give their employees paid vacations that summer and sizeable wage increases to boot caused labor costs to rise rapidly with no compensating increases in production. Rather than causing the hoped for return of investment capital from abroad, the troubled situation encouraged additional flights of capital from the economy, creating a serious crisis for the franc. By September 1936 it was clear that the Popular Front economic experiment was failing badly.

Nothing remained but to devalue the franc. Blum was not personally opposed to devaluation and, as Colton notes, had publicly asserted as far back as 1934 that it was inevitable.[19] The popular aversion to any further tampering with the franc, the residue of the experiences of the 1920s, was fully appreciated by Blum, however, and as premier he had declared that his government was "resolutely hostile" to any devaluation. Secretly he knew better (as he later claimed), but he banked on the long shot: an economic recovery of sufficient proportions to attract capital back into France, thereby preserving the value of the franc and providing the necessary investments to allow economic expansion. His first four months in office having witnessed the opposite effect, Blum had now to renege on his promise. The blow was meant to be cushioned by the placement of the devaluation of the franc in the context of a tripartite agreement with Britain and the United States in which those two countries accepted as desirable the "adjustment" of the franc, and all three governments agreed to work together to stabilize their currencies and prevent further difficulties of this kind. The September devaluation nevertheless aroused intense hostility in the press and in parliament; even the Socialists' allies, the Radicals and the Communists, were angered (one of the PCF electoral promises had been the maintenance of the existing value of the franc).

Regrettably, the devaluation did not render its full share of financial and economic benefits to the government. As the Treasury's gold reserves were low because of the crisis of the franc, the revaluation of gold relative to the franc produced a comparatively small amount in profit to the government. In accordance with the stipulations of the tripartite agreement, most of this was placed in a new Exchange Stabilization Fund to support the franc in the event of future currency difficulties. Mysteriously, the government then allocated the remaining sum not to easing the budget, which was strained by the cost of the social reforms, but to repaying, quite needlessly, provisional advances that had been made by the Bank of France to both it and previous governments. Finally, owing again perhaps to "excessive scruples,"[20] the devaluation law provided that gold could only be exchanged for francs at the old exchange rate, so that those who had speculated against the franc would not be rewarded; but the effect was to destroy any incentive to repatriate gold that the devaluation might have created.

These negative features of the implementation of the September 1936 devaluation of the franc should not be used to mask its most significant quality: for a time it worked. After September, for a period of six months, production levels increased, unemployment fell, the balance of trade improved, and the economy generally was on the upswing. Naturally this situation could last only as long as the circumstances that made it possible. The comparative price advantage provided by the devaluation proved, however, to be temporary; prices were rising fast and so was the cost of labor because of the progressive implementation of the forty-hour week. Moreover, according to Greene, the additional income received by the workers was spent on basic commodities such as food and consequently did not function to stimulate industrial production.[21] The shorter workweek, because of the strict way it tended to be interpreted, also prevented the expansion of production even where business conditions warranted it. In such a situation it is perhaps not surprising that the anticipated return of capital into the economy failed to materialize; the hard-pressed government, facing immense expenditures, including those for rearmament, had to compete with a recovering private sector for ever scarcer credit resources. The increasing pressure on the Treasury ultimately set off renewed currency difficulties and by January 1937 the entire balance of the Exchange Stabilization Fund had been expended to shore up the franc. By late winter of 1937 the second phase of the Popular Front economic experiment, too, had ended in failure.

In March 1937 Blum announced a partial surrender: the "pause." The pause consisted of the abandonment of intended reforms covering unemployment relief and workmen's compensation, the elimination of numerous new governmental expenditures, especially on public works, the rescinding of the provision making gold exchangeable only at the old franc rate, and a further renunciation of exchange controls as a method of preventing speculative attacks on the franc. Further, three conservative bankers were appointed to head the Exchange Stabilization Fund in order to reassure financial circles. As Colton notes, "The mild flirtation with deficit funding and pump priming ended."[22]

Again the effect of this change in policy was salutary to begin with. The exchange markets quieted, and a national defense loan to finance rearmament was rapidly oversubscribed by the public. However, a clash between right-wing and left-wing activists in Clichy, a suburb of Paris, that inexplicably resulted in the police firing on the leftists and killing six, shook the political atmosphere and helped provoke a new round of labor unrest and demonstrations. The policy of nonintervention in Spain continued to anger the Communists and contributed to the same end. But most important, the economy started to worsen: the balance of trade fell into the red once again, production declined and, consequently, so did tax revenue. The Treasury was again in difficult straits and confidence was so lacking that even Treasury bonds could find no market. Rumors of a new devaluation abounded and a near-panic flight from the franc erupted. The opposition in the Chamber and the Senate clearly saw the pause as a retreat on the part of the Popular Front government and became more and more aggressive. The three bankers who headed the Exchange Stabilization Fund resigned over the government's failure to adopt deflationary policies to save the franc. The Blum government was once more in the midst of grave difficulties.

The government made rapid preparations to meet the new crisis. Plans were drawn up for tax and postal rate increases, for tougher measures to be taken against tax evasion (a chronic problem in France), and for a new bond issue to cover the immediate needs of the Treasury. The decision was taken by the cabinet to undertake the exceptional step of asking parliament for pleins pouvoirs to permit the government to deal with the crisis with whatever measures it might deem necessary, and the implication was that these measures might be drastic. To appease the opposition, however, Blum committed the government to the promise that the measures would include neither a devaluation nor exchange controls, although he was vague as to what might be included. We have already commented on the reaction in parliament: twice the bill passed in the Chamber of Deputies and twice the Senate rejected it by responding with its own bill that would have placed numerous restrictions on the government's freedom of action. It seems that at this point the Radical ministers in the cabinet, after a separate meeting, informed Blum that they were unwilling to prolong this constitutional crisis, for that was what it had become, in view of the grave financial and international situations facing the nation. Blum decided to resign. According to Greene, "Blum simply had no reason to hang on to power: unless the liberal capitalistic institutions were to be altered drastically—and the time was not one for revolutionary alterations—enactment of further reforms was impossible."[23]

The Post-Blum Experience

The remainder of the Popular Front experiment, which lasted from June 1937 to December 1938, saw four different Popular Front governments. As symbolized by the selection of the very moderate Radical Camille Chautemps to head the first two of them, the reforming drive of the Popular Front was very much in decline. An indicator of the fact that this was appreciated by the parliamentary Right was the rapid granting to Chautemps of the pleins pouvoirs that Blum had been denied by the Senate. The basis of Chautemps' formula for restoring the nation's finances was another devaluation, increased taxes, and further expenditure cutbacks—hardly the sort of economics that the Popular Front had stood for at the outset. Blum's attitude to these developments was that, while not much was to be expected of the Chautemps government, the Popular Front coalition had to be held together to protect the regime and the major reforms, such as the forty-hour week, that had been legislated; he persuaded his party to support the government on this basis and accepted the post of vice-premier.

At first things were fairly quiet. But by the fall of 1937, the alienation of the PCF from the Chautemps government because of its economic policies and its inaction on the Spanish question in spite of the blatant violations of nonintervention by the Axis powers—an alienation that the PCF had hitherto managed to suppress—began to manifest itself in an increase in worker strikes and demonstrations. "For some reason," notes Brower, "the protection of the Soviet alliance was no longer felt to justify a policy of complete social and political restraint."[24] In addition, the rise in prices that had more or less eradicated the wage increases the Blum government had won for the workers and the desire on the part of labor for the renewal by management of the collective work contracts, which were due for renegotiation, were also important factors in the union militancy. On the side of management, the bitterness surrounding industrial relations expressed itself in a second abandonment by the employers of joint CGPF-CGT talks relating to the establishment of conciliation and arbitration procedures; but in one of the few areas where Chautemps stood by the Blum government's lead, a final version of an arbitration and conciliation law was eventually passed (albeit with some compromises to the Senate at the expense of the Communists in such matters as cost of living increases). Nevertheless the labor unrest, the continuing trade deficits caused in part by a high rate of domestic inflation, and, of course, the perennial budget problems had in the meantime encouraged a resumption of currency instability. Chautemps' openly expressed view was that the blame for this new crisis was attributable solely to the labor unrest, despite the employers' recalcitrance as evidenced by their abandonment of the labor relations conference—an interpretation which provoked the PCF decision to abstain in a vote of confidence for the government. When Chautemps countered that he did not want Communist support because, he intimated, he could look to the opposition for support, this clear violation of the Popular Front principle obliged the Socialists to resign from the government, thereby bringing about its fall in January 1938.

There followed considerable searching about for a different governmental formula, including an attempt by Blum to form a broadened coalition that would include all but the far Right, but in the end no viable alternative could be found to another Chautemps government. This time the Socialists refused to participate in the government but agreed to support it in the Chamber. Perhaps the chief consequence of the Socialists' participation in the preceding government and their support of this one was the frustration of a strong Radical desire to modify the forty-hour law; moreover with Socialist support the arbitration and conciliation bill was finally enacted by this government. Little else of note, however, was accomplished, in part because the government was quickly faced with the same financial and economic difficulties that had plagued the previous government—the bankruptcy of the Treasury, the poor balance of trade, and the troubled exchange-market situation. By March 1938 the Chautemps government found itself again having to ask parliament for pleins pouvoirs to cope with a financial and monetary crisis. When the

Socialists expressed uneasiness over this and asked for assurances that the Popular Front program would be respected, Chautemps seized the opportunity to resign without a vote. The cabinet had been too narrowly based to have lasted long in any case; whether the resignation was also inspired by the worsening international situation remains debatable. The very next day, the Nazis moved into Vienna.

Upon the demise of the Chautemps cabinet, Blum made a more determined effort to form a government of "national unity" in view of the growing danger that Germany posed to the nation. His impassioned overtures to the opposition were, however, ultimately rejected. Colton regards this turn as decisive:

> Blum's failure was a watershed in the history of the Third Republic. Never again did the opportunity for a true "national unity" cabinet arise, one that had a place in it for the working class political parties. . . . From the summer of 1938 on, the working class political parties and trade union organizations no longer had a voice in the national political community or in the national defence effort. A "national unity" cabinet . . . would have guaranteed that a united France would have faced Hitler's challenges in 1938.[25]

Blum had no choice but to fall back on the already dated formula of a Popular Front cabinet; it was to last less than a month.

The area of industrial relations was in desperate straits. The collective contracts of 1936 had already been extended by the government the maximum two times and had to be renegotiated. The employers, however, were unwilling to cooperate with the government's mediators or with the unions; the unions themselves were responding to the advent of a new Socialist-led government with increased militancy. A rash of strikes, fed by the workers' hopes of getting the Blum government to end the embargo on arms shipments to Spain, broke out and further damaged the government's credibility.

The near impossibility of the government's survival was well appreciated by Blum. With little to lose he embarked on an ambitious program to tackle the difficulties facing the nation. By this time Blum had read and been influenced by Keynes; furthermore he was now openly comparing his economic thinking to that that lay behind the Nazi economic miracle. The result was an economic strategy of heavy deficit spending centering on rearmament, with the possibility of a limited control of the exchange markets in the event of the customary flight from the franc and consequent loss of gold.

Such a program stood little chance in parliament. Blum's bill passed the Chamber with only a narrow majority; the more conservative

Senate naturally rejected it. Large-scale demonstrations in favor of the government took place, but Blum was again reluctant to utilize the massed pressure of labor, particularly as it was a time when the international situation necessitated domestic social harmony. Once more Blum yielded to the Senate and resigned.

The fifth and final Popular Front government was formed by the Radical Daladier. The Socialists, who again refused to participate, agreed to support the government despite the presence of some right-wing deputies in the cabinet. Daladier soon demanded and was granted limited pleins pouvoirs in the financial and economic spheres by the Chamber and the Senate. Gradually the industrial relations crisis began to subside as the major employers started to settle the strikes, often on the very basis that had been proposed by the Blum government. This plus a third devaluation of the franc and an easing of the forty-hour law to allow more overtime at low rates helped the economic situation somewhat, although the economic performance in 1938 was to be significantly poorer than in 1937. The tougher stand taken by the Daladier government against the strikes was not appreciated by the Socialists and the Communists.

The signature of Daladier to the Munich Agreement, which surrendered the Sudetenland to Germany in late September 1938, further compromised what little remained of the Popular Front. When Daladier upon his return from Munich demanded and received a strengthening of his pleins pouvoirs, and used this authority to promulgate decrees sharply compromising the forty-hour law and setting very low standards for overtime pay, the split between the Marxist parties and the Radicals was complete. It needed only to be formalized by a December 1938 vote of confidence in the Chamber of Deputies in which the SFIO and the PCF went into opposition; Daladier survived with the support of the Right, and the Popular Front was officially finished.

Economic Aspects of the Popular Front Experiment

Without doubt the most compelling image that the history of the Popular Front experiment projects is one of repeated economic and financial crises frustrating the efforts of the various Popular Front governments to proceed with their increasingly milder programs. The first stage in our investigation of the nature and causes of the failure of the Popular Front experiment will therefore concentrate on the attempts that have been made to account for the inability of the coalition to cope with the economic situation in a more satisfactory fashion.

One common approach to the problems of the pre-1945 French economy has attempted to characterize the "economic culture," if that is the term, of French capitalism and to see in this culture the roots of the slow economic growth, poor adaptability, and susceptibility to stagnation that marked the French economy in those years. The main point of this line of inquiry is that the French approach to industry and business has traditionally been conservative, lacking in entrepreneurial skills, or, in the most common epithet, "Malthusian." As such, it lacked the resources to respond to the innovative attempts at economic stimulation provided by the Popular Front.

Some authors have attributed the origin of this type of economic ethos to the penetration of nonentrepreneurial values into the bourgeois world of industry and finance. Unlike in England, where the aristocracy has been held to have adopted commercial values and practices very early in the development process,[26] in France the noncapitalist values of the old aristocratic tradition prevailed well into the industrial era. According to Pitts, "The man of aristocratic values, bringing to industry the attitudes which elsewhere bring him prestige and power, is not primarily interested in applied-science aspects of production or in the problems of adding value to the goods and services produced."[27] This man's sense of his own superiority precludes any possibility of salesmanship, for that would entail the subjection of the value of his product to the judgment of someone else, the customer. Similarly, the necessity of narrow specialization or of catering to the needs of mass consumer-demand was not acceptable in the aristocratic tradition, and the requirement of keeping costs at a minimum was an inappropriate objective: "because for him perfection and not price was the measure of the worth of an object or deed."[28]

Among the bourgeoisie, envy of the position and prestige of the aristocracy apparently caused the adoption of these aristocratic values and goals. In addition, its hard-fought struggle to acquire economic power and status of its own led it to prefer business practices aimed above all at the preservation of its wealth and position. For the bourgeois:

> Property ... is a symbol of family relationships, but it is also the proof of the family's rootedness and the guarantee of its status.... Everything possible is done to preserve the continuity of the bourgeois family by maintaining it as an island of integrity and order in a disorganized and unprincipled world.... The bourgeois protects himself from the threats of the world by favoring those careers where safe revenue is assured. A family firm is managed so as to minimize market risk. A bourgeois investor feels a great respon-

sibility not to lose money, for that would be a crime against his family.[29]

In Sawyer's view, the basic nature of French society complemented these nonentrepreneurial values. Because the society was geared to tradition and continuity, he believes, resistance to the newer products of mass production and the new methods and relationships involved therein was widespread. Moreover, in a society caught between "a declining aristocracy and a rising socialism" the role of the business-man never became "legitimate" and consequently could not attract outstanding talent. There was a marked lack of a drive to innovate, and little consideration was given to the possibility of increasing the consumption of the mass public. Instead, production was geared toward "inelastic and class markets, markets defined in terms of social classes rather than present or potential income groups."[30] He, too, credits much of this economic style to the overriding necessity of preserving the status and honor of the bourgeois family:

> Given the structure of the family as an enduring entity enjoying an established place, the motivation has typically been to run the busi-ness so as to assure the preservation over time of the family status and the family honor involved with it . . . . This has motivated businessmen toward caution, thrift, security, tradition, avoidance of risk.[31]

The result of this family orientation in French business was an economy characterized by the coexistence of a large number of small family firms servicing more or less fixed markets and never really attempting to compete or expand at the expense of others. The ability of this type of undynamic economy and economic culture to bring an end to a major depression is presumably limited.

The much-noted proliferation in prewar France of small family firms that seemed to operate on the principle of "live and let live" rather than "dog eat dog" was not the only salient characteristic of the economy, however. As Bettleheim has pointed out, this mass of small enterprises masked a marked propensity to cartellization and mono-polization.[32] The small size of the domestic market, limited both by the absence of attitudes that would foster its expansion and by the huge percentage of the population that comprised peasants or small farmers with relatively few industrial needs and not much disposable income, contributed to this tendency in two respects. First, it weak-ened France's economic competitiveness and thereby necessitated high protective tariff barriers; second, it made possible control over dif-ferent sectors of industry by small groups of industrialists and financiers. Safe from foreign competition and free to charge the high prices that the small enterprises had to charge to survive, the larger enterprises were able to maintain a substantial profitability without heavy investment in machinery. Moreover, by restricting credit for the small and middle-sized businesses on the grounds that their profit margins were much smaller than those of the large industries, the banks functioned to preserve the untouchable position of the large enterprises, to which they had become intimately linked. Thus risks were small and profitability assured for the oligopolies because the absence of competition guaranteed their markets and because they enjoyed particularly close relationships with the banks; and the incentive to invest and expand was thereby minimized. In Bettleheim's view:

> This sort of industrial structure, dominated by monopolistic groups which, in alliance with the bankers, held the key positions in the economy and allowed the small and middle-sized enterprises little more than the recovery of their costs, is the source of the stagnation of our productive forces and our economic decline.[33]

The high degree of concentration of industry and its close ties with the banks, in particular its domination of the governing councils of the Bank of France, also inspired the left-wing political doctrine of the malevolent control of French politics by the Two Hundred Families, or the "Wall of Money," which gained wide currency in the 1920s and 1930s.

The import of these observations from the point of view of explaining the economic problems of the Popular Front era would seem to be that the Malthusian ethos, supported by both small- and large-scale enterprise, failed to meet the harsh economic challenges of the interwar years and especially of the Great Depression. In Landes' opinion:

> Once the World War had changed France's economic problem from one of conservatism and leisurely growth to one of reconstruction and replacement, this lack of dynamism became a force for retardation and strangulation. This was all the more true because the simultaneous collapse of the franc, after over 100 years of stability, was utterly demoralizing in a society whose greatest economic virtue was thrift.[34]

Is the thesis that the French economy was basically Malthusian valid, and, if so, can it contribute in any way to the explanation of the economic difficulties that repeatedly beset the Popular Front?

Concerning the first part of this question, the answer would seem to be largely in the affirmative. It is unquestionable that the French economy was characterized by the simultaneous existence of a mass of small businesses and a few large cartels and conglomerates, each of which, for its own reasons, chose to maintain a posture of defense or preservation rather than of growth or expansion. It is also the case that in broad comparison with the British, German, and American economies of the nineteenth and early twentieth centuries, the French economy developed slowly. However, this latter point can be misleading, for the rate of growth of the French economy in this period was far from uniform. Instead, it seemed to fluctuate between periods of virtually complete stagnation and periods of rapid economic growth such as occurred during the reign of Louis-Napoleon (1851–70), during the early years of the twentieth century leading up to the First World War, and, as we have noted, during the latter half of the 1920s.

On the assumption that the economic Malthusianism thesis has some validity, we seem to be faced once again with a historical situation characterized by periods of both relative success and relative failure under the broad umbrella of a certain set of cultural and institutional limitations. We are therefore led to respond to the Malthusianism thesis in a manner that reflects our earlier line of reasoning concerning the Third Republic itself. While not rejecting out of hand the utility of these observations concerning the obstacles to recovery and growth in the French economy in accounting for the persistence of the Depression in the face of the Popular Front's efforts, we conclude in view of previous periods of economic growth that causal agents are needed that apply in a more specific sense to the situation of the 1930s and the failure of the Popular Front.

One possible agent that has received considerable attention in the literature is the influence of the politically motivated, anti-Left activities of big business and finance. This approach has certain features that make it attractive. For one thing, it follows readily from the interpretations of the French economic culture just presented. Surely, the argument goes, an industrial and financial class as traditional and conservative as the one we have just described would have been led to resist any left-wing government, especially a governing coalition whose goal was to aid the working classes beyond all precedent and to pay for its share of the cost through unorthodox and unprecedented measures such as deficit spending in a time of depression. Moreover, the thesis of the influence of the Wall of Money on French politics in the interwar period has a certain amount of empirical support. According to Larmour:

The money powers were a great bogey, but that should not prevent their being taken seriously. The financial circles wanted . . . to maintain a sound currency; and to ensure this they felt they had to keep the Socialists out of the government. Since the budget was always out of balance, the government had to borrow to finance itself. Control of the money market, therefore, gave the financial world a weapon of great subtlety and strength: when the financiers were discontented, the market for Treasury bonds suddenly dried up, the Bank of France placed conditions on advances to the Treasury's account, and gold began fleeing the country.[35]

Thomson has pointed out that evidence for the reality of the influence of high finance on governmental affairs can be found even in the Bank of France's own statements. He quotes, for example, from an incredible Bank of France communiqué of 1935:

M. Flandin's government has some praiseworthy actions to its credit. . . . Its economic measures—though a little less certain— still deserve a good mark, in view of the difficulties of the situation. This good mark has been given to M. Flandin in the form of credit facilities. These credit facilities may not prove sufficient. He will ask for more credit. Our reply will then depend on whether we are satisfied with the actions of the government during the first respite we have given it as a reward for its present determination to defend the currency.[36]

More important, this interpretation seems to accord with many of the facts and events of the Popular Front experiment. Consider the currency and financial difficulties that plagued the Popular Front governments. Blum believed that the increased government expenditures resulting from the social reforms would be paid for ultimately by an augmented tax income. The additional tax money would come from an upturn in industrial production to meet the greater demands of a lower-class citizenry with significantly more purchasing power. But he and his successors were stymied by a business psychology that responded to budgetary deficits with flights of capital abroad. As Colton puts it, "Only in France could an announcement of government defence expenditures lead to a panic in investment circles, such as occurred in September 1936."[37] The Blum tenure of power was in a certain sense a gamble; repeated assurances that the Popular Front would act legally and not indulge in structural reforms, plus promises to safeguard the franc, were counted on to restore enough confidence among the monied interests so that the 60 billion francs estimated to be "missing" in June 1936 would flow back into the economy. The reluctance to impose exchange controls, although motivated in part by the Radicals' opposition to them, was also in large measure an attempt to create confidence in the "safeness" of the Popular Front. The failure of the money-holders and the speculators to respond other than negatively to this attempt was the immediate precondition of several Popular Front governmental crises and defeats, as we have noted. In Colton's judgment, "The sitdown strike of capital, which outlasted the sitdown strikes of labor, in the long term proved decisive in the failure of the Blum experiment."[38]

The harmful reactions of the industrial-financial oligarchy were not solely monetary either. We have noted the intransigence, at several stages in the Popular Front's history, of the employers and their organization (the CGPF) in their intent to frustrate the government's reforms and thereby to recoup some of the losses they suffered by signing the Matignon Agreement in the pressured atmosphere of the strikes and factory occupations in June and July of 1936. A case in point would be the sequence of events that began with the overhaul of the CGPF and the firing of its president, who had signed the Matignon Agreement, and led to the open condemnation of that agreement and the abandonment of the joint talks with organized labor on arbitration procedures in the autumn of 1936. Even after the pause, designed to win their confidence, the employers refused to negotiate with the unions; instead they maintained their resistance to the Popular Front's industrial relations policies throughout the 1936–38 era.

This attitude, it is argued, applied not only to labor negotiations but extended into the whole area of management. In Lorwin's view, "Management responded not by increasing efficiency, as the reform and recovery theory implied, but by raising prices. It was unwilling to invest in modernization."[39] In fact, as Ehrmann points out, several important industries even decided to discontinue retooling and normal maintenance rather than to try to cover the wage increases by technological advances. Moreover, the excuse that reforms paralyzed production by suppressing profits is questionable; Ehrmann notes that in many industries profits actually rose.[40] It was Blum's failure to win over the *patronat* that led, according to Dupeux, to his giving up so easily before the Senate.[41] Wolfe summarizes the argument: "Just as the French speculator refused to be cajoled into acceptance of the exchange value of the Auriol franc [i.e., the Blum devaluation], the French industrialist refused to expand his output except on his own terms."[42]

Needless to say, not everyone sees the events in this manner. Prost, in his study of the nature and effects of sit-down strikes, attributes a considerable degree of blame for the subsequent economic troubles to the behavior of the workers, who were never able to regain their previous work discipline after the explosive release of the strikes.[43] Lorwin, too, acknowledges that "labor was indifferent to the need for higher productivity to accompany shorter hours,"[44] and Kindleberger agrees that the lack of a strong, responsible labor movement played a part in the economic failure.[45] The occurrence of the most serious labor unrest during the time of the Blum governments is a good example of how labor hurt the chances for success of its most faithful defender by contributing to a downward turn in the economy and by feeding the employers' opposition to Blum.

The objections of those who reject the thesis that the Popular Front's economy policy failed because of resistance from the patronat have involved more than mere blame of the workers, however. In the opinion of Jeanneney, the real problem behind the economic troubles was quite simply that Blum's theory of "reflation" was wrong. Blum believed that the higher wages would increase consumption, thereby reducing the unit cost of goods, increasing production and profits, and encouraging investments. A more likely approach would have been to devalue heavily right away and keep the costs of production (that is, wages) down. This would have increased exports, caused capital to return, reduced interests rates, created new investments, and finally allowed wage increases. For Blum's theory to work:

> it would have been necessary for the managers to have accepted on faith the success of this policy and decided that their best interests lay in preparing to increase their production and therefore in investing in stocks and fixed assets when, at the time, the wage increases had reduced their profits or even placed their companies in danger.[46]

Whether this view is substantially correct or not, it loses sight of two important considerations. First, it seems certain that the sit-down strikes could not have been ended without the immediate implementation of significant wage increases. Second and more important, the original economic strategy had in essence been abandoned in September of 1936 when the franc was devalued. And, as we have noted, this devaluation did have beneficial effects on production, which rose throughout the fall and winter of 1936–37.

The question now becomes, why did these production increases come to a halt and the recession that endured until the end of the Popular Front begin? For Sauvy the forty-hour workweek was to blame.[47] His careful study has revealed that, as the forty-hour week was progressively implemented in industry after industry, production in the affected industries dropped accordingly. Regrettably, the government did not watch industrial indices or seasonally adjust employment figures; as a result it was unaware of the increase in production and drop in unemployment following the devaluation until after the forty-hour week had been fully implemented. Moreover Blum seems to have been under the erroneous impression that the major factories were working less than forty hours per week (as had been the case in the United States when the reform was introduced), when in actuality the average workweek was 44.5 hours; consequently, he did not appreciate the adverse effect this reform would have on production. And, as Asselin has pointed out, with unemployment at well under 10 percent at this time, even if all the jobless could have been taken on, the expanded labor force still would not have been able to compensate for the 10 percent reduction in the length of the workweek.[48]

Much blame has also been given the labor unions. The unions generally insisted that the only way to ensure proper enforcement was to have a workweek of five eight-hour days; this meant that plants had to shut down for two days a week. Since the shortage of skilled workers made shift work impossible, and since productivity was not increasing, production levels could only be maintained through overtime. Yet the unions preferred to interpret the forty-hour week not as a norm for wages, as was the case in the United States, but "as a legal maximum on hours with exemptions difficult to secure."[49] Even firms with full order books could not boost production. On no account, therefore, was the production reversal due to the export of capital:

> The export of capital in 1936, although morally reprehensible, caused a loss of gold but not of production. It was the decrease in industrial production, for a completely different reason, that brought on the fall of the Blum government. With a production level of 100 or 110 and the increased tax revenue that would follow, the political victory would have been assured.[50]

This conclusion, too, has not gone unrebutted. Wolfe, in asserting that "it is doubtful that the manufacturer who refused to increase production in the face of rising prices during the first half of the Blum regime would have acted much differently if the forty-hour week had never been enacted,"[51] directly contradicts the contention of Sauvy that production had been rising quickly enough after the devaluation to have assured the success of the Popular Front. The question can be resolved by an examination of the production figures given in table 2. On the basis of the upward trend in industrial production levels after the devaluation, it can reasonably be projected that, if the forty-hour week had never been implemented, the record high levels set in the late 1920s (1928 forms the base figure of 100 for table 2) would have been surpassed well before the end of 1937. The halt in these increases coincides too closely with the progressive implementation of the forty-hour week to doubt the impact of this reform, as Sauvy has demonstrated.

Table 2   Industrial Production Levels during the First Blum Government (1928 = 100)

Reflation		Devaluation		Forty-Hour Week	
1936		1936–37		1937	
June	80	October	88	April	92
July	82	November	90	May	89
August	76	December	91	June	89
September	81	January	92	July	85
		February	93		
		March	94		

SOURCE: A. Sauvy, *Histoire Économique de la France Entre les Deux Guerres*, 2 vols. (Paris: Fayard, 1965), 2:528.

The line of reasoning we have followed in this section leads us to the following conclusions. The industrial-financial oligarchy, by responding to governmental pump-priming not with increased production and investment but with panicky "flights from the franc" that reflected not only the particular state of economic culture and reasoning prevalent at the time but also an eagerness to damage the Popular Front experiment, must bear considerable responsibility for the economic difficulties that plagued the Popular Front governments. On the other hand, the success of the theory of reflation depended to a large extent on Blum's ability to win the confidence of right-wing business and financial circles at a time when all that was happening was negative from their viewpoint: higher wages, paid vacations, shorter hours, serious budgetary deficits, and so on. When a measure more clearly beneficial to the economy—the devaluation of the overvalued franc—was adopted, neither their political opposition to the Popular Front nor their economic opposition to a further lowering of the franc's parity with gold prevented substantial economic recovery. What killed this recovery, it seems most likely, was the gradual implementation of the forty-hour work-week in a most disadvantageous manner. We noted earlier that the forty-hour week had never been part of the Popular Front program and that Blum himself regarded a shorter workweek as a reform that should be introduced very gradually and internationally through the auspices of the International Labor Organization. The sit-down strikes forced his commitment to the forty-hour week, but could he not have stalled or even reneged, as he did on his promise not to devalue? The answer seems to reside in the simple fact that neither Blum nor anyone else realized the extent to which the economy was recovering after the devaluation and the forty-hour week was erasing these gains. In fact, even in retrospect Blum never admitted the adverse impact of the forty-hour week, and a principal function of his party's support of the two Chautemps governments was to preserve the inviolability of this particular reform long after the Radicals wanted it weakened or ended.

Political Aspects of the Popular Front Experiment

Our discussion of the Popular Front era has thus far been dominated by the economic and financial problems that repeatedly cropped up and precipitated governmental crises. This orientation should not be taken to indicate, however, that the fate of the Popular Front can be cast entirely in economic terms. To establish this point, we need only recall the defeat of the first Blum government. Granted that much of the blame for the failure of the Popular Front's economic policies can be attributed to errors in theory and implementation (especially the forty-hour week), it remains the case that on this occasion, as on the occasion of the fall of his second government, Blum was proposing or implying radical departures from the prevailing economic policies. Yet in each instance he was defeated. Many authors have indicated that these defeats were brought on by an opposition on the part of the Radicals and other moderates in the Popular Front that manifested itself covertly in the Chamber of Deputies and overtly in the Senate. But what was the basis for this opposition? At least three plausible answers can be suggested: disillusionment because of the economic failures; disillusionment that encompassed not just the economic sphere but the whole Popular Front experiment; not disillusionment with the actual results of the Popular Front policies so much as the logical working out of serious ideological and policy differences that existed within the Popular Front even before it took office. To understand the Popular Front it is important not only to know that the economic strategy failed, and why this was so, but also to discover the nature of the commitment of the various parties to the Popular Front to begin with and how this commitment became affected by such events as the financial crises. In other words, the Popular Front must be studied both from the perspective of the effects its policies had on the country and the economy, and from the perspective of what was happening within the coalition itself. The former aspect having been exhaustively researched elsewhere and briefly reviewed in the previous section, it is to the latter end that the remainder of this study is primarily directed.

The value of the more political line of investigation that we are proposing can best be illustrated if we make reference to two significant theses that bear upon the Popular Front. The first relates to the general nature of the party system in the Third Republic and how it evolved through time, while the second more specifically concerns the attitudes and actions of the Radical party during the Popular Front era.

One of the first points made in this chapter was the difficulty that the parties of the parliamentary Left in France found in trying to ally themselves to the extent of forming viable and lasting governmental coalitions in the interwar period. The fundamental stumbling block, it is said, was that the Radicals were considered, and considered them-selves, to be of the Left, using the pre–World War I definition of the term as meaning pro-republican, at a time when the majority of the Right had been reconciled to the regime and when an immense rift had developed between the Marxist parties and the non-Marxist parties (including the Radicals) over the causes and remedies of the financial and economic troubles that plagued these two decades. As Larmour put it:

> The Radicals looked on themselves as men of the left, yet their inter-ests were on the center or on the right—the classic French conflict between the heart and the pocket-book. In a tranquil era this tension was not serious; in a period of crisis it became disastrous.[52]

The consequence was that in both 1926 and 1934, a left-wing Chamber of Deputies came to support a right-wing government because of the impossibility of finding a common core of agreement on financial and economic policy among the major parties of the Left, in particular among the Radicals and the Socialists; and, as we have seen, a similar falling-out was to take place in the Popular Front in 1938.

In 1936, however, it looked as if something new was occurring. After all the weakness and confusion of the previous decade and a half, the entire Left, including the Radicals with their more conservative social and economic opinions, had united behind a detailed, explicit program aimed at defending the republican regime and instituting sweeping reform. The immense excitement that the Popular Front movement attracted at the time and the equally impressive amount of attention it has received from scholars since then testify to the enormity of the obstacles that had to be overcome for this unity to be achieved.

Yet one may well wonder, given the course the Popular Front experiment was to take, to what extent the unity was in fact achieved. Had the Radicals, in their own electoral statements written on the eve of the 1936 elections, in fact overcome the obstacle of their hypothesized ideological mélange of political leftism and socioeconomic conservatism and accepted the strongly reformist posture of the Marxist parties and of the Popular Front program that bore their party's signature? What does their subsequent voting behavior indicate in this regard—cohesion with the Marxist parties or significant defections? If the latter, when did they take place and what specific issues provoked them? Divisions in the roll-call voting of the Popular Front related to specific aspects of the Popular Front program, especially if explicable by means of significant ideological differences in the electoral statements of these deputies, would clearly point to an explanation of the Popular Front's political problems in terms of ideological divergences. If the nature of those cleavages matched the substance of the alleged ideological dividing line between the Radicals and the Marxist Left, this would constitute evidence for the existence and importance of this fault-line in the French Left. On the other hand, it could be that any voting defections that did occur within the Popular Front should be attributed to disillusionment with the failure of the legislative program to put the economy back on its feet rather than to ideological disunity as such. If this interpretation is correct, one would expect to find that the voting dissension within the coalition was diffuse and not tied to specific issues. More important, voting defections would not be connected to any ideological or policy differences within the Popular Front that might appear in the electoral statements of the Popular Front deputies. Instead, such defections would presumably suggest a gradual disillusionment with the movement as the Blum government ran into serious setbacks, perhaps coupled with strong support for the more moderate Radical governments that succeeded Blum.

A second thesis that our investigations are intended to bear upon has been put forward by Larmour. It, too, concerns the Radical party in the Popular Front era, but the argument advanced is somewhat different. One of the main points argued by Larmour is that the defection of the Radical party from the Popular Front coalition was not the result of the extremism of the coalition's program or even of the failure of the reforms to revive the economy. Rather, he notes, "in October, 1936, the Popular Front was assaulted, battered and almost overthrown by the [Radical party] Congress of Biarritz, long before the financial and economic failure of the Blum government was clear."[53] Moreover, the Radicals, "whatever their secret feelings may have been," never publicly repudiated the reforms. Indeed, Larmour feels that the Radicals tended to regard the Popular Front program as not significantly different from their own. As time passed, "the Radicals' attachment to the program, if anything, increased";[54] the only exception in this regard was their hostility to the forty-hour week.

The real source of the alienation of the Radicals from the Popular Front was therefore not the Popular Front reforms or their disappointing consequences but the realization, stemming from the sit-down strikes and the subsequent chronic labor unrest directed at the policy of nonintervention in Spain, that "their Communist playfellows had turned into a mass of striking men":[55]

> By the fall of 1936, the traditional domestic sources of controversy were definitely subordinated to foreign policy or transformed into a dispute over anti-Communism that became progressively more detached from specific issues. In such conditions, the actual performance of the Blum experiment played a secondary role in the estrangement of the Radical party from the Popular Front.[56]

With this thesis, the full extent of the polarization of the literature on the Popular Front is revealed. From critiques of the economic policies of the Popular Front which implied that the fate of the experiment would have been the reverse of what it was, had a few mistakes such as the implementation of the forty-hour week been avoided (Sauvy: "It was the decrease in industrial production . . . that brought on the fall of the Blum government")[57], we have reached a point where the virtual irrelevance of the Popular Front's policies or policy failures to the progressive disunity of the coalition is being seriously advanced (Larmour: "Economic issues never became very important in the attacks on the Popular Front within the Radical party").[58] It is for this reason that we regard as problematic the easy leap from the study of the economical and financial failures of the Popular Front policies to an assumption of disillusionment leading to dissension and defection among the moderates in the coalition on this score.

Although the history of the Popular Front has been well studied and the economic problems thoroughly documented, much needs to be discovered about the nature of the coalition, its constituent elements, and the behavior of these elements over time before something resembling a complete picture of this critical segment of twentieth-century French history is available. In particular, there seem to be two interpretive dilemmas in the literature on the Popular Front that warrant study. First, was the Popular Front's failure a failure of economic strategy that led to a gradual disintegration of the coalition, or was the coalition divided to begin with? Second, if the coalition was divided, was it a division between Marxists and non-Marxists on questions of social and economic reform, and did this cause its difficulties, or was the cause something quite different, such as a new fear of communism on the part of the Radicals, as hypothesized by

Larmour? The next three chapters, which present the findings of a quantitative analysis of samples of the roll-call votes and electoral statements of the deputies of the 1936 Chamber, are devoted to the empirical investigation of these questions. The final chapter will then attempt to assimilate the understanding of the Popular Front that this data analysis provides into the broader perspective of the nature and history of the Third Republic itself.

Chapter Three

A Roll-Call Analysis of
the Blum Experiment

The chief motivation for the quantitative analysis of the electoral statements and roll-call votes of the French deputies during the Popular Front tenure of power is the existence of several alternative interpretations of the political fate of the Popular Front experiment, as we have indicated. Accordingly, it seems appropriate before we actually discuss the findings to indicate briefly in what manner an analysis of this data can be expected to contribute to the evaluation of these interpretations.

To begin with, since we have selected a random sample of ninety-three roll calls extending over the entire Popular Front period, we can investigate the degree of cohesion of the coalition as evidenced in its roll-call voting.[1] Did the Popular Front's unity decline with the gradual appearance of serious difficulties and failures in the economic sphere or was the coalition's cohesion level basically constant regardless of the effect of its policies? Conversely, was the parliamentary Right unified in opposition to the Popular Front or was there a time trend of increasing unity with the appearance of these setbacks? These questions can be readily answered by an examination of the trend lines of cohesion among the Popular Front and opposition deputies, which will be undertaken in the next section.

Investigation of the extent of Popular Front disunity is only part of the story, however. We must also determine whether any divisions on roll-call votes were indiscriminate with respect to issues or whether they only occurred on certain bills or issues. Policy-specific divisions within the Popular Front might indicate the preexistence of ideological divisions within the coalition rather than a disillusionment over policy failures in general or a culturally based fragmentation as the likely explanation of dissension within the Popular Front. This would particularly be the case if policy-specific divisions arose which concerned bills introduced into the Chamber to implement reforms mentioned in the Popular Front program, rather than over makeshift measures such as the 1936 devaluation bill (the "loi monétaire"), which was a response to the failure of these reforms. These points will be investigated in the remainder of this chapter.

The course of Popular Front divisions can be further explored by comparing their nature and extent during Blum's premiership with the situation after the leadership fell into Radical hands. Was there a decline in defections from the coalition's position with the change in leadership or perhaps a significant change in the nature of these defections, say from a general opposition to the government by some elements of the coalition to an opposition over specific issues only, either of which would indicate that the Socialist leadership of the Popular Front government, not the government's reform policies, was the prime source of dissension? On the other hand, a constant opposition to certain types of Popular Front policies over the entire era would refocus attention on a programmatic explanation of Popular Front disunity rather than on disillusionment over economic setbacks. These considerations will be examined in chapter 4, which presents an analysis of the roll-call voting after the fall of the first Blum government and the relationship of that voting to the voting in the Blum period.

Analysis of the roll calls in our sample should provide significant indications of the direction in which these matters will be resolved. There are, however, equally significant limitations on what the voting data can tell us. In large part this derives from the nature of roll-call data. Roll calls are often valuable for indicating the locus and strength of the divisions in a legislature but are somewhat less valuable as a source for the interpretation of these divisions. At best, roll calls are rather vague and complex stimuli that may evoke similar responses among legislators for a wide variety of different reasons.[2] Therefore the real test of the ideological-cleavage (of whatever form) versus disillusionment-over-policy-failure debate can only come from an examination of the electoral statements of the deputies. How much agreement was there among the deputies of the Popular Front, as evidenced in their electoral statements, concerning what policies should be pursued and what reforms instituted by a future coalition government? If there was disagreement, what was its nature and significance? Most important, can the roll-call vote divisions within the Popular Front be explained by ideological or policy disagreements expressed in the electoral statements, statements made *before* the Popular Front assumed power and ran into economic and financial difficulties and the possibility of disillusionment? Because of the inherent limitations of roll-call votes, the analysis presented in this and the next chapter will be most valuable for arriving at precise measurements of the voting divisions in the Chamber and, more particularly, in the Popular Front coalition that can be used for subsequent analysis and only secondarily for providing explanations of these divisions. This latter goal will be the objective of chapter 5, where we take these measures of the vote divisions in the Chamber and attempt to account for them by means of such dimensions of ideological disagreement as the analysis of the electoral statements may produce.

In broad outline, we propose to investigate these questions in the following manner. We shall rely to a large extent on principal-components (factor) analysis to decipher the dimensions of vote and ideological cleavages among legislators. The nature of principal-components analysis, as well as of the other statistical techniques employed in this study, is developed in appendix A. Our justification for the use of this technique is largely pragmatic: we believe that the analyses undertaken in this study have given meaningful results for the data and have only very occasionally found need for recourse to other forms of analysis such as cumulative scaling. In addition, we argue in the methodological appendix that the roll-call data, coded trichotomously in the manner indicated, may reasonably be considered as equal to the level of measurement assumed by parametric statistics. Of course, the question of whether to use interval-level statistics or techniques such as cumulative scaling that assume less of the data is basically one of trade-offs: scaling techniques such as Guttman scaling on the basis of Yule's Q's can involve a considerable loss of information or reduced potency of explanation, but parametric statistics can create artifacts by assuming more of the data than is actually justified.[3] To put it somewhat differently, if the argument that the trichotomously coded roll-call data can be considered to be interval in level of measurement seems specious to the reader, he must consider that to analyze roll calls by means of Q-scaling requires that they be dichotomous, in other words reduced to a nominal level of measurement. At certain points where the hypothesis of cumulative scalability becomes particularly relevant, we have in fact relied on Q-scaling. But in general we have taken the assumption of intervality and believe the results justify that decision; the reader must of course judge for himself.

The basic direction of the roll-call analysis that we undertake in this chapter is from the general to the more particular. First we shall present the results of a principal-components analysis of the whole Chamber on the Blum era roll calls, then we shall consider the findings of a principal-components analysis of the Popular Front coalition alone. In addition, we have singled out the Radical party for a separate principal-components analysis in view of its critical role in the Popular Front; the findings from this analysis will be given following the Popular Front analysis. The same order of presentation is also used for the analysis of the post-Blum roll calls in the next chapter. Finally, to relate the various principal components or factors produced for different groupings of roll calls and different groupings of deputies, we shall rely on correlation analysis.[4]

The utility of this procedure can be illustrated if we briefly discuss the results we expect from it. First, the principal-components analyses of the entire Chamber should bring to the fore the overall divisions of the Chamber, the most important of which we would expect to be that between the Popular Front and the opposition. In factor-analytic terms, this means that roll calls that show a fairly clean division between the Popular Front and its opposition, for example, should occupy proximate positions in factor space (that is, have similar loadings) even though their subject matters may differ substantially. When we move to the Popular Front or the Radical party, on the other hand, this fundamental division no longer exists, and the finer cleavages within these collectivities should become more apparent. Presumably, at this point the issue composition of roll calls that make up particular principal components will become more salient, and interpretation of these factors in terms of the issues or ideological stances they may represent will be possible. The purpose of correlation analysis is then to relate the particular to the general; that is, to examine the way in which particular issue-cleavages in the Popular Front or the Radical party relate to the overall divisions of the Chamber.

As we indicated, the vote dimensions derived from the roll-call analysis, while useful for the light they cast on the viability of the various hypotheses we have outlined, are likely to be more valuable as dependent variables to be explained from the electoral statements data. In chapter 5 we analyze the electoral statements, again with principal components, and use the various dimensions so produced to account for the theoretically significant vote dimensions by means of multiple regression (path) analysis. But first let us turn to the Blum roll calls and what they can tell us about the fate of the Popular Front in the Chamber of Deputies.

The Patterns of Voting Cohesion

Perhaps the best introduction to the roll-call data of the Blum period can be achieved by a consideration of the time trends in bloc and party cohesion that the roll calls provide. This choice of starting point is dictated both by the fact that roll-call analysis must by its very nature be concerned with questions of cohesion and division as well as by the substantive importance that the matter of party and bloc unity has for our understanding of the Popular Front. From the trend lines of bloc cohesion, we shall be able to assess (a) the relationship between the varying degrees of cohesion of the Popular Front and of the opposition, and (b) the changes in cohesion of these blocs over the course of the Blum experiment. The analysis of the party cohesion lines can then be utilized to indicate the party sources of the unity or dissension that we have discovered within each bloc and how this varies over time. This should give an overview, albeit limited, of the nature of the data and what they can reveal about the Chamber of Deputies under Blum, a topic which our subsequent analyses will explore more thoroughly.

    The first set of findings, the trend lines of cohesion for the Popular Front and opposition blocs, is given in figure 1. To simplify the presentation, we have chronologically grouped the sixty Blum roll calls into twelve sets of five roll calls each and calculated the average size, in percentages, of the majority vote within each bloc in each of these roll-call sets. Needless to say, the data-points on the trend line for the right-wing opposition always represent the percentage of deputies voting opposite to the way the majority of the Popular Front deputies voted, as indicated by the Popular Front trend line.

    The behavior of the trend lines is suggestive in both respects mentioned above. Apart from an initial degree of disunity on the part of both blocs, the pattern is one of high Popular Front cohesion and a considerably less impressive right-wing cohesion during the first half of the Blum experiment. There is one major exception to this, however. The fifth set of roll calls shows a slight dip in the Popular

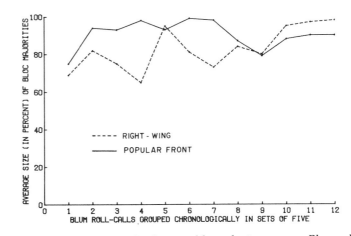

Figure 1.   Popular Front and right-wing bloc cohesion rates on Blum roll calls

Front cohesion level and a sharp rise in the opposition's cohesion level. Since four of these five roll calls concern the loi monétaire which legislated the September 1936 devaluation of the franc, it appears that negative feelings towards the devaluation was one of the very few topics about which the Right was able to unite in its opposition to the Blum government in 1936. Except on this occasion a basically solid Popular Front faced for much of its life a less united opposition with, presumably, significant defections to the Popular Front on the majority of roll calls that came up in the Chamber in this period.

This trend disappears towards the end of the Blum era, however, and is completely reversed in the last few roll-call sets. The last four data-points show a steady climb in the levels of cohesion in the opposition bloc to a point where the Right becomes virtually unanimously opposed to the Blum government. The Popular Front coalition, on the other hand, loses its previous very high level of cohesion around the beginning of 1937 (roll-call set 8) and seems to establish a fairly steady but lower cohesion rate of about 90 percent. This rate is still high, certainly high enough for the Popular Front to dominate the Chamber of Deputies, but it suggests that a noticeable minority of Popular Front deputies may have become permanently alienated from the coalition during the last six months of the Blum government, so alienated in fact that this minority was willing to resist the sanctions against overt breaks with the coalition and express its feelings in roll-call votes.

To establish the party sources of this behavior, we present the party

trend lines for the twelve parties of the legislature in figures 2A and
2B.[5] For simplicity's sake, we have further grouped the sixty Blum roll
calls into six sets of ten each in these diagrams. The patterns for the
Popular Front parties (figure 2A) are quite distinctive. The most
cohesive group of deputies were the Communists (PCF), who generally maintained a 100 percent support of the Blum government,
closely followed by the Socialists (SFIO), who only twice fell below 90
percent support of the Popular Front position. Next in order of
cohesiveness are two small left-wing parties, the Union socialiste et
républicaine (USR), a group composed largely of dissident Socialists,
and the Gauche indépendante (GI). Finally, there are the Radicals
who, as one might expect, are the least supportive of the coalition.

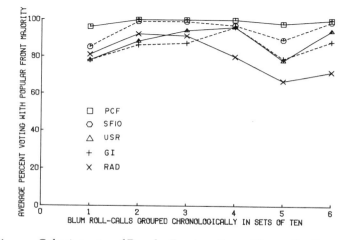

Figure 2A.   Cohesion rates of Popular Front parties on Blum roll calls

In general these trend lines tend to parallel each other at levels
reflecting the leftism of the parties they represent, but there is one
significant perturbation in the pattern. The Radical trend line for the
first three data-points is closely bunched with the USR and GI lines,
but after that it sharply drops off and averages for the remaining half
of the Blum government a cohesion rate of only about 70 percent. In
addition, whereas the trend lines for the SFIO, USR, and GI parties all
go up at the last data-point, when Blum was facing the onslaught of a
financial and currency crisis and the opposition of the Senate, the
Radicals failed to rally significantly to the government's cause. Here
we have a clear indication that some Radical opposition to a confrontation with the Senate did express itself not just privately but in

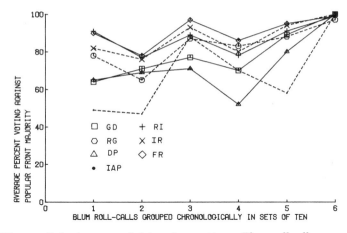

Figure 2B.   Cohesion rates of right-wing parties on Blum roll calls

open defection from the Popular Front in the Chamber of Deputies. Since this level of defection exists throughout the second half of the Blum roll calls, however, it is uncertain whether it indicates that a certain subset of Radicals were opposing the government on all issues or whether different Radicals were defecting on different issues. This can only be discovered by our principal-components analyses; we simply note here that enough dissidence does appear to have occurred in the roll-call votes of the Popular Front, and in particular in the Radicals' votes, to make them a worthwhile and intriguing object of investigation.

The trend lines of cohesion for the opposition parties (figure 2B) present a much less clear pattern. At certain points they do behave uniformly; thus at the time of the September devaluation of the franc (set 3) and again during the final roll calls one finds a high degree of right-wing unity in opposition to the government. But there are significant divergences elsewhere. The three most conservative parties, the Indépendants républicains (IR), the Républicains indépendants (RI), and the Fédération républicaine (FR), generally vary together at a high level of cohesion, but the four moderate right-wing parties tend to deviate from this pattern quite noticeably. This is particularly true of the Indépendants d'Action populaire (IAP) and the Démocrats populaires (DP), which are closest to the Popular Front in their voting behavior. It would be a digression to attempt to unravel these complex patterns of right-wing voting any further; what is important for our purposes is simply the fact that the lower cohesion of the opposition for most of the Blum experiment that our data reveals results from quite distinct patterns of voting behavior by different subsets of these parties. A solid bloc of right-wing parties united in their opposition to the Blum government clearly did not present itself in the Chamber of Deputies until very near the end of that government.

The basic pattern that figures 2A and 2B present may be summarized as: (1) for the first half of the Blum government, a solid Popular Front accompanied by sizeable defections from the moderate right-wing parties, with the one exception of the devaluation roll calls which caused both blocs to be cohesive and opposed to each other; (2) for the remainder of the Blum experiment, an increasingly united right-wing in opposition to a much less cohesive Popular Front, with defections to the opposition coming principally from the coalition's most moderate constituent part, the Radicals. If one were to speculate on the interrelationship of the roll calls that would yield such a pattern, the most likely conclusion would be that the majority of roll calls constitute just one Guttman scale representing a Left-Right continuum of roll calls and deputies. The reasoning that leads to this conclusion is as follows. Under the hypothesis that there is just one left-right continuum dominating the Chamber, one would expect some roll calls to divide the Popular Front and the opposition fairly cleanly (the devaluation roll calls), others to group the Popular Front and the most moderate elements of the opposition in one voting bloc (the early roll calls), still others to group the whole opposition and the most moderate of the Popular Front deputies (the later roll calls), but none to divide both the Popular Front and the opposition at the same time. This is the basic logic of Guttman or Q-scaling, and for the majority of data-points in the trend lines it seems to apply.

In conclusion, the trends of bloc and party cohesion in the roll-call votes of the Chamber of Deputies during the first Blum government suggest two significant findings. First, the cohesion of the Popular Front, and in particular the Radical party, decreased over time and that of the opposition increased, implying a loss of allegiance and stamina in the Popular Front and a corresponding increase in these properties in the opposition as the Blum experiment wore on; second, there may be a certain scalability or unidimensionality of a left-right sort in the majority of roll calls. In the next section we shall investigate this latter area, the general nature of the voting patterns in the Blum roll calls, including the hypothesis of unidimensionality, leaving to subsequent sections the question of the nature and evolution of support and defections from the Popular Front coalition.

The Principal Components of Voting in the Blum Period

In this chapter we will interpret the results of three different principal-components analyses of the Blum era roll calls. Given that the number of roll calls in these analyses can range up to sixty, the complexity of this design poses serious problems of data presentation. To aid the reader in understanding the findings, we have given brief descriptions of each roll call in appendix B. In the main body of the study, however, we shall limit our presentation of data almost entirely to scatterplots of the roll-call loadings and the deputy scores which accompany the text. This graphic approach should make the nature of the principal-component solutions more readily comprehensible, especially as it possesses the advantage of consistency with the methodological appendix, where principal-components analysis is introduced in geometric terms. The principal-components solutions of chapters 4 and 5 will also be presented in this manner.

When the votes of a sample of deputies on the sixty Blum era roll calls were subjected to principal-components analysis, four factors (principal components) with eigenvalues greater than 1.0 were produced.[6] Of these the fourth factor, which accounts for just 1.9 percent of the variance in the correlation matrix, will not be interpreted. The first three factors, which together account for a very high 84.7 percent of the variance, do prove to be amenable to justifiable interpretation, however, and will be retained.

The outstanding characteristic of the initial solution is unquestionably the distribution of variance among the three factors, for the first factor alone accounts for 76.5 percent of the total variance, leaving the second and third factors to account for just 5.1 percent and 3.1 percent of the variance respectively. It is rare in factor analysis for three-quarters of the total variance to be accounted for by all the significant factors together, much less by one. The intriguing question arises, is this first factor interpretable as it now stands; if so, what can it be?

The best way to approach this matter of interpretation is by first considering the kinds of dimensions that would be most useful for our purposes. Comparison of the axis locations that maximize these criteria with those produced by the initial solution should then give us some basis for tackling the delicate and uncertain matter of whether (and how) to rotate the factors to yield a different solution than this initial one.

To begin with, since we are dealing with roll calls in a legislature formed of two opposing blocs of parties, it would seem appropriate to look for an axis or factor that may be interpreted to represent "bloc loyalty." By so doing, we would be able to evaluate roll calls according to the extent to which they manifested pure divisions between the Popular Front and its opposition and to distinguish deputies according to their degree of solidarity with their blocs in the roll-call voting, thereby creating two very valuable measures. MacRae has found, however, that, generally speaking, there are no analytic methods of factor rotation that are likely to produce an axis justifying this interpretation.[7] One solution MacRae has used in his studies of the United States House of Representatives is to locate an axis directly through the roll-call vote for the speakership, since that vote apparently produces a pure Democratic-Republican split on a matter presumably devoid of ideological content. This solution will not work in our case, however, as the vote that gave Édouard Herriot the presidency of the Chamber did not evoke a pure Popular Front–opposition split (the vote was 377–150). But the principle of searching for one or more roll calls that cleanly divide the Popular Front and opposition deputies to locate a bloc-loyalty factor is still valid. The form of cross-tabulation that this involves is illustrated in table 3. In this ideal-typical relationship of vote and bloc affiliation, the entire Popular Front is located in the "For" column and the whole of the right wing in the "Against" column, producing a perfect opposition of the blocs. By performing this cross-tabulation on the roll calls of our sample and calculating on each a measure of association such as lambda (asymmetric), which approaches the value 1.0 as the cell entries approach the ideal configuration, we can assess the degree to which the actual roll calls are characterized by bloc loyalty. A axis located in factor space as close as possible to the roll calls having the highest lambda coefficients would presumably then be a summary measure of this property.

Table 3	Hypothetical Cross-Tabulation of Bloc Affiliation by Roll-Call Vote Showing a Perfect Relationship of Bloc-Loyalty		
Bloc Affiliation	For	Abstain	Against
Popular Front	100%	0%	0%
Right wing	0%	0%	100%

With the use of this criterion for determining bloc loyalty, the factors produced by the initial solution were scrutinized. When we did this, it turned out that we needed to look no further than the large first factor, for a careful comparison of the lambda coefficients for the Blum roll calls with their loadings on this factor revealed a very strong positive relationship: the higher a roll call's loading on the first factor, the higher its lambda value. To cite an example, roll call 8, which has loadings of -.968, -.002, and -.126, indicating that it is virtually entirely accounted for by the first factor, also reveals a relationship of near perfect bloc loyalty, as table 4 shows. To verify in a more precise way the generality and importance of this relationship, we calculated the correlation coefficient between the lambda coefficients and the loadings on the first factor. It turned out to be .945, affirming that the interpretation of this factor as a measure of the degree of bloc loyalty of the roll calls is indeed justified.

Table 4   Bloc Affiliation by Vote on Roll Call 8

Bloc Affiliation	For	Abstain	Against
Popular Front	99.4%	.3%	.3%
Right wing	.7%	.9%	98.4%
Lambda asymmetric = .973			

An examination of figure 3, which is a scatterplot of the deputies' scores from the first factor, stratified by party, adds further weight to this interpretation. In the figure not only are the Popular Front parties distinctly separated from the opposition parties by a large gap but the distribution of the deputy-points by party also follows very closely the patterns of party cohesion that were noted in figure 2. Thus the most solid supporters of the Popular Front position are shown by the first factor to be the Communists and the Socialists, then the USR and GI parties, and finally by the party least cohesive with the Popular Front, the Radicals. Among the right-wing parties, the conservative RI, IR, and FR parties reveal the most solid opposition, while the moderate IAP and DP parties occupy positions closest to the Popular Front, and the GD and RG parties are in between.[8]

On the basis of these sets of evidence, we conclude that the first unrotated factor can be taken to measure bloc loyalty. Since this factor accounts for over three-quarters of the voting behavior of the Chamber of Deputies, the implication of this finding is that the Chamber under the first Blum government was characterized to a very considerable extent by the opposition of two reasonably cohesive voting blocs, the Popular Front and the parties of the right-wing opposition. This fact, which can be observed in a crude way in the trend lines of bloc cohesion, has now been established and measured in a much more precise manner by the principal-components technique. Moreover this measurement of bloc loyalty has the valuable property of allowing us to relate it quantitatively both to other vote

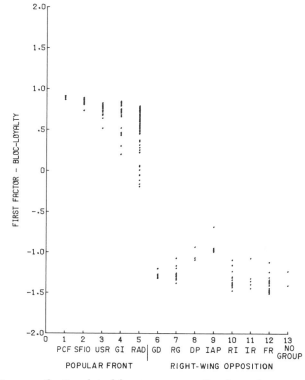

Figure 3.   Scatterplot of deputy scores on first factor by party, Blum roll
calls

factors that may be derived and, more important, to factors derived
from the electoral-statements data which we shall use as explanatory
variables. To the extent that the fate of the first Popular Front
government can be accounted for in terms of varying degrees of
loyalty on the part of its adherents, the fact that we can measure this
property will prove to be of paramount significance.

If a high loading on the first factor indicates a clean split between
the two blocs, how do we interpret roll calls that do not closely fit this
pattern? Consider the scatterplot of the Blum roll calls on the first and
second initial factors, given in figure 4. The majority of roll calls are
located in this figure close to the end of the bloc-loyalty axis. This of
course is a reflection of the fact that the bloc-loyalty factor accounts
for a very high proportion of the variance in the Blum roll calls.
Despite this clustering, however, the general shape of the display of
roll calls does resemble to some extent an arc with tails trailing off

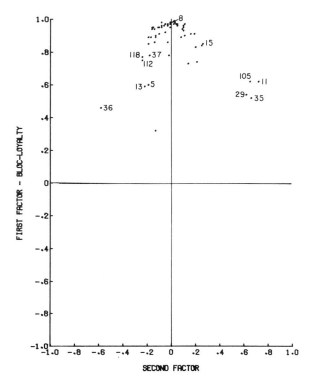

Figure 4.   Scatterplot of loadings on unrotated first and second factors, Blum roll calls

from the first axis in the direction of both ends of the second axis. To understand the nature of this "trailing off" process, let us examine roll calls 15 and 37, which occupy positions at the right and left bounds of the large cluster of roll calls around the bloc-loyalty axis. Cross-tabulation of their vote distributions with bloc affiliation yields the relationships shown in table 5. Clearly the cross-tabulations show that roll call 15 has defections principally from the opposition, while roll call 37 has defections mainly from the Popular Front. In fact this, too, proves to be a general relationship true of virtually all the roll calls: those to the right of the bloc-loyalty axis in figure 4 show the Popular Front to be solid, with defections coming from the right wing; those to the left of the bloc-loyalty axis reveal just the reverse.[9]

We still do not know very much about the nature of these defections, however. There is one aspect deriving from our earlier discussion of the patterns of bloc and party cohesion that especially

Table 5   Cross-Tabulations of Bloc Affiliations by Vote on Roll-Calls
15 and 17

	Roll Call 15		
Bloc Affiliation	For	Abstain	Against
Popular Front	99.4%	0.6%	0%
Right wing	15.8%	9.1%	75.1%
	Roll Call 37		
Popular Front	69.1%	9.5%	21.4%
Right wing	0%	1.0%	99.0%

warrants investigation. This is the question of whether the alignment of roll calls in an arc in figure 4 reflects a more systematic pattern in the defections from one bloc to the other than has thus far been revealed; in particular, do the roll calls scale? We tested for this property of cumulative scalability by constructing a matrix of Yule's Q's from sixty roll calls. This matrix need not be considered in detail here because the pattern it yields is surprisingly straightforward: of the sixty roll calls entered, only one (13) does not fit a single-scale pattern, using a high cutting-off point of .9. This does not mean that the unidimensionality this finding suggests is everywhere perfect, however. For instance, roll call 36 has the most right-wing parties voting with the Popular Front against the moderate opposition parties—clearly not a left-right split—yet largely by virtue of the fact that the Popular Front is united on this issue roll call 36 fails to have a scale relationship with only six of fifty-nine roll calls. But this type of roll call is exceedingly rare, and in general we appear to be dealing with a single voting continuum: as one moves to the right along the second axis from the zero point (the bloc-loyalty factor) in figure 4, the roll calls become progressively more "right-wing" in the sense that more and more of the moderate Right sides with the Popular Front, isolating an increasingly smaller hard core of opposition; whereas moving to the left along the second axis from zero reveals the opposite process, with the hard-core left wing being increasingly isolated.

This neat relationship seems strongly to indicate that the second factor should be interpreted as representing a left-right dimension—a very valuable finding if it holds up. The validity of this interpretation can be clarified by examining a scatterplot of the second and third factor loadings, presented in figure 5. The top half of the diagram, as it turns out, does fulfill these expectations. The cluster of roll calls at the positive end of the second axis (11, 29, 35, and 105) includes those roll calls with the most defections by opposition deputies to the government position, and in general the amount of right-wing defections decreases as one examines roll calls closer and closer to the third axis. Moreover roll calls 27 and 114, which very strongly exhibit pure bloc splits with minimal defections on either side, are located close to the juncture of the two axes. But beyond this point our expectations belie themselves, for the rest of the roll calls forms an arm or column that shoots off at right angles to this first column, so that the loadings on the second axis for these roll calls increase only slightly, even for roll calls with the most left-wing defections (roll calls 13, 104, 112, and 118). That they increase at all is the explanation of the relationship noted in the plot of the first and second factor loadings whereby roll calls located to the left of the bloc loyalty axis exhibit defections from the Popular Front. But it is easy to visualize that a rotation of the axes in figure 5 so that the second axis passes through the cluster formed by roll calls 11, 29, 35, 105 (and 36) and the third axis through the cluster formed by roll calls 13, 104, 112, and 118 would immediately eliminate this relationship and produce a second axis that aligned the roll calls solely according to the extent of their right-wing defections and a third axis that aligned the roll calls solely according to the extent of their left-wing defections (such a rotation is sketched in figure 5).

While it may seem odd at first that we do not have a single factor representing left-right ideology, this finding of two right-angled factor axes is in fact confirmation of the finding noted earlier that the traits of defections from the Popular Front and from the opposition do not often occur in the same roll call, in other words that the roll calls form one cumulative scale of a left-right sort. This point can be elucidated by drawing upon the methodological discussion of appendix A. For a left-right scale to exist, the Popular Front must be solid when the opposition is not, and vice versa. For instance, if there were a roll call in which the moderate Right decided to side with the Popular Front, one should not find defections within the Popular Front itself since its deputies should all have been further to the left than those moderate right-wing deputies who were defecting to the Popular Front position. What makes it possible for the Blum roll calls to scale is this very property of a lack of co-occurrence of left-wing and right-wing defections in any one roll call. In statistical terms, this means that the one type of defection is always constant (zero) when the other varies, in other words that the two types of defections are statistically independent. But as we point out in the methodological appendix, statistical independence is represented in vector geometry by the location of vectors or axes at right angles. Hence we find in a plot of the second and third factors that two distinct columns of roll calls at right angles to each other are produced—one column containing roll

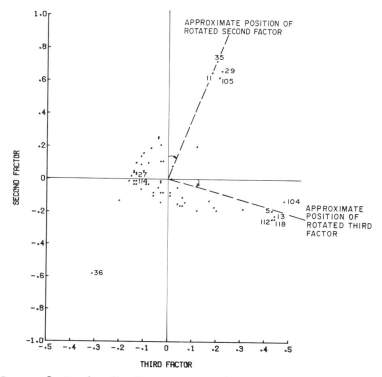

Figure 5.   Scatterplot of loadings on unrotated second and third factors,
Blum roll calls

calls with a solid Popular Front and opposition defections, the other
roll calls with a solid opposition and Popular Front defections.

A preferred solution would therefore be one which left the first axis
(bloc loyalty) where it is but rotated the second and third axes so that
each passed through the cluster of roll calls at the end of the nearest
column of roll calls in figure 5. This would leave the second and third
axes more or less orthogonal to each other but would have them both
oblique or correlated with the bloc-loyalty axis. We can see from
figure 4 that the first and second axes so rotated would have to be
oblique with respect to each other. But we can reason out this point as
well. Since the loadings on the second and third factors generally
show one bloc solid and the other less solid, they always have
something in common with the roll calls close to the bloc-loyalty
factor, which show both blocs solid. Thus there must be some
correlation between roll calls of these two types and, hence, of axes

that pass close by them. An oblique rotation of the initial factor loadings did in fact produce a solution that approximated very closely this preferred solution, yielding factors or dimensions that we shall refer to as: (1) bloc-loyalty, (2) Right-Wing Defection (RWD), and (3) Left-Wing Defection (LWD).

The nature of the rotated solution can perhaps be appreciated more fully through a consideration of the scores that are generated for the deputies from the second and third rotated factors. Since the RWD and LWD factors consist of roll calls that isolate an ever-diminishing number of the most right-wing or left-wing deputies respectively as their loadings increase on these factors, the two dimensions should align the opposition or the Popular Front deputies according to their general "right-ness" or "left-ness," whichever the case may be. Each of these factors should leave the deputies from the other bloc relatively undifferentiated, since it is only the voting behavior of the deputies of their own bloc that varies. Thus the RWD factor should align the deputies of the right wing in an ideological continuum of greater/lesser right-ness but should not greatly affect the Popular Front deputies, and conversely for the LWD factor.

We present in figure 6 the scatterplot of the deputy scores on the LWD and bloc-loyalty factors. In the figure, our expectation that the Popular Front would be spread out widely while the opposition deputies would be left comparatively undifferentiated is met. Also, the order of the parties is in line with what we know about their general ideological leftism. Thus at the extreme positive end of the LWD axis are located the Communist and Socialist parties. They are followed for the most part by the more moderate USR and GI parties. Finally, at the negative end of the axis, are the Radicals. It is interesting to note that those Radicals who deviated most in the direction of the opposition on the bloc-loyalty factor are also the deputies located furthest down on the negative end of the LWD axis. This plus the basic ordering of the parties suggests a strong correlation between the two factors, which our analysis of the roll-call loadings also led us to anticipate. The correlation coefficient between the two factors is in fact a strong -.686.

A very similar pattern was found to exist in the scatterplot (not presented) of the RWD and bloc-loyalty factors. Basically, that scatterplot shows the Popular Front deputies closely grouped together and the right-wing deputies distributed in accord with the general rightism of the parties to which they belong, as indicated by the time trends of levels of cohesion and by their positions on the bloc-loyalty axis. The solidly anti–Popular Front parties, the IR, RI, and FR, occupy the negative end of the RWD axis, while the parties showing the greatest proximity to the Popular Front on the bloc-loyalty axis, the IAP and DP parties, are located at the positive end of the RWD axis. As with the LWD axis, however, the RWD axis has a much greater capability of discriminating among the deputies and their parties than does bloc loyalty. Thus among the solid opponents of the Popular Front on the bloc-loyalty axis, the RWD axis is able to sharply separate the most right-wing party, the Fédération républicaine (FR), from the others at the negative end of the RWD axis. Unlike the previous situation, however, the correlation between the RWD and bloc-loyalty factors turns out to be a much more modest -.254.

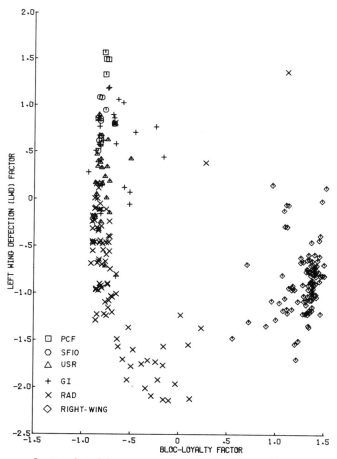

Figure 6.   Scatterplot of deputy scores on bloc-loyalty and left-wing defection dimensions, Blum roll calls

At this point we shall sum up the main findings of the principal-components analysis of the sixty roll calls of the first Blum government. First, it must be emphasized that the predominant characteristic of the legislative voting of this period is bloc solidarity. This is illustrated by the clustering of the roll calls high on the first factor, a factor which accounts for 76.5 percent of the variance and which we were able to identify as representing "bloc-loyalty" in the roll-call voting. By contrast the second and third dimensions explained only small amounts of variance, but they nonetheless proved to be interpretable, the former as aligning roll calls according to the extent of dissidence among the opposition deputies, the latter according to the extent of dissidence among the Popular Front deputies. We refer to these two factors as Right-Wing Dissidence, or RWD, and Left-Wing Dissidence, or LWD factors. Second, the general shape of the scatterplots presented—the location of almost all roll calls in an arc in figure 4 and in two columns meeting at right angles in figure 5—also proved to be highly significant. The first configuration implied scalability, or "unidimensionality," which was supported by a Q-scaling of the roll calls. The second was also consistent with this judgment, in that the right-angled alignment of the columns of roll calls proved to be a geometrical representation of the fact that roll calls that exhibited right-wing dissidence had solid Popular Front voting, and vice versa.

A very sensible pattern thus emerges from the principal-components analysis, consistent with the interpretation of the political spectrum of the Chamber of Deputies in this period as dominated by a single Left-Right continuum of deputies, grouped into two strong and cohesive blocs. While the roll calls do produce a unidimensional scaling pattern, however, the existence of three distinct factors does suggest the possibility of significant substantive differentiation among the roll calls that load highly on each. The question occurs, why it is that some roll calls, those that loaded highly on the LWD dimension, attracted the support or opposition of the extreme ends of the left wing only, while others, loading highly on bloc loyalty, divided the blocs so cleanly? The investigation of the substantive basis for this distinction will come to the fore in the remainder of this chapter, where the Popular Front coalition will be analyzed separately and consequently in more detail.

The Principal Components of Popular Front Voting

It was noted earlier that there was one exception to the randomness of the selection of the sample of roll calls: no roll calls with less than 7 percent dissidence were included. This is, of course, a consequence of the fact that what one actually examines in roll-call analysis is the dissidence that is present in the roll-call votes; hence, unanimous or near-unanimous roll calls are inappropriate for study by the means at our disposal. Although the sixty Blum roll calls that were selected for the sample all had 7 percent or more dissidence, however, it does not follow that they all elicited as much dissidence within the Popular Front coalition. Indeed, this would hardly be consonant with the substantial amount of bloc voting that we know occurred in the Popular Front. Therefore, the principal-components analysis of the Popular Front coalition that we shall undertake in this section will be based on those roll calls that were divisive enough, by the reasonably slack 7 percent criterion, to be amenable to the research techniques we have chosen to employ. As it turns out, only twenty-five roll-calls fit into this category.

In effect we are putting aside those roll calls that did not divide the Popular Front internally in order to concentrate on those that did. The elimination of most of the Blum roll calls has the advantage of allowing us to narrow our focus considerably in the quest for an understanding of the nature of the issues that produced divisions within the majority coalition.

The principal-components analysis of the twenty-five roll calls on which the Popular Front revealed 7 percent or more dissidence produced three principal components or factors that were retained as important enough, in terms of variance explained, to bear inter-pretation. The solution is quite good in that 63.8 percent of the variance is accounted for by the three factors, although this amount of explained variance is somewhat below the figure achieved in the last section. This is to be expected, however, since we have narrowed our focus and thereby increased the weight that minor amounts of unique variance will have. It is noteworthy that 40.5 percent or two-thirds of the explained variance is attributable to the first factor. In the previous analysis we found that 76.5 percent was accounted for by just one factor, but it represented the division between Popular Front and opposition that was by far the dominant element in the Chamber's voting patterns. Since this division is no longer present when we examine the Popular Front by itself, what could such a strong dimension be? Could it be related in any way to the bloc-loyalty factor? Much of the discussion in this section will center around these questions.

As no a priori notions concerning what kinds of dimensions we would like the final solution to contain suggested themselves, the first step we took was to rotate the three factors in the quest for a solution that would render the task of interpretation as simple as possible. As before, an oblique rotation was chosen for this purpose, for reasons that will become evident. The rotated factors shall be referred to, for brevity's sake, as PF1, PF2, and PF3, "PF" indicating that they derive from the principal-components analysis of the Popular Front by itself.

Given that we are dealing with a population of politicians that is usually identifiable in partisan and ideological terms, it will often hold true that we can tell as much or more about the nature of a factor by the distribution of deputies it produces than by the sometimes difficult to interpret roll calls that load highly on it. This proved to be particularly true of the second factor, PF2. Inspection of the deputy scores revealed that PF2 is entirely concerned with separating out a small, compact group of Socialists and Radicals from the rest of the Popular Front deputies. The reason for this became evident when we recognized that this small group of deputies happened to be the Blum cabinet. Concerning the subject matters of the roll calls that so separated the cabinet from its followers, it turns out that three involved inquiries into the election of particular deputies (roll calls 2, 10, and 119), and a fourth a minor change in the rules of the Chamber (roll call 36). In short, what is happening is that the nature of these roll calls was such that the Blum cabinet felt obliged to abstain, although in general the rest of the Popular Front adopted a bloc-cohesive stance in its voting. As this factor hardly seems of great theoretical importance, we may turn to the more interesting scatterplot of the scores for the Popular Front deputies on the PF1 and PF3 axes, which is presented in figure 7.

Figure 7 shows a display of deputy points which also has a distinctive and interpretable pattern. In the figure, the Communist and Socialist deputies and the bulk of the USR and GI parties are located close to the position of the Blum cabinet near the origin of the two axes. The variance that does appear in this scatterplot seems to be almost entirely attributable to the Radical deputies, who display two distinct types of deviation from the main body of the Popular Front. On the third factor, PF3, it is clear that virtually the entire Radical party, with the exception of those Radicals in the cabinet, are at variance with the Popular Front position. PF1, on the other hand, selects from these deviant Radicals a much smaller subgroup of Radical defectors. They are accompanied to a lesser extent by a handful of GI and USR deputies who do not (unlike the Radicals) defect on PF3. In short, we appear to have unveiled two different types of defections from the Popular Front during the Blum era, each

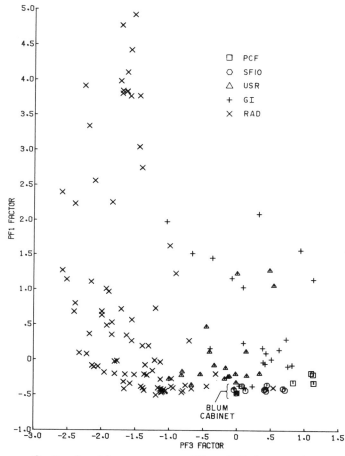

Figure 7.   Scatterplot of deputy scores on PF1 and PF3 factors, Blum roll
calls

of which involves principally the Radicals. That the Radicals are the
main defectors is, of course, consistent with the finding reported
earlier that the Radicals had the lowest cohesion with the Popular
Front of any of the five Popular Front parties. But now that we have
isolated the factors that measure the defections, we are in a position to
attempt to identify them in substantive terms.

The discussion of the substance of the roll calls of PF1 and PF3 that
produced these patterns of defection within the Popular Front will be
undertaken with the aid of figure 8, which plots the roll calls
themselves. Because of the difficulty of sketching an oblique solution,

we have displayed the roll calls according to their initial loadings, with the approximate positions of the oblique axes indicated with dotted lines. It is clear from the figure that the roll calls principally align themselves into two clusters. The larger of the two is located high on the first unrotated axis and accounts for the large proportion of variance (40.5 percent) attributed to that factor. The second cluster, consisting of just five roll calls, is positioned roughly halfway between the two initial axes. Since our criterion for rotation of axes is that they should as much as possible pass through clusters of roll calls so as to summarize their behavior, it is evident from the proximity of the two clusters that an oblique solution was preferable. The consequence of the rotated axes passing through these two clusters of roll calls is that the small subset of, mainly, Radicals who were shown in figure 7 to be deviant on PF1 defected on the roll calls of the larger cluster, while the defectors on PF3, which included virtually the whole of the Radical party, defected on only the handful of roll calls clustered around that axis.

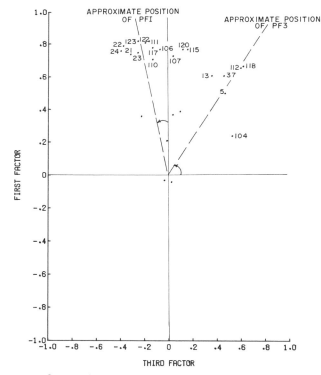

Figure 8.   Scatterplot of loadings on unrotated first and third Popular Front factors, Blum roll calls

We shall begin our attempt to decipher the meaning of these factors with the smaller of the two, PF3. In appendix B we have provided brief descriptions of the nature of each roll call. Inspection of the descriptions of the roll calls that load on PF3 quickly reveals that there seems to be no clear-cut pattern to their subject matters. Roll calls 118 and 112, which load most heavily on the factor and concern the defense of the rights of the landowner over those of the tenant farmer and the possible reduction in one type of social benefit, could quite plausibly be interpreted as indicating a desire on the part of the defectors to protect the propertied farmers and the middle-class "haves" over the farm and industrial working-class "have-nots" (the defectors were in favor of both measures). Indeed, if one stretched the point, so could roll calls 13 and 37, which involve protection for French farmers against agricultural imports and an attempt to limit speculative profits resulting from the September 1936 devaluation of the franc (the defectors were for the first and against the second measure). Roll call 5, involving an election inquiry in which a right-wing candidate's claim was favored over that of a Communist's, although devoid of issue content, is not inconsistent with this interpretation, either. Yet we are reluctant to force such an interpretation at this early point in the analysis; instead we merely wish to point out one highly significant fact about these roll calls, namely, that none involve key Popular Front issues or policy positions. In fact all but roll call 5 are amendments, one to reinsert a provision eliminated by the Senate (37), one to adopt a Senate amendment (13), one brought by a Popular Front deputy to correct a perceived flaw in a piece of government legislation (112), and only one (118) brought by the opposition and carried with the aid mainly of the Radicals. And all are concerned with relatively small points. Clearly the Popular Front deputies that defected on these issues, and they included the bulk of the Radical party, were confining their opposition to minor points only and sticking with the Marxist parties when it came to the more important roll calls.

This is in marked contrast to the voting behavior represented by PF1, which, it will be remembered, involved defections from a much smaller subgroup of those deputies than defected on PF3 but which is nevertheless more important in the sense that it loads many more roll calls highly. In deciphering the nature of this factor from the roll calls that load highly on it, we shall start with the left-most roll call in figure 8 and move to the right; such a course has a substantive logic to it that will become evident in our discussion. Proceeding in this manner, our initial observation is that the first four roll-calls (21, 22, 23, 24) all concern the loi monétaire, which was the bill authorizing the devaluation of September 1936, a turning point in any history of the Popular Front. When we add the two roll calls close by them (122 and 123), which were on the government's demand for pleins pouvoirs in the economic and financial sphere that brought its defeat in the Senate, we begin to sense the great significance of this dimension: it registers the two crucial junctures in the history of the Blum experiment when crises on the exchange markets caused by a lack of confidence by financial interests in the economy and government forced Blum to take measures—the devaluation and the request for emergency powers—that marked serious departures from Popular Front policy. The presence of both types of roll call on this factor indicates that those Radicals who were unwilling to support Blum in his demand for emergency powers, and who were a considerable part of the cause of his not challenging the Senate's defeat of his government, were by and large the *same* group of Radicals whose opposition to unplanned economic measures had emerged in the votes for the loi monétaire nine months previously.

Conceivably the defectors on the devaluation roll calls were a hard core of opposition that was increasingly joined by other Popular Front deputies as the Blum experiment wore on, culminating in the bill requesting pleins pouvoirs that brought the government's ultimate defeat. The close proximity of these roll calls in factor space makes this unlikely at least as far as they are concerned, however, and a check on the marginals of the roll calls confirms that there was no increment in the numbers of defectors. This finding brings into question the thesis of an increasing loss in confidence by the Radicals and other moderates in the Popular Front over the course of the Blum experiment. Or more precisely, our data indicate that the loss in confidence, to the extent that it shows itself in the roll-call votes, began as early as September 1936 with the devaluation of the franc and remained essentially the same in numbers at the end of the Blum experiment in June 1937, despite the decline in the intervening period of the government's fortunes.

Turning to the remaining roll calls that load on PF1, we note that, unlike the financial crisis roll calls that we have just discussed, these roll calls do involve issues of declared Popular Front policy. The first roll call, 111, is an objection to the failure to provide for an appeals procedure in illegal price-raising cases, evidently judged by some as too severe. The next roll-call, 110, also deals with the legislation against price-raising. This time it is an attempt to get farm producers exempted from the regulations. All the rest of the roll calls extending to 120 also deal with agriculture and include such matters as trying to get the same tariffs for farm products as industrial goods and trying to keep control over the setting of farm prices with the Chamber and not with the cabinet. As such they are not all that dissimilar from some of the PF3 roll calls; indeed one roll call, 117, concerns the compensation due a tenant farmer from the landowner for improvements made on the property, and thus is very close to roll call 118. But in general they do deal with more significant aspects of Popular Front legislation and perhaps because of this evoke less dissidence within the majority coalition.

If we consider for a moment the nature of these other PF1 roll calls in a more abstract sense, it is significant that they constitute a considerable proportion of the remaining roll calls in figure 8 and that they all took place during the later phases of the Blum period. This indicates that the Popular Front dissidence in the period after the devaluation, and consequently the decline in the Radicals' and the Popular Front's trend lines of cohesion that we noted in the latter half of the Blum period, can be attributed by and large to one group of defectors—those indicated by PF1. To be completely accurate, we should point out that the location of these roll calls between the devaluation and emergency powers roll calls at one extreme and the cluster of PF3 roll calls on the other does mean that the original core of PF1 defectors (those who defected on the financial measures) were being joined on these roll calls by some of the PF3 defectors (more Radicals) and that this increases with the proximity of the roll calls to the PF3 factor. Thus there is in this principal-components solution some evidence for an increased body of defectors after the devaluation. But the essential point is that these extra defectors returned to the fold in the crunch—the pleins pouvoirs bill that led to the government's defeat before the Senate—while the original defectors on the devaluation roll-calls, those who form the basis of the PF1 factor, did not.

To recapitulate, our interpretation is that this very important first factor, PF1, tends to represent the dissidence of a subset of those Popular Front deputies (mainly Radicals) who opposed the government on the PF3 roll calls, this subset being motivated by opposition to emergency government actions to ameliorate financial crises and secondarily by some aspects of government interventionism, particularly where it affected prices and tariffs in the agricultural domain. This opposition originated with the devaluation of September 1936 and continued with the same core-membership throughout the remainder of the Blum experiment, including in particular the pleins pouvoirs bill that was the immediate cause of the Blum government's demise. Moreover, it accounts to a large extent for the lower levels of cohesion in the Popular Front in the latter part of the Blum experiment that was noted earlier. The consequence of its significance is that a large part of our attempt to account for the fate of the Blum experiment by means of the electoral-statements data will be concentrated on the explanation in terms of beliefs or ideology of the voting behavior measured by this factor.

There is one final point about this solution that bears mentioning. We have more than once noted the fact that the defectors on PF1 were a subset of those deputies that had defected on PF3. This finding suggests a relationship between the two factors not just of correlation but also of scalability. In other words the PF3 roll calls seem to represent the "easy" items in that a large number of deputies defected on them, while the PF1 roll calls are the "hard" items on which only a subset of these PF3 defectors saw fit to defect. We found in the previous section that fifty-nine of the sixty roll calls do scale when taken over the entire Chamber of Deputies. Could this mean that PF1 and PF3 bear some relation to the bloc-loyalty and LWD factors?

This hypothesis can readily be tested by means of correlations. The correlation coefficient between LWD and PF3 turns out to be .942, indicating that the two factors are virtually identical. A comparison of figures 5 and 8, showing the same cluster of variables to be the principal ingredient in both factors, explains why this is the case. In addition, the correlation coefficient between bloc loyalty and PF1 is a lower but still substantial .807, also indicating considerable comparability. The implications of these correlations would appear to be as follows. First, there are two types of voting patterns that have emerged from the analysis of the whole Chamber and that bear on the Popular Front. One of these, measured by the LWD factor, represents numerically the most serious losses for the Popular Front; it is mirrored in the factoring of the Popular Front by PF3 and, as the analysis has attempted to show, involves relatively minor roll calls only. The other factor, bloc loyalty, represents roll calls with divisions that approximate clear-cut Popular Front–opposition confrontations. Those roll calls closest to this pattern have, of course, been eliminated from the analysis of the Popular Front because they show too little dissidence within that bloc, but there are others that show defections from a fairly small subset of deputies composed principally of Radicals. These defections are few enough in comparison to the size of the entire Chamber for these roll calls to load highly on bloc loyalty, yet great enough to appear in the factoring of the Popular Front. There they constitute the roll calls of PF1 and cause its fairly strong correlation with bloc loyalty. While these defections are numerically small, they are substantively very important. They indicate that those deputies who deserted the government in the end also deserted the government as early as September 1936 on the issue of the devaluation of the franc and on a number of roll calls, especially those concerning agriculture, that took place in between. Despite the sanctions against open dissidence from the Popular Front coalition, some opposition did occur in the roll-call votes on critical issues. It emerged early, appears to have involved more or less the same *core* of deputies, and remained fairly intact throughout the remaining nine months of the Blum experiment. As we have indicated, considerable attention will be devoted in this study to the better understanding of this internal opposition to the Popular Front government of Léon Blum.

The Radical Party

During the course of this discussion we have tended to emphasize the role of the Radical deputies in the interpretation of the dissidence within the Popular Front coalition. This is quite essential in the case of the PF3 factor since it basically consists of the majority of the Radical party in opposition to the majority of the rest of the Popular Front. Moreover, if we examine the roll calls that loaded highest on the PF1 factor we find that, of an average of 38.5 deputies who did not vote with the government, about three-fourths were Radicals. This should not be taken to mean, however, that the voting behavior of the dissident Radicals is perfectly mirrored in the interpretation of the PF1 factor. A significant discrepancy could easily have been produced in the following manner. According to the 7 percent cut-off point for dissidence, only roll calls with about twenty-seven dissident Popular Front deputies were deemed to have enough dissidence to justify inclusion in the principal-components analysis of the Popular Front. Yet, since the average number of Radicals defecting on the roll calls of PF1 was only 28.3, it is not hard to imagine that many roll calls could have evoked the opposition of a sizeable percentage of Radicals but few others, and consequently that these roll calls were excluded from the analysis of the Popular Front as having less than 7 percent dissidence. In oher words, there could be roll calls on which the Radicals had more than 7 percent dissidence but which have less than 7 percent dissidence over the whole Popular Front. The best way to explore this possibility is to examine the Radical party itself.

    When the thirty-four roll-calls on which the Radical party exhibited 7 percent or more dissidence were submitted to principal-components analysis, three factors explaining a total of 55.3 percent of the variance were retained as significantly large and rotated obliquely. A plot of the roll calls in the two-dimensional space defined by the first two factors is given in figure 9, which also indicates the initial and approximate rotated axis positions. The first point that comes to mind with respect to this figure is the large number of roll calls loading highly on the first axis, an axis which, in its initial form, accounts for 40.6 percent of the variance. In this discussion we shall concentrate on its interpretation.

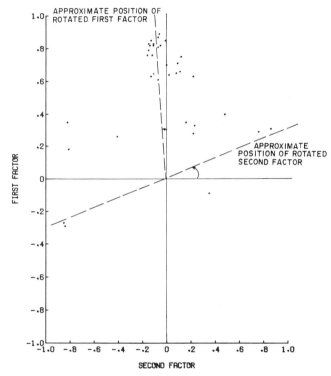

Figure 9.   Scatterplot of loadings on unrotated first and second Radical factors, Blum roll calls

A major indication of the interpretation of this first factor is provided by its near perfect correlation with PF1 of .982. This means that the same subset of Radicals who defected on the roll calls of PF1 also defected on the roll calls of this Radical factor. Why this is the case can be readily comprehended when one realizes that all thirteen of the roll calls that loaded highly on PF1 also load highly on this factor. But there is one important difference: the Radical factor also has high loadings from nine other roll calls that were not significantly present on PF1. In short, these two factors manifest the same voting patterns but the Radical factor loads 70 percent more roll calls on it.

As our introductory remarks imply, the explanation for this lies in a consideration of absolute numbers. Unlike the thirteen roll calls that also load on PF1, the roll calls unique to the Radical factor have an average dissidence of just 18.1 deputies, of whom 15.6 were Radicals. In other words, these roll calls generally had too little dissidence to be included in the principal-components analysis of the Popular Front but enough Radical party dissidence to be included in the principal-components analysis of the Radical party—hence, their presence on the first Radical factor with loadings generally lower than PF1 roll calls. This leads to an interesting inventory of the postdevaluation roll calls. Of the forty in this category, twenty-two load on the first Radical factor. A further seven load highly on the second Radical factor, three are right-wing defection roll calls (that is, these roll calls saw the Popular Front and most of the opposition aligned against the extreme right wing of the opposition), and two have dissidence that is not accounted for by the two Radical factors. This leaves just six roll calls that were not right-wing dissidence roll calls on which the Radical party was united in support of the cabinet. And since the defectors on the first Radical factor are likely to have defected along with most of the Radical party on the second Radical factor, as far as a small group of Radicals—an average of sixteen—is concerned, the issue specificity of PF1 (the fact that the dissidence it registers was centered on two main issues, emergency financial measures and some aspects of agricultural policy) more nearly approaches an opposition in principle that manifests itself on most of the postdevaluation roll calls in our sample. This helps to explain the persistently lower level of Radical cohesion in the post-devaluation period that the trend lines revealed.

We shall conclude this section by mentioning one implication of our findings of particular relevance for the rest of the study. It was noted in the principal-components analysis of the whole Chamber in the previous section that the bloc-loyalty and LWD factors ordered the parties of the Popular Front in essentially the same way, with the Communists at one extreme and the Radicals at the other. This fact helps to account for the substantial correlation between the two factors. But why two dimensions instead of one? The answer to this dilemma is now clearer. The LWD factor, mirrored in the separate analysis of the Popular Front by PF3, is formed of roll calls of a relatively minor nature that evoked widespread defections among the deputies of the Popular Front, in particular among the Radicals. Although the dissidents on the bloc-loyalty factor and its correlates, PF1 and the first Radical factor, also defected on LWD (PF3), the nature of the defections on the first set of factors is nonetheless different. For the roll calls that loaded on bloc-loyalty and PF1 were much more central to Popular Front policy and survival; and the fact that over the whole Chamber they tended to show near perfect splits between the Popular Front and the opposition only serves to highlight the critical nature of the defections that they register. In other words bloc-loyalty and PF1 really do measure loyalty to the Popular Front on roll calls that were essential to its success, and by removing the type of defection represented by LWD (PF3) we have been able to isolate this property for subsequent analysis and explanation.

Summary and Implications

This chapter has consisted of a rather large amount of statistical manipulation of a sample of sixty roll-call votes of the Chamber of Deputies under the first Blum government and a correspondingly sizeable outflow of descriptive information on the Chamber and its component parts. While none of this was, we believe, unnecessary for the pursuance of our investigation of the Popular Front in power, the key aspects of our findings with respect to that goal can in large measure be concisely outlined as follows.

First, the Chamber of Deputies of this period can be characterized in terms of its voting behavior as a single left-right continuum of deputies, sharply divided into two blocs, the Popular Front and the right-wing opposition. This finding of a single continuum accords with the classic interpretation of French party politics that has existed since the Revolution.

Second, the most important deviation from this pattern of bloc solidarity within the Popular Front came from a small number of moderates who defected on: (a) the devaluation roll-calls, (b) the emergency-powers roll calls that brought Blum's defeat in the Senate, and (c) a number of agricultural and price-control roll calls in the intervening period. That the financial crises that figure so large in our historical account of the Blum experiment did provoke internal opposition means that the hypothesis of dissension resulting from Popular Front policy failures in the financial and economic spheres receives some support in our data analysis. This conclusion must, however, be tempered by two other considerations that emerge from the analysis: (1) certain Popular Front *policies* (the agricultural and price-control roll calls) also triggered the opposition of this same group of dissenting deputies, plus some others, when they were being introduced in the Chamber; (2) apart from the small increase in defectors on the agricultural roll calls, this opposition remained quite constant and did not significantly swell in size with the downward slide of the Blum experience over time. Thus the impression left by the cohesion trend lines of a progressive disintegration of the Popular Front over the course of the Blum government is only partly correct; for although the dissidence did become more frequent towards the end, it remained (except for a small number of Radicals) issue-specific and of fairly steady membership. The crisis that led to the September 1936 devaluation may have been a trigger that set off this dissidence, but its constant composition together with its appearance on policy as well as "economic failure" roll calls leaves open the possibility that an ideological predisposition unfavorable to the Popular Front among certain of its moderate members, not just particular economic and financial difficulties, lay behind these defections.

In general, these findings illustrate both the advantages and limitations of roll-call analysis. We have discovered which deputies defected from the blocs and on what bills, but we cannot say with certainty why they defected. Did the PF1 defectors simply have some doubts over some aspects of Popular Front agricultural policy and a preference for the strict adherence by the government to the economic measures of the Popular Front program that precluded deviation towards unforeseen measures such as devaluation of the franc? Or was there a more fundamental ideological rift between them and the rest of the Popular Front that explains these defections? Our analysis of the electoral statements of the deputies will address itself to this issue, but first we shall turn to the logically prior question of whether these patterns of solidarity and defection were specific to the Blum government or whether they persisted throughout the entire Popular Front experiment.

Chapter Four

A Roll-Call Analysis of
the Post-Blum Experience

The Chamber under the Subsequent Popular Front Governments

The defeat of the first Blum government has almost universally been considered as marking the beginning of the end of the Popular Front. Several interesting questions occur with respect to this thesis. For instance, was there a noticeable change in the predominant pattern of bloc-voting with the accession to power of the Radical senator Camille Chautemps, or did the highly bloc-cohesive pattern that was discovered in the Blum roll calls persist throughout the remaining period of Popular Front rule? Did the deputies who defected on certain important financial and agricultural measures—in particular the emergency financial powers roll calls—return to the fold once Blum had been removed from power (which would suggest that the opposition was mainly to the Socialist premier and his leadership of the Popular Front), or did the basic pattern of dissidence continue despite the change in government? In short, can we determine if the Popular Front's divisions were based on disagreements over specific reform-policy issues, or was it a more diffuse disillusionment with the coalition's program and actions, or perhaps even a question of personality?

The period we are dealing with stretches from Blum's first defeat in June 1937 until December 9, 1938, the date when a confidence motion expressing support for the Daladier government saw the Socialists and Communists move into opposition to the Radicals, who survived in power with the support of the Right. Although the period is longer than Blum's year in office, the roll calls of our sample number only thirty-three, an indication of a marked decline in Popular Front legislating. Of the thirty-three, fourteen took place under Chautemps' first Popular Front cabinet (June 22, 1937–January 14, 1938), twelve under Chautemps' second cabinet (January 18, 1938–March 10, 1938), five under a very brief return to power of Blum (March 13, 1938–April 8, 1938), and just two under the much longer period of office of Daladier (from April 10, 1938). The reason for the small number of Daladier roll calls is that he was able to get the emergency powers Blum had again been denied by the Senate; Daladier was to govern in this fashion until 1940. The uneven distribution of roll calls makes it impossible to contemplate examining the roll calls of each government separately; instead we shall analyze them as a unit but take note of any differences in the principal component loadings that might be related to the government they were held under rather than to their subject matters.

We begin the analysis with an examination of the trend lines of party cohesion on the thirty-three roll-calls of the post-Blum period.[1] In figure 10, the roll calls have been grouped chronologically into sets of five, with the exception of the final eight roll-calls, which are grouped into sets of seven and one. The reason the last roll call is isolated is that it marked the final disintegration of the Popular Front, with the realignment of the moderate Left and Right into a governing majority and the slide of the Marxist parties into opposition. Apart from this roll call, however, there appear to be only minor changes in the cohesion patterns from the Blum period. Within the Popular Front (figure 10A) the most noticeable deviation is the decline in the Communists' rate of cohesion from a previous 99 percent to 88 percent. This is counterbalanced, however, by a sharp increase in the cohesiveness of the Union socialiste et républicaine (USR) party and a return of the Radicals' cohesion rates to the levels of the first half of the Blum government. These concurrent changes would seem to indicate that the Popular Front's orientation may have shifted to the Right with the removal of the Socialist Blum from the premiership. As for the Socialists and the Gauche indépendante (GI), their cohesion levels average about the same as before, but, as befits a coalition in some uncertainty after the fall of its first government, there is considerable crisscrossing of the trend lines generally.

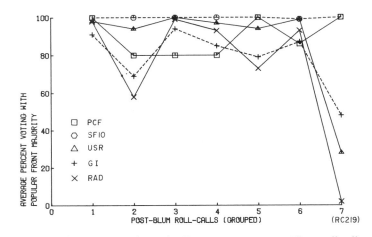

Figure 10A.   Cohesion rates of Popular Front parties on post-Blum roll calls, grouped chronologically

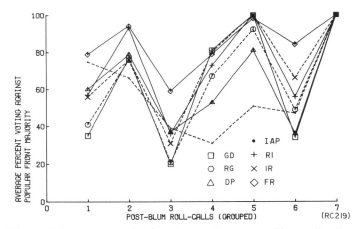

Figure 10B.   Cohesion rates of right-wing parties on post-Blum roll calls, grouped chronologically

If the patterns within the Popular Front have become more complex, those of the opposition (figure 10B) have simplified to some extent. The predominant trait is the almost perfect colinearity of the trend lines of the four parties that occupied a middle position, ideologically speaking, between the Indépendants d'Action populaire (IAP) and the Démocrats populaires (DP) parties on the one hand and the Fédération républicaine (FR) on the other. The Fédération républicaine, the most conservative party of the Right, seems to reflect the pattern of these four parties but at a considerably higher level of cohesion, as one would expect. As for the IAP and DP parties, which were the parties closest to the Popular Front in the Blum roll calls, their deviation from the rest of the Right has become even more pronounced in these roll calls.

What is the overall meaning of these cohesion patterns? Concerning the Popular Front, there is the possibility, mentioned above, that the removal of Blum from power had the effect of balancing, or was coincident with the balancing of, the coalition so that the interests of the more moderate elements were better accommodated and those of the extreme Left less so. This proposition is difficult to prove, but it receives indirect substantiation from the fact that, while the Popular Front's overall solidarity remains approximately the same, the cohesion of the opposition is significantly lower than during the Blum period; only the FR party approaches its former level of bloc-voting. Whether this interpretation can be sustained or not, it is clear from the cohesion levels of both blocs and from the lack of any clear-cut time trend of increasing Popular Front defections and increasing opposition cohesion in this set of roll calls that an interpretation of the Popular Front's decline as marked by an increasingly belligerent and united opposition attacking an increasingly incoherent and incohesive governing co-alition is not borne out by the data.

The Principal Components of Voting in the Post-Blum Period

One of the most pervasive themes of this chapter is the similarities between the Blum and post-Blum roll calls, a property of the findings that is particularly evident in the principal-component solutions of the whole Chamber. As we found for the Blum roll calls, the analysis of the thirty-three post-Blum roll calls produced four factors (principal components) with eigenvalues greater than 1.0, of which the first, which accounts for 65.7 percent of the variance, is by far the most important. The second, third, and fourth factors account for 10.6 percent, 6.5 percent, and 3.1 percent of the variance, respectively, to give a total explained variance of 86.0 percent, a very high figure by any standard.

We can best visualize the nature of this solution by considering a scatterplot of the loadings of the first two factors in figure 11. The most striking aspect of the scatterplot is the large number of roll calls that cluster high on the first axis to form the center of an arc that trails off in both directions. It immediately reminds one of the scatterplot of the unrotated loadings of the first two factors of the Blum roll-calls

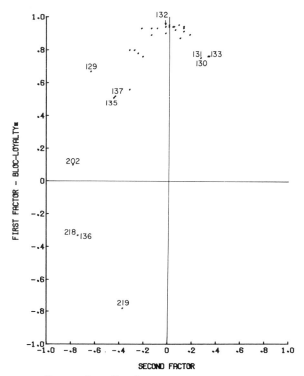

Figure 11.   Scatterplot of loadings on unrotated first and second factors, post-Blum roll calls

solution and suggests a similar interpretation. Inspection of cross-tabulations of bloc affiliation by vote for the thirty-three roll calls affirms that an interpretation of the first factor as "bloc loyalty" is indeed justified. To cite an example, roll call 132, which has loadings of .940, -.011, -.104, and -.165, has the relationship of bloc affiliation to vote, shown in table 6, of near-perfect bloc loyalty. The similarity of this factor with the previous bloc-loyalty factor becomes all the more striking in the plot of the deputy scores on it by party in figure 12. As did the first bloc-loyalty factor, this factor, which we shall label "bloc loyalty*," also orders the Popular Front parties—from the Socialists and Communists, the parties most cohesive with the coalition, to the more dissident Radical party.[2] Moreover, it strongly separates all the Popular Front parties from the opposition parties, which reveal a pattern of bloc loyalty very similar to their pattern for the Blum roll calls. We need have little hesitation in identifying this first dimension as bloc loyalty*.

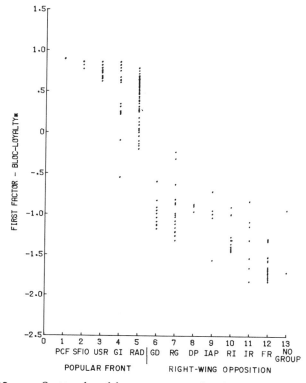

Figure 12.   Scatterplot of deputy scores on first factor by party, post-Blum
roll calls

As one moves from the first axis to an examination of the roll calls
in the clusters at either end of the arc in figure 11, the pattern of
deviations from bloc loyalty that we discovered in the Blum roll calls
repeats itself. Roll calls in the cluster at the right-hand end of the arc
(roll calls 130, 131, 133) show a solid opposition and sizeable
defections from the Popular Front while those in the cluster at the
left-hand end of the arc (roll calls 129, 135, and 137) reveal a cohesive
Popular Front and massive defections from the Right. To illustrate
these relationships, one example of each type (roll call 130 and roll call
137) is given in table 6.

The next stage in the analysis is the determination of whether the
voting splits in the roll calls, in particular those in the arc centering on
the bloc-loyalty* axis, display a cumulative or unidimensional scaling
relationship. To test for this property, a Q-matrix of the thirty-three
roll calls was computed. Again, because of the simplicity of the

Table 6   Bloc Affiliation by Vote, Roll Calls 132, 130, and 137

| | Roll Call 132: Bloc Loyalty | | |
Bloc Affiliation	Against	Abstain	For
Popular Front	.6%	1.1%	98.3%
Right wing	97.0%	.5%	2.5%
	Roll Call 130: Left-Wing Defections		
Popular Front	25.1%	1.1%	73.8%
Right wing	98.0%	1.0%	1.0%
	Roll Call 137: Right-Wing Defections		
Popular Front	0%	.3%	99.7%
Right wing	18.9%	8.2%	72.9%

matrix, we need cite here only the basic finding: with the exception of roll call 202 and possibly 131, all the roll-calls form one large Guttman scale. In the light of our findings in the previous chapter, the scalability of the post-Blum roll calls makes it very likely that they will align themselves in factor space in two columns located at right angles to each other, one representing right-wing defections and the other left-wing defections. Investigation of the loadings on the third and fourth factors suggested a relationship of this sort, and the oblique rotation that we applied to the initial solution produced a third factor clearly representing right-wing defections and a fourth representing left-wing defections. These factors will be referred to as RWD* and LWD*, respectively. To sum up, we find that the period after the first Blum government is characterized by two traits: (1) the arrangement of roll calls in a single Guttman scale and in two right-angled columns in factor space in accordance with the classic interpretation of politics as dominated by a left-right ideological dimension, and (2) the location of a large number of roll calls very high on the bloc-loyalty* axis, indicating that they tended to approximate clean Popular Front/right-wing splits. It will be remembered that both traits match those found in the Blum roll calls.

Thus far in the discussion, in an effort to emphasize the marked similarities between the solutions of the Blum and post-Blum roll calls, we have tended to pass over the small differences between them. For instance, in figure 11 there are a few roll calls that are located nowhere near the arc of roll calls at the top of the diagram. In addition, while we originally extracted four significant factors explaining 86.6 percent of the variance from the Blum roll calls and four factors explaining 86.0 percent of the variance from the post-Blum roll calls, only in the case of the post-Blum solution did we retain all four factors for interpretation. Since we matched the bloc-loyalty, LWD, and RWD factors of each solution, the one remaining post-Blum factor to be interpreted, the second, seems unique to these roll calls. The rotated loadings reveal that only three roll calls load highly on it, 136, 202, and 218. Interestingly, these roll calls constitute three of the four that do not fit into the arc of roll calls in figure 11. What is their interpretation? Examination of the vote by bloc affiliation cross-tabulations for each of these roll calls reveals one common element: in each case they separate out the Communists from the rest of the Chamber, including the Socialists. This voting pattern is not entirely new to this period, however. For if we reexamine the hitherto uninterpreted fourth factor of the Blum roll-calls solution, the roll call that loads best on it, 104, also fairly cleanly divides the Communists from the rest of the deputies. In other words, the second factor of the post-Blum roll calls also has a counterpart in the Blum roll calls, the difference being that it has grown to such importance as to merit inclusion in our interpretation. Indeed, by appearing as the second largest factor, explaining 10.6 percent of the variance in its unrotated form, it is probably largely responsible for the drop in the amount of variance (from 76.5 percent to 65.7 percent) attributable to bloc loyalty.

We have now disposed of the relationship implicit in the location of most of the thirty-three post-Blum roll calls in an arc centering on the bloc-loyalty* axis in figure 11 and of three of the four roll calls located some distance from this arc. But what of the remaining roll call, 219? Its position is easily explained; it is the roll call that marked the formal destruction of the Popular Front. With it, Communists and Socialists moved into opposition to the Radical Daladier's government, which survived with the support of the Right.

In sum, the main finding of this section is that, with the exception of the emergence of a sizeable amount of Communist dissidence, the dimensions of voting behavior in the post-Blum Chamber are strikingly similar to the situation under Blum. This high degree of continuity would seem to cast doubt on the hypothesis that certain moderate Popular Front deputies in the Blum period were moved to defection because of the Socialist leadership of the government. Yet the decrease in dissidence from the moderate wing of the coalition and the increase in Communist dissidence suggests that the more moderate leadership of the government may have appeased the moderates at the expense of the Communists. The crucial test of these alternate hypotheses can only come with an examination of the sources, issue-content, and issue-specificity of the roll calls that did produce defections within the Popular Front coalition in this period.

The Principal Components of Popular Front Voting

Of the thirty-three post-Blum roll calls, fifteen, or 45.5 percent, proved to have enough Popular Front dissidence by the 7 percent criterion to warrant analysis (as compared with 41.7 percent of the Blum roll calls). The principal-components solution of these fifteen roll calls produced three factors with eigenvalues greater than 1.0, explaining an impressive 78.7 percent of the variance. The three factors, which we shall call PF1*, PF2*, and PF3*, were rotated obliquely. Of the three factors, the second gives the readiest interpretation. Roll calls 136, 202, and 218, which have already been noted to be characterized by Communist opposition to the rest of the Chamber, load highly on this factor, as does 129, which also sees Communists opposed to the rest of the Popular Front (in this case the Communists receive some opposition support). Concerning the subject matter of the bills, two concern the government's desire for delays in debates involving foreign affairs, the area which saw the Communists most at odds with the Popular Front government policy, while the other two are more diverse; 202 was a motion to prevent deputies from holding positions in private corporations, and 136 was an effort to reduce the allowable rate of increase of rents on a certain type of housing below that which the government itself had proposed. We can couple this last measure with roll call 104 of the Blum period, which was a Communist attempt to sharply restrict the seller's rights in a situation where the purchaser of a small business had become financially unable to repay, to produce a common element of Communist defense of the financial interests of the less privileged. This, plus concern for the government's conduct of foreign affairs, seems to be the core of the Communists' opposition, and in no instance did it involve dissidence on a major aspect of government legislation.

Turning now to the first and third factors, PF1* and PF3*, we shall begin our interpretation with a consideration of a scatterplot of the deputy scores on these two dimensions, presented in figure 13. The nature of the scatterplot—PF1* separating out one group of dissidents composed principally of Radicals and PF3* separating out a larger group of Radicals—is strongly suggestive of the corresponding scatterplot for the Blum roll calls (figure 7) which had the same characteristics. It is evident from a comparison of the two scatterplots that PF3 and PF3*, which both divide the bulk of the Radical party from the rest of the Popular Front, must be closely related; the correlation coefficient is in fact -.819. But are the smaller groups of dissident Popular Front deputies that PF1 and PF1* separate from the rest of the coalition composed of the same individuals? The correlation coefficient between these two factors, which is -.827, substantiates this hypothesis as well. Thus the thesis that the critical defections of PF1 represented an opposition to the Socialist leadership of the Popular Front seems unlikely, for clearly these defectors persisted in their dissidence even after the first Blum government had been defeated. It would seem, therefore, that the critical factor must be issues, and the question becomes, what are the issues that caused the continuation of the defections represented by PF1 into the post-Blum period?

In accordance with the importance of strikes and labor unrest in this period, the predominant issue in the PF1* roll calls involved labor

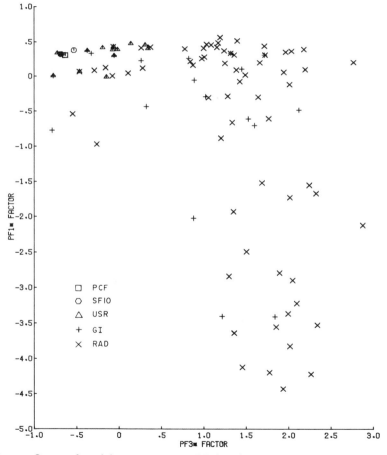

Figure 13.   Scatterplot of deputy scores on PF1* and PF3* factors, post-Blum roll calls

relations. Examination of the roll calls that load above .4 on PF1*
reveals that of the six in this category, four (roll calls 208, 209, 210,
and 211) concern the Popular Front legislation on conciliation and
arbitration. The Conciliation and Arbitration bill was unquestionably
the most important piece of legislation of the Chautemps period, a
reform measure that the premier himself, despite his moderate views,
quite sincerely supported. It constituted the main instrument of the
Popular Front attempt to realign the field of industrial relations to the
benefit of labor, and it can be fairly said that it made up the principal
line of Popular Front endeavors and was probably the most controversial and fiercely contested issue after Blum's defeat.

That the PF1 defectors by and large continued to defect in the
post-Blum period on these roll calls, which were held during the two
Chautemps governments, does indeed discredit the hypothesis that the
opposition during the Blum period was opposition to the Socialist
leadership of the coalition rather than to the specific issues involved.
This is not to say, however, that this opposition took place entirely
under Radical premiers in the post-Blum period, for the two remaining
roll calls that load highly on PF1* (214 and 216) did occur under
Blum's brief return to power in 1938. Moreover, both of these roll
calls concern an agreement with the Bank of France under which the
state's borrowing privileges were extended, a measure necessitated by
the worsening bankruptcy of the Treasury, and as such they have an
obvious similarity with the emergency financial-powers bill that
evoked opposition in the Blum period. Thus one can surmise that in
both periods a particular group of Popular Front deputies showed a
tendency not to trust Blum on financial measures associated with crisis
situations—devaluation, emergency powers, further loans from the
Bank of France—a finding consistent with our historical account of
the Popular Front. But the essential point is that this opposition did
not emerge solely when Blum was prime minister but extended to other
Popular Front governments on the rare occasions when they attempted
to introduce social reform legislation. Even under the Blum governments the opposition measured by the PF1 and PF1* factors was
concerned more with issues than with the leadership of the Popular
Front governments.

Turning now to the PF3* factor, we find that just two roll calls have
loadings above .4 on it. They do not concern the same subject matter
and, more significantly, they are both of a minor nature. As we noted,
they both tend to evoke the dissidence of most of the Radical party. In
these two important respects they resemble the Blum roll calls of PF3,
and we may apply the conclusion reached at that point: there were a

few roll calls of a minor nature in this legislature that did not challenge Popular Front policy seriously and on which the majority of Radicals and some other moderate deputies of the coalition were willing to defect from the government position; this opposition did not for the most part carry over to the more significant roll calls concerning Popular Front legislation and therefore need not overly concern us.

Having discovered, to the extent that we can, the nature of the Popular Front factors, the question of their relationship to the bloc loyalty* and LWD* factors naturally arises. Again correlations can help us with this point. The correlation between bloc loyalty* and PF1* is a sizeable .711, while LWD* correlates -.963 with PF3*. This pattern of correlations is identical with our findings for the Blum roll-calls factors and points to the same interpretation that we gave to the Blum roll-calls data; namely, that the defections on the critical roll calls of the first Popular Front dimension (PF1*) correspond in the overall principal-component solution to a lesser degree of bloc loyalty, while the more widespread defections on PF3* reflect the left-right alignment of the Popular Front parties on the LWD* factor. Finally, we pointed out that the second factor of the solution for the entire Chamber and the second factor of the Popular Front solution both represented dimensions along which the Communists deviated from the rest of the Chamber or from the Popular Front parties. This, too, is reflected in the correlation of the two factors, which yields a coefficient of .999.

In the discussion of the principal-component solution for the Blum roll calls, it was pointed out that the issue-specificity of the roll calls that load highly on PF1 tended to evaporate when we considered the Radical party alone. This was a consequence of the fact that a smaller subgroup of the PF1 defectors defected on a number of other roll calls as well, suggesting that for them it was an opposition in principle to the government, or its legislative efforts, rather than merely opposition to particular issues or policies. We factored the Radical party's dissident post-Blum roll calls to see if this tendency persisted. Examination of the rotated loadings of the twelve divisive roll calls for the Radical party showed, however, that the loadings on the first factor matched the pattern of the PF1* loadings very closely—just one new roll call, 125, is added. The close similarity of the two factors is confirmed by their intercorrelation, which is .964. This would seem to indicate that the small amount of virtually constant Radical opposition to the Blum government was indeed specific to that government rather than to issues and that the advent of the more moderate Chautemps governments appeased this opposition. Our conclusion, then, is that while the PF1 defectors continue to defect after Blum's departure, suggesting an issue-specific opposition, for a small part of the Radical party there was an opposition in principle to the Blum government that disappeared in response to the more moderate stance of the Chautemps governments.

In sum, the main finding of this section has been the remarkable continuity of the lines of division within the Popular Front between the Blum and post-Blum periods. This conclusion has implications of considerable importance. For instance, it seems quite clear, both from the issue-specificity of the PF1 and PF1* roll calls and from the fact that to a large extent they involved the same deputies under Chautemps as under Blum, that the critical defections under Blum were for the most part not the result of an opposition to Blum or the Socialist leadership of the Popular Front. Rather, in this legislature there were an important set of issues, the Popular Front reforms in the fields of agriculture and labor relations, to which a subset of Popular Front deputies, mainly Radicals, objected. To be sure, these deputies also objected to Blum's efforts in handling financial crises, but these vote defections, too, were issue-specific and most likely reflected a conservatism on financial matters that emerged especially when things went wrong rather than an all-pervasive anti-Socialist or anti-Blum reaction per se. To these defections must be added the tendency for most Radicals to defect on certain minor points of fairly diffuse subject matters. These defections, plus some Communist defections on minor issues and some Cabinet abstentions, constitute the sole systematic breaks in the dominant pattern of bloc solidarity in the voting behavior of the Popular Front deputies throughout the Popular Front era.

Yet an interpretation of "no change" between the two periods is not entirely justified. If we have evidence that the same lines of division emerged under Chautemps as under Blum, we also have evidence from the cohesion trend-lines in figure 10 that the Communists were less supportive, and the Radicals and the right-wing parties more supportive, of the later Popular Front governments. This finding is mirrored in the principal-components analysis, where the existence of the PF2* factor, which represents Communist dissidence, is an indication that the line the government was taking on some, at least, of the minor roll calls was less leftist than before. We also found that the indiscriminate opposition to Blum by a small group of Radicals disappears in the post-Blum roll calls and that even the first-factor opposition within the Radical party is issue-specific. In short, the evidence of a strong, united Popular Front from 1936 to 1938, coupled with the same kinds of defections and the same defectors after Blum as under Blum must be tempered with the knowledge that the ideological fulcrum of the coalition may well have shifted to the right under more moderate leadership in the post-Blum period.

Implications of the Roll-Call Analysis of the Popular Front Experiment

The major finding concerning the Popular Front that emerged from the analysis of the Blum roll calls was that there existed a hard core of internal opposition related to policy failures in the financial and economic spheres but that, because these defections also occurred on roll calls concerning the introduction of reforms that were not beyond the scope of the Popular Front program, a difference of political belief or ideology within the Popular Front could not be ruled out as the cause. The failure of this type of dissension to increase in numbers over time with the Popular Front's failures also suggested this conclusion.

The analysis of the post-Blum roll calls furthered the investigation of this point significantly. First, it revealed that the solidarity of the Popular Front continued to maintain itself throughout the post-Blum period; there is no evidence of a gradual disintegration as the "policy failure leading to disaffection and defection" thesis would imply. This might be explained by a rightward shift in the government's political orientation, which the cohesion trend lines tend to support, but on the other hand the same basic set of defectors seems to have emerged in these roll calls as well, and once again the basis for their defection was both financial difficulties and a specific policy area, the Popular Front labor legislation. This rules out the possibility that the dissidence of the Blum period was motivated solely by the fact of the Socialist leadership of the government. Moreover, it strongly supports the thesis that while policy failure in the economic and financial areas did lead to defection, this failure seems principally to have provoked defection among deputies already predisposed to defect for policy or ideological reasons. A milder stance by the post-Blum governments might have appeased many moderates, but it failed to bury the basic division between the PF1 defectors and the rest of the coalition that the Blum roll-call analysis uncovered.

Thus we come to a perplexing point concerning the basic question posed by this study. Is the Popular Front experiment a counter-example or simply a more unusual exemplification of the hypothesis of an ideological basis for the fragmentation of the Left in twentieth-century France? In the sense that it lasted two and one-half years with a remarkably high level of voting loyalty it was exceptional; yet through the screen of the public voting solidarity we have discovered unmistakable traces of the sort of internal issue divisions that have been posited as central to any explanation of the failures of the Left or of the regime's parliamentary system generally. But beyond this point roll-call analysis cannot help us, and it is for this very reason that we shall next investigate the political ideologies, or belief systems, of the deputies as portrayed in their electoral statements.

Chapter Five

Political Ideology and
Legislative Voting, 1936–1938

There are two characteristics of the analysis of the Popular Front governments presented in the two preceding chapters that are quite typical of the literature on legislative voting analysis. The first is the method of analysis. The exact combination of methodological choices is perhaps unique, but the general line of inquiry—principal-components analyses of a sample of roll-call votes—has been frequently followed in previous studies. The second characteristic is a property of the type of data used. There is a fundamental difficulty in legislative voting analysis of really knowing what a given roll call means to the legislators who voted on it—to know, in other words, what the legislators thought they were voting on. As a result we were obliged to follow the norm by being quite cautious and limited in our interpretations of the dimensions of voting. To discover more about this legislature, however, we shall now venture upon a mode of analysis that violates both of the characteristics just mentioned. This mode of analysis is new, in some senses less firmly based, but will allow, one hopes, much greater scope for reaching conclusions about the Popular Front. In this chapter we shall attempt: (1) to analyze in a quantitative fashion the statements of political belief and opinion (*professions de foi*), as published by the French government, of a sample of the victorious candidates in the 1936 general elections, and (2) to relate the results of this analysis to our findings from the roll-call votes. Because these aims are somewhat ambitious, we shall begin this introductory section with a discussion of the nature and limitations of this source of data.

The first and most important point in this regard is that, in comparison with the roll-call votes, the opinions data are "soft" in the extreme. About ninety categories of political opinion were developed and used in the analysis in a quite pragmatic fashion, and while we believe that the bulk of the "significant" political sentiments were covered, no claim to completeness in the strict sense of the term can be offered. Moreover, in the coding of these electoral statements we not uncommonly found instances where it was ambiguous as to exactly what the candidate in question meant or in which category the opinion should be placed. Judgments in these cases were intuitive and, needless to say, occasionally inaccurate. All that can be claimed with certainty is that ambiguity was never consciously resolved to improve the supposed or hoped-for results of the statistical analysis; as a consequence, error of this sort should have only weakened such relationships as do exist among the opinions variables or between them and the vote factors.

It should also be borne in mind that we have coded the electoral platforms of a sample of just under one-half (294) of the victorious candidates for the 1936 legislature. The principal elements of the reasoning behind the sampling design are these. The Communist and Socialist parties both published party platforms of considerable length; presumably because of this, it was often the case that the candidates of these parties discussed very little of national political interest in their personal statements. This required the insertion of a coding of the party platforms as a supplement for all the Communist deputies and for about three-fifths of the Socialist deputies. Since we have previously noted the high degree of bloc-voting among the deputies of these parties, it seemed clear that both their opinions and their voting behavior could be represented by a very small sample (one-sixth). On the other hand, the remaining three parties of the Popular Front coalition, in particular the Radicals, revealed the defections and deviations in voting behavior that concern this study the most; we therefore took a 100 percent sample of these deputies. Finally, a 50 percent sample of the opposition, stratified by party to enhance accuracy, was used. Appropriate case weights were then introduced to restore the correct party proportions.

We have tested the representativeness of this sample on the roll-call voting data by conducting the principal-components analyses reported in the previous two chapters on both the sample of deputies and the full legislature; the results always appeared to be essentially equivalent. This was confirmed by calculating correlations between factor scores for the sample of deputies derived from solutions based on the whole population and those derived from solutions of the sample. They, too, showed corresponding factors to be virtually identical. This was our warrant for reporting the results derived from the sample of deputies in the roll-call analyses; and it gives us reasonable hope that the opinions data coded for the sample are equally representative of all the deputies of the 1936 legislature.

Lastly, a note on the presentation of the data. We again have to deal with a large number of variables, most of which will have little significance to the reader. There is provided in appendix C a complete list with descriptions of each of the opinion variables, but in the main text we have tried to curtail detailed discussions of the nature and individual interrelationships of large numbers of separate opinion variables. Instead, the intention has been to discuss the nature of only those factors or dimensions that we regard as important and in this manner to make a large and complex amount of data digestible for the reader.

Given the limitations of this data base, what can we reasonably hope to gain from its analysis? First, we believe that the electoral statements, or professions de foi, can be said to constitute reliable sources of information on the deputies in the Popular Front legislature. Our impression in coding these statements is that, as a rule, the policies, actions, and political philosophies most ardently favored or detested by each deputy are quite frankly noted. This seems to follow from the fact that we are dealing with a multiparty system where the basic electoral concern is not so much to appeal to the greatest number of voters by moving to the political center as to precisely delineate one's own or one's party's particular creed and how it differs from all the others in the political arena. This is not to say that errors of omission—the ignoring or downplaying of certain points of view deemed unappealing to some sections of the electorate—are absent. Rather, we merely wish to point out that a cynicism that regards political platforms as entirely unreliable indicators of subsequent behavior is probably out of place here, a conclusion that the findings from the data analysis tend to bear out.

Another reason for the value of these electoral statements derives from the date of their preparation. Because they are essentially campaign platforms, representing the hopes and beliefs of the deputies before any of the events of 1936–38 or even the Popular Front victory were known, we are afforded an opportunity of further investigating perhaps the most central question of this study: did the crucial dissidence that we noted among a small subsection of moderate Popular Front deputies emerge as a consequence of the events of the Blum tenure of power, perhaps over disappointment with the results of the legislated reforms, or were the seeds sown much earlier in fundamental policy or ideological differences that were recorded even before the Popular Front came to office?[1] In addition, because these statements avoided the full extent of coalition discipline evident in the roll-call votes, we may also determine if this small group of critical vote-defectors was only the visible tip of a much larger mass of moderates who had strong reservations about the Popular Front and its program of reform, a finding that certainly would explain much about the fate of the Popular Front and the behavior of Léon Blum in particular that the roll-call analyses could not explain. For both of these hypotheses, the underlying issue is whether the bases for defeat—or at least severe problems—predated the Popular Front experiment itself. Our understanding of this exceptional period in French history will be considerably advanced if our analysis can meaningfully address itself to this issue.

Ideological Dimensions of the 1936 Chamber of Deputies

Following our usual procedure, we shall begin the examination of the deputies' political opinions with a principal-components analysis of the entire sample of deputies for all the opinions of sufficient dissidence that were coded. This procedure should enable us to reach conclusions concerning certain matters of considerable relevance for the overall understanding of the Popular Front's fate in the Chamber of Deputies. For instance, what is the degree of similarity between the patterning of the deputies that emerges from the analysis of the electoral statements and the patterning of the Chamber that the dimensions of roll-call voting produced? In particular, how close are the Radicals and the other moderates in ideology and policy prefer-ences to their Marxist allies in comparison to their ideological closeness to their right-wing opponents? Was the moderate wing of the Popular Front, or some part of it, maintaining a voting discipline that merely concealed this wing's basic ideological distance from the Socialists and Communists and its proximity to the right wing? We will explore these issues by first ascertaining the dimensions of political opinion and belief in the Chamber and then relating these dimensions to the dominant pattern of roll-call voting, the bloc-loyalty factors.

It is worth pointing out, before the actual results are presented, that in this analysis we shall have to deal with a serious matter of possible measurement artifact. In the previous section we noted that the lack of detailed individual electoral statements from all the Communist and many of the Socialist deputies necessitated the coding of the party platforms as supplements to the deputies' own expressed opinions. Since the party platforms were much lengthier than individual statements, however, one would expect a large number of opinions to have been mentioned only or principally in the platforms. It seems likely that opinion variables most closely approximating this situation would be minor items that appeared at all only because of the greater comprehensiveness of the party statements. It would not be justified, therefore, to attribute such opinions to the individual deputies for whom the party statements were used as supplements. The question is, can we in some manner control opinion variables to the extent that they reveal this property, or is our data analysis doomed to be contaminated by some degree of coding artifact of this sort?

With this possibility in mind, let us turn to the actual findings. The significant features of the principal-components solution of the opinion variables can be discovered by a consideration of the scatterplot of the first and third unrotated principal-component loadings given in figure 14.[2] The most striking characteristic in this figure is undoubtedly the large cluster of variables around the first axis that gives it a sizeable explained variance of 38.8 percent. The first explanation we must consider in accounting for this result is the sort of potential measurement artifact just mentioned. And, indeed, it turns out that a number of the opinions in this cluster are mentioned chiefly in the platforms of the two Marxist parties. But a more careful study of the cluster indicates that the variables generally lying to the right of the first axis are those most closely approximating a division between, on the one hand, those Communists and Socialists for whom party platforms were coded and, on the other, the rest of the deputies. If one examines those opinion variables to the left of this axis, one finds that they are more likely to unite the Communists, all the Socialists, and various members of the remainder of the Popular Front against the rest. The first axis itself seems to mark a middle position where the Communists and most or all of the Socialists are opposed to the rest of the deputies. It appears, then, that this factor is partially but not completely affected by the method of coding the opinions of the Marxist deputies that the nature of the data forced upon us.

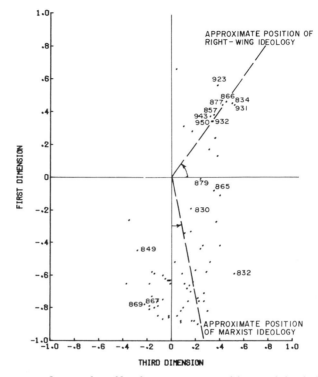

Figure 14.   Scatterplot of loadings on unrotated first and third ideology dimensions

The nature of this factor can be clarified by an inspection of the deputy scores produced by it, plotted against party. This is given in figure 15. Quite clearly the Communists and part of the Socialist party are sharply differentiated from the rest of the legislature. Moreover, the remainder of the Socialist party, those deputies for whom their party's platform was not added as a supplement, are on average the closest of all other groups to them, as one would expect. However, the other three Popular Front parties do not seem to be greatly differentiated from the parties of the Right. Does this mean that ideologically these parties were closer to the Right than to the Marxist parties, giving us an ideological picture of the legislature fundamentally different from that derived from the roll-call votes?[3] Or, is it simply an undesirable artifact of our method of coding the opinions of the Communist and Socialist deputies?

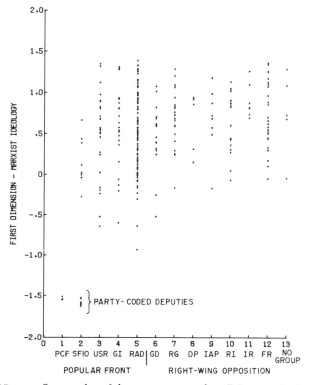

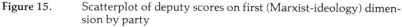

Figure 15.   Scatterplot of deputy scores on first (Marxist-ideology) dimension by party

There are two approaches to the resolution of this sticky question. The first, which will be dealt with in this section, consists in the continuation of our consideration of the scatterplot of the first and third factors in figure 14. The configuration of variable points in this scatterplot seems to be one of two main clusters—one at the negative end of the first axis, the other in the upper right-hand quadrant—linked by a thin string of variables. We have already remarked that, as one moves from left to right within the cluster around the first axis, one finds that the variables increasingly isolate the extreme Left. What happens if one continues along the configuration in this counter-clockwise direction? As it turns out, examination of the cross-tabulations of party affiliation by opinion variable shows that this trend of isolating the extreme Left persists but with the difference that, as one moves up the string of variables linking the two clusters, the extreme Left tends to be joined by parts of the Right on many of these opinions. This process continues until, by the time one has reached the variables in the cluster in the upper right-hand quadrant, the left-wing support has dropped off completely, leaving only support from right-wing elements in the legislature.

The nature of this patterning of variables in these two dimensions can be better appreciated if we next consider the scatterplot of the scores for the deputies on both factors. To do this optimally we must first decide upon a rotation of the two factors that is most meaningful for our purposes. Based on the line of reasoning presented in the methodological appendix (appendix A), our principal criterion is to try to place axes as nearly as possible through clusters of variables, where these exist. Since the two clusters that are distinguishable in this scatterplot do not appear to be located at right angles to each other, it was decided to employ an oblique rotational solution. Plotting the deputy scores that this solution yields gives the pattern presented in figure 16.

The scatterplot of deputy points in this figure reveals that the consequence of the semicircular patterning of variables in figure 14 is a semicircular patterning of deputies. In addition, because the first factor loads variables that generally separate the Marxist deputies from the rest, and the third factor loads variables that separate varying elements of the right wing from the rest, we find that the two factors together cleanly separate the Popular Front from the right wing. Thus the inclusion of the third factor, which we shall term the "right-wing ideology" dimension, produces the result that the first, or "Marxist ideology," dimension could not alone produce; namely, the clear differentiation in ideology between the Popular Front and the right wing that one would have expected to exist. Moreover, it is evident from the scatterplot that it is the right-wing-ideology dimension which contributes most to this result. But by principally registering opinions mentioned by sections of the right wing, this factor is basically free of the coding bias that seems to affect the Marxist-ideology factor. In other words, we can already foresee that the possibility of coding bias will not prohibit us from bringing opinions and opinion factors to bear on the roll-call voting divisions in the legislature in a substantively meaningful way. In the next section we shall reexamine the Marxist-ideology dimension and, by attempting to break up the large cluster of variables on it, come to grips with its partial contamination due to the coding problem. For the moment, however, let us concen-

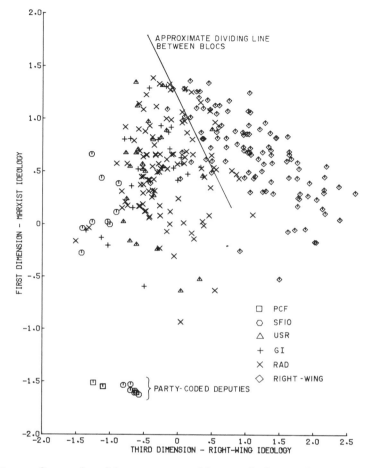

Figure 16.   Scatterplot of deputy scores on Marxist-ideology and right-wing-ideology rotated dimensions

trate our discussion on the highly discriminatory right-wing-ideology dimension.

If the large number of variables loading highly on the Marxist-ideology dimension represents opinions that various elements of the Popular Front coalition advocated and that the Right generally did not advocate, the smaller set of variables on the right-wing-ideology dimension constitutes the opposite: they are for the most part issues which right-wing deputies actually put forward in opposition to the ideas of the Left. The opinions loading highest on this factor[4] fall into three categories: economic, political, and, for want of a better term, "moral." The economic demands were fourfold. One, not surprisingly, was the desire to persist in the (disastrous) policy of strict budget-balancing and economizing on government expenditure known as deflation. In line with this was the second economic demand, which was that the existing parity of the franc be maintained. This reflected a distrust in the Anglo-American solution of devaluing the currency to improve one's competitive position and, like the call for continued deflation, represented for them a traditionalist, conservative response to an unprecedented economic calamity.[5] The third demand is more suggestive. It was a call for increased reliance on the National Economic Council, an organization of representatives from all fields of industry, commerce, and labor formed to advise the government on economic problems and legislation. This demand was frequently couched in terms strongly implicative of corporatism, and, where this was the case, it can be said to be the sole new idea that the Right put forward to alleviate the intense distress caused by the persistence of the Depression. Finally, there was a marked lack of agreement among the Right with the suggestion, supported in the Popular Front, that the Bank of France and other credit institutions be brought under greater control.

Under the rubric of "political" opinions are seven items, five of which were right-wing suggestions. These were: (1) a call for a stronger executive, for the restoration of the authority of the state, for the use of the executive's legal right to dissolve the Chamber and call new elections when the executive was thrown into a minority; (2) the advocacy of an end to partisan rivalry and strife; (3) sentiments of support for the formation of a "union républicaine" or "concentration républicaine," terms used at the time to denote majority coalitions of the Right with the aid of the Center; (4) the expression of opposition to the Popular Front; and (5) fear of the "Communist danger," the "threat of communism," or words to that effect. On a more negative note, there was a significant lack of support among the Right for the suggestions that the extreme right-wing paramilitary leagues be dissolved and that it was imperative to defend republican liberties and republican institutions against their enemies (that is, the extreme right wing). The reason these two opinions loaded negatively on this factor more strongly than on the Marxist-ideology factor is that they tended to elicit the support of most of the Popular Front, not just of the two Marxist parties. Finally, there are two items which may loosely be categorized as moral: an advocacy of moral regeneration or improvement of French society, and a demand for a concerted policy to protect the family (a concern related not only to traditional standards of social organization but also to a worrisome problem of a declining population in a time of international troubles).

Taken together, these opinions constitute a good empirical definition of what distinguished the Right from the Left in prewar France: traditionalism in economic and moral matters, and politically the desire for a stronger state led by the Right, united and in opposition to communism. Given this set of beliefs, it is evident why the (negative) Marxist-ideology factor should correlate both positively and highly with this factor ($r = +.513$), for it logically implies the negation of almost everything that the Marxist parties in particular were advocating. It is also interesting to note the tone of this set of right-wing beliefs. Although the beliefs have authoritarian implications, one cannot really conclude that the parliamentary Right was antirepublican. Even though these right-wingers did not believe in the danger to the republican regime from the extreme Right that had done so much to unite the Left, their professed desire was in the direction of a stronger but nonetheless democratically elected executive more than it was in dictatorship. Of course some right-wing deputies may have felt the need to disguise their authoritarian or fascist tendencies—a proposition that naturally cannot be tested—but the findings tend to support the general belief that right-wing antirepublicanism was, with few exceptions, not represented inside the Chamber of Deputies.

In the discussion of the nature of the display of variable points in figure 14, we remarked that there was an area that contained opinions on which the extreme Left and Right seemed to unite against the middle. The scatterplot of the deputy scores in figure 16 reflects this: note the way the opposition deputies' scores seem to become lower or closer to the position of the Communists and Socialists on the Marxist-ideology dimension as they become higher or more supportive of the items in the right-wing-ideology dimension. Let us briefly consider some variables that cause this to be the case. One (865), which concerns the demand to defend the franc, drew support from the Communists, who thought a devaluation would hurt the workers, as well as from elements of the Right who felt that it would hurt the middle classes. A second variable (879), a call for the reconciliation of all Frenchmen, is similar in that the extreme Right and extreme Left were united in support of it but for different reasons: the Communists believed the unifying principle should be communism, while the Right had something more traditional in mind. A third opinion variable (832), advocating electoral reform, especially proportional representation, drew support from both extremes because each saw itself as underrepresented in favor of the center. A final example (830), representing the advocacy of more honesty and less financial scandals in government, received support from both extremes as it generally was the more centrist parties and politicians who held power and hence were susceptible to corruption.

The effect of the joint operation of the Marxist-ideology and right-wing-ideology dimensions is to give us a pictorial representation of the 1936 legislature that is suggestive in two respects. First, as we noted, the presence of these "both-ends-against-the-middle" roll calls causes the configuration of the deputy-points in the figure to resemble to some extent a semicircle and would have done so even if the problem of coding the Marxist party platforms had not occurred. Second, although the Popular Front and right-wing blocs are clearly separated, as one would expect if the measures of political opinion are valid, the gap or hiatus between the blocs that the bloc-loyalty factors exhibited has disappeared. Two observations merit consideration in regard to these findings. First, the semicircular patterning of the legislators has precedents: a study of roll-call voting in some Third Republic legislatures of the late nineteenth century revealed a trend whereby a clear-cut left-right division among deputies just following an election came more and more to resemble a semicircle due to the increasing number of "both-ends-against-the-middle" roll calls.[6] It now seems quite possible that there is a natural tendency in French parliamentary life, and perhaps in all multiparty legislatures, for extremes to occasionally be in agreement against the (usually ruling) middle and hence to form a hemispherical political spectrum. Naturally such a situation cannot occur when the governing coalition is well to the left of center and incorporates even the extreme Left. Thus, we find in the roll-call voting in the 1936–38 period that the Popular Front defections, thanks to the PCF's voting discipline and the Radicals' lack of it, came mainly from the right wing of the coalition. But the tendency for extremes to unite on some matters could and did crop up in the less disciplined atmosphere of election promises and commitments, as figures 14 and 16 illustrate, suggesting that this tendency may be the norm.

The second point is that our observations concerning the properties of the principal-components solution can be used to make certain guesses about the overall goodness of fit of these two ideology dimensions with the important bloc-loyalty factors from the roll-call analysis. Thus from the unmistakable differentiation between the Popular Front deputies and the right-wing deputies in figure 16, we can postulate that the degree of correlation between the ideology dimensions and the bloc-loyalty factors may well be quite high.

Moreover, of the two ideology dimensions the right-wing ideology should be the dominant influence since it is the better discriminator of the two voting blocs. However, the semicircular patterning of the ideology deputy scores which was produced by variables exhibiting an accord between the extremes that is unique to the ideology data strongly suggests that the fit will be less than perfect. This is also indicated by the lack of a large hiatus between the blocs in figure 16 that was very much present in the bloc-loyalty deputy scores. The fit between the ideology dimensions and the bloc-loyalty factors can therefore be anticipated to be good but not perfect. Because of the importance of assessing the ability of ideological dimensions to account for significant vote dimensions such as bloc loyalty, we shall test these suppositions by means of path analysis.

We present in figure 17 two simple path models, one attempting to statistically account for the bloc-loyalty factor derived from the Blum roll calls, the other for the corresponding bloc-loyalty* factor from the post-Blum roll calls. In these models, numbers attached to curved, doubled-headed arrows are unanalyzed correlation coefficients between the factors so connected, while coefficients associated with straight, single-headed arrows are the standardized beta weights derived from ordinary multiple regression. The magnitudes of these coefficients are indicative of the net amount each predictor variable contributes to explaining the dependent variable, independent of the other predictor variable.

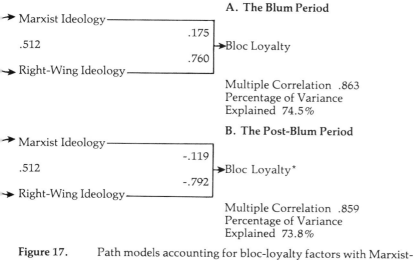

A. The Blum Period

→ Marxist Ideology

.512   .175

→ Right-Wing Ideology   .760

→Bloc Loyalty

Multiple Correlation .863
Percentage of Variance
Explained 74.5%

B. The Post-Blum Period

→ Marxist Ideology

.512   -.119

→ Right-Wing Ideology   -.792

→Bloc Loyalty*

Multiple Correlation .859
Percentage of Variance
Explained 73.8%

Figure 17.   Path models accounting for bloc-loyalty factors with Marxist-ideology and right-wing-ideology dimensions

The models make absolutely clear two fundamental points. First, the electoral statements, as we have coded and analyzed them, do bear a remarkably high degree of association with the important bloc-loyalty factors from the roll calls. While the opinions data naturally must contain a certain amount of idealizing and propaganda, it is evident that the ideological positions that deputies outlined for themselves are nonetheless strongly associated with their general left-right position as it emerged over the course of two years of legislative roll-call voting. From the finding of a semicircular patterning of the deputy-points and the lack of a hiatus between the blocs, we may assume that the 25 percent of variance that is unaccounted for in these path models is largely attributable to these unique properties of the two opinion factors. Second, the path models reveal that by a ratio of more than 4:1 the right-wing-ideology dimension, whose substantive content was just described, is the best predictor of the deputies' positions on the bloc-loyalty factors. This accords with our expectations and confirms our earlier argument that the necessity of coding the lengthy party platforms as supplements to the personal statements for most of the Socialist and all of the Communist deputies need not create an artificial correspondence between opinion and vote. Indeed, the degree of correlation of the right-wing-ideology dimension with the dependent variables would by itself render a percentage of explained variance of 72 and 73 percent on the Blum and post-Blum bloc-loyalty factors respectively, very close to the 74 to 75 percent that both ideology dimensions together account for. And, as we have emphasized, the right-wing-ideology dimension by its very nature would have existed as it is even if we had codable individual electoral statements from all the Marxist deputies.

In sum, the findings of this section point to two conclusions of significance for the analyses that follow. The first is that the electoral statements of the legislators clearly do delineate political positions that strongly predict subsequent legislative voting behavior and thereby allow us to comprehend that behavior more thoroughly than would otherwise be the case. In specific terms, we found that the bloc-loyalty factors discovered in the roll-call analysis can be accounted for statistically by agreement or lack of it with a set of items stressing social, economic, and political conservatism or traditionalism, coupled with antagonism to the "communist" Popular Front, and that it can be accounted for to a lesser extent by the related rejection or acceptance of a large number of proposals supported by the Marxist parties, the SFIO and PCF. Second, much more than with the roll-call votes, the political-opinion spectrum of the Chamber of

Deputies resembles a continuum rather than a dichotomy, suggesting that the view of French politics in this period in terms of two hostile coalitions or camps is probably overdrawn. One would have expected an ideological continuum in a normal French election in normal times; it is somewhat surprising that the extraordinary circumstances of the 1936 elections did not alter this expectation as much as is frequently assumed.

The implications of these findings are as evident as they are crucial. If the centermost part of the Popular Front coalition was as close or closer ideologically to the centermost part of the right wing as it was to the Marxist parties, and if ideological positions are readily translated into behavior in the Chamber of Deputies, the possibility of actual or threatened defections to the opposition on ideological or policy grounds must be judged considerable. And if this possibility manifested itself even before the Blum government took office, what chance would this government have when the going got tough?

Ideological Dimensions of the Popular Front

In the roll-call analysis in the preceding two chapters, we discovered that significant but nonetheless numerically fairly small defections from the Popular Front did occur on certain key roll calls. In this section we shall undertake the task of discovering the extent to which the ideological diversity within the Popular Front that we have unveiled is related to these vote defections and, equally important, what particular areas of political belief or ideology are involved.

The first step in this process is to come to terms with the Marxist-ideology dimension, a dimension which appeared to be problematic in that it represented to some extent the possibly artificial distinction between party-coded and individually coded deputies. One solution would simply be to exclude all items mentioned only in the party platforms on the grounds that they are probably minor items that appear at all only because of the greater length of the party platforms. Unfortunately, few items meet this criterion perfectly. What is really required is a statistical means of separating out items to the extent that they appear only in the party platforms. As it turns out, principal-components analysis provides a means of doing this. In roll-call analysis, it is not an uncommon experience for a factor that emerged in the analysis of the entire legislature to be broken down into finer components by analyzing the blocs or factions of that legislature separately. Since the Marxist-ideology dimension contains items supported by varying numbers of the Popular Front deputies, the possibility exists that a principal-components analysis of the Popular Front alone may result in a breakdown of this factor that would allow us to control the problem of coding bias.

The principal-components solution of the Popular Front deputies' opinions produced four sizeable factors accounting for a total of 57.6 percent of the variance. Of the four, the first and the fourth factors proved to be of special importance, for it so happens that both these factors correlate highly with the Marxist-ideology dimension, the coefficients being .930 and .782 respectively.[7] More importantly, however, these two Popular Front opinion factors together account for virtually all (98 percent) of the variance in the Marxist-ideology dimension. Quite clearly, then, the large first dimension produced by the analysis of the opinion variables over the entire sample of deputies, a dimension which we labeled Marxist-ideology and which we shied away from interpreting in the last section, can be broken down into two correlated components (r = .529). Moreover, because the variables loading highly on the Marxist-ideology dimension generally elicited only the support of elements of the Popular Front, the fact that we are confining our breakdown of this factor to the Popular Front does not handicap the analysis. What we need to know now is how these two component factors themselves divide the Popular Front and whether any substantive significance can be attached to it.

Consider the scatterplot of the deputies' scores on these two factors shown in figure 18. Despite the sizeable intercorrelation of the two factors (and their high correlations with Marxist-ideology) it is evident that the two factors do partition the Popular Front in different ways. The first factor, for instance, clearly separates those PCF and SFIO deputies who had their party's platforms coded as their own from the individually coded deputies, much in the manner of the scatterplot of the Marxist-ideology dimension by party (fig. 15). But the fourth axis produces a quite distinct pattern. Here all the Socialists, whether they had their party platforms coded or not, are located at roughly the same place, separated off with the Communists from the three other Popular Front parties in varying degrees. In other words, the distinction we made in the previous section to the effect that the cluster of variables on the Marxist-ideology axis included both variables reflecting the division between the party-coded deputies and the individually coded deputies and variables not so constituted is now transmuted into two distinct factors. It becomes important now to investigate these factors more closely to see if there is a substantive basis for this contrast.

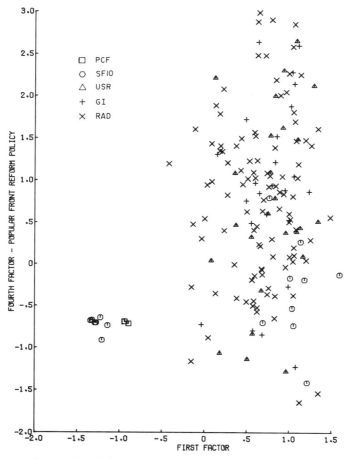

Figure 18.   Scatterplot of deputy scores on first and fourth rotated ideology dimensions, Popular Front deputies

In general, the twenty-one opinions that had loadings higher than .45 on the fourth factor can be said to come close to the heart of the Popular Front reform program—its concern for and measures to remedy the acute social and economic distress caused by the Depression, and its political stance of antifascism at home and peace through collective security abroad. Included in the first category are such welfare items as the need to fight unemployment, to shorten working hours and improve the pay and vacations of workers, to initiate a massive public works program, to defend the rights of unions and to increase social security allocations. Also included in this category are items dealing with financial inequities and abuses, such as the intention to tax the rich more, to end the policy of deflation and cuts in payments to various pensioned segments of society, to fight the "Wall of Money" (i.e., the power of big business and high finance), to regulate or nationalize the Bank of France, and to fight fiscal fraud. The political aspects also went to the heart of the Popular Front cause: the need to fight the fascist menace and to destroy the right-wing paramilitary leagues, to check the "merchants of death" by nationalizing the war industries, and externally to support the League of Nations, collective security and international joint disarmament. Finally, there is a diversity of other projects, such as support for the creation of a Wheat Board, the defense of the secular state and secular education, and increases in educational spending. These, then, are the opinion differences within the Popular Front that cannot be blamed on coding artifact: generally speaking, they elicit the support of all the Socialists and Communists, no matter how they were coded, but only to a lesser extent the USR, the GI, and the Radicals. The proximity of the subject matter of the variables on this factor to the very core of the Popular Front movement indicates a great deal of substantive importance for this component of the Marxist-ideology dimension, which we shall term the "Popular Front reform-policy" dimension. Its predictive importance will be tested presently.

What is more frequently left out in the statements of the individually coded Socialists as well as the three parties to their right are the twenty-two opinions loading highly (above .45) on the first factor. Given that the most reform-oriented of these four parties, the SFIO, was an urban working-class party, it is perhaps not surprising that eleven of the opinion variables on this factor deal with agriculture (only one agricultural variable, which concerned the creation of the Wheat Board, loaded on the fourth factor). These variables include such matters as increasing agricultural tariffs, rural construction, welfare to agricultural workers, protection against natural disasters, lowering transportation costs and agricultural taxes, protection of peasant property from the trusts, and the need to unionize agriculture. Thus what the PCF and SFIO party platforms covered but what tended to be ignored by those Popular Front deputies, including Socialists, who gave detailed individual statements are a number of agricultural proposals plus a smattering of other proposals and beliefs. Where there was good agreement among the individual Marxist deputies' platforms and those of their parties is on the more central issues of social and economic reform, an end to right-wing extremism, and the continued support of peace through the League of Nations.

Earlier we made an argument about the relative nonimportance of the coding bias that resulted from the necessity of coding party platforms for many Marxist deputies by pointing to the weak role played by the factor susceptible to this bias, the Marxist-ideology dimension, in accounting for the bloc-loyalty factors. To this we can now add the second and more conclusive argument for the validity of our findings. Not only does the Marxist-ideology dimension really have two components—a fact we suspected from the data in the last section— but it turns out that the most important component in substantive terms is *not* the one that mirrors the break between party-coded and individually coded deputies.

Our analysis to this point has revealed three opinion dimensions: (1) a right-wing-ideology dimension that impressively divides the right wing from the Popular Front; (2) a Popular Front reform-policy dimension which loads many of the key socioeconomic reforms and political beliefs of the movement and tends more or less to align the Popular Front parties in a left-right continuum with the Marxist parties at one extreme and mainly Radicals at the other; and (3) a "Marxist party-platform" dimension, containing agricultural reforms and other issues of less importance mentioned only in the Communist and Socialist party platforms for the most part and dividing the party-coded deputies from the rest for that reason. In the subsequent analysis we shall concentrate on the first two dimensions, which are both theoretically more meaningful and free of the possibility of coding bias inherent in the third dimension.

In the analysis of the roll-call votes, it will be remembered that the basic finding as far as the Popular Front coalition is concerned was that there were two types of defections: one involving almost all the Radical party plus some deputies from the small GI and USR parties but taking place only on a small set of fairly minor and heterogeneous roll calls (the PF3 and PF3* factors), and a second involving a smaller subset of these deputies but occurring on key roll calls in the area of economic and labor policy—especially the devaluation, the demand for full economic and financial powers, and in the post-Blum period the legislation on labor arbitration and conciliation (the PF1 and PF1* factors). If we were to consider just how the opinion dimensions should relate to these vote dimensions, our reasoning might run as follows. It is commonly argued of the Radicals in particular that they were leftist in political orientation, by which is meant that they were ardent defenders of the republican regime, its democratic and civil liberties, its secular character, and so on, but that they were quite conservative or "bourgeois" in their social and economic thinking.

Social reformism existed among them but so did such classical economic ideas as laissez-faire, and notions approaching those that we would associate with the welfare state were quite rare. Some have held this to be the fundamental problem of the Third Republic and of this unique exemplification of its will to survive, the Popular Front experiment; the roll-call analysis in the last two chapters has added some confirmation to this view. This leads us to suspect, first, that both the Popular Front reform-policy and right-wing-ideology dimensions would be moderately strong predictors of the PF3 factors that separate the Radicals from the rest of the Popular Front. In other words, we hypothesize that the set of fairly strong social and economic reform measures of Popular Front reform-policy would not have been supported by some of the Radicals at least, and that right-wing-ideology contains items which some moderates might have found persuasive. The role of these dimensions in explaining the PF3 dimensions should, however, be limited by the fact that the Popular Front reform-policy items are so close to the Popular Front program (which the Radical party had accepted) that there must have been some Radical support for them; the explanatory role of these dimensions should also be limited by the fact that many items in right-wing-ideology are very distant from Popular Front policy and, in some cases, are even inconsistent with the supposed political leftism of the Radicals. Thus the Radicals, the party most closely identified with the Third Republic, would not have been very likely to have agreed to any sizeable extent with a fundamental constitutional change such as the increasing of the executive's authority at the expense of the legislature; nor could they, believing themselves to be a party of the Left, easily urge the victory of a right-wing coalition and the defeat of a left-wing one. On this reasoning we therefore anticipate that the PF3 factors would be accounted for no more than moderately well by both the right-wing-ideology and Popular Front reform-policy dimensions.

The path models testing this hypothesis are presented in figure 19. These path models do indeed show that our reasoning was basically justified. When the two opinion dimensions were simultaneously entered into regression equations to account for the PF3 factors, they both proved to have fairly large path coefficients (beta weights), with the right-wing-ideology dimension being the somewhat stronger influence. Figure 19 also shows that the two opinion dimensions together explain a respectable amount of variance in the PF3 factors (about 50 percent), a further confirmation of our position that the kinds of belief and opinion coded from the electoral statements do have much to do with the subsequent voting behavior of the deputies who wrote them.

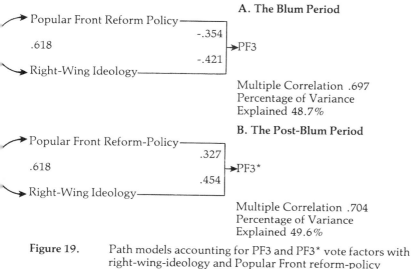

A. The Blum Period

Popular Front Reform Policy

−.354

.618   PF3

−.421

Right-Wing Ideology

Multiple Correlation .697
Percentage of Variance
Explained 48.7%

B. The Post-Blum Period

Popular Front Reform-Policy

.327

.618   PF3*

.454

Right-Wing Ideology

Multiple Correlation .704
Percentage of Variance
Explained 49.6%

Figure 19.   Path models accounting for PF3 and PF3* vote factors with right-wing-ideology and Popular Front reform-policy dimensions

Turning now to the explanation of the PF1 factors, our expectations are somewhat different. It seems reasonable to make the assumption that, ideologically, the right-wing-ideology dimension is noticeably more "right-wing" than the Popular Front reform-policy dimension. It is one thing to fail to mention in one's electoral statement certain key policy positions of one's coalition, but it is quite another thing to actually support counterproposals and beliefs put forward by members of the opposing bloc. Since the PF1 vote factors represent a more extreme opposition to the Popular Front in the sense of an opposition to key rather than peripheral roll calls—an opposition that tended to compromise the Popular Front coalition itself—we anticipate that the right-wing-ideology dimension would therefore be the dominant explanatory variable. This expectation was put to the test by means of path analysis, with results as presented in figure 20.

Quite clearly the path diagrams of figure 20 do conform to this expectation. In both cases right-wing-ideology substantially outweighs Popular Front reform-policy in its importance in accounting for the PF1 factors. Indeed, Popular Front reform policy is practically reduced to substantive insignificance in the post-Blum era, a finding that most likely reflects the increasing irrelevance of the Popular Front program as the exercise of power wore on. Our earlier observation that the PF1-type defections represented a fundamentally different and more serious split in the Popular Front than did the PF3-type defections is thus supported by their differing relationships with the ideology dimensions.

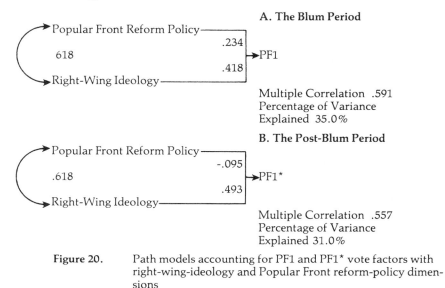

A. The Blum Period

Popular Front Reform Policy

618

Right-Wing Ideology

.234

.418

PF1

Multiple Correlation .591
Percentage of Variance
Explained 35.0%

B. The Post-Blum Period

Popular Front Reform Policy

.618

Right-Wing Ideology

-.095

.493

PF1*

Multiple Correlation .557
Percentage of Variance
Explained 31.0%

Figure 20. Path models accounting for PF1 and PF1* vote factors with right-wing-ideology and Popular Front reform-policy dimensions

The conclusions to be derived from this series of findings are twofold. First, since the basic nature of the PF3 factors is to separate out the Radicals in varying degrees from the rest of the Popular Front, we can conclude that the Radical party, or a large part of it, was significantly less likely to mention in their electoral statements the core reform ideas of the Popular Front program and that there was even substantial support for aspects of the counterideology of the right wing. This conclusion is hardly surprising; in fact, it could have been deduced from the scatterplots of the deputy scores on the two dimensions without resort to path analysis. But what the scatterplots could not have told us is that for the more critical PF1 defectors the mere nonmentioning of the Popular Front reform-policy items was far less important in comparison with the positive support for the items of the right-wing-ideology dimension. For some of the Radicals at least, those that caused the critical defections of PF1 and PF1*, their political beliefs and policy positions were very far indeed from the Popular Front program. This adds considerable substantiation to the view that the Radicals were to some extent misplaced in the Left in this era and supports the interpretation, which we set out to test, that the ideological distance from the Marxist parties of these moderates is significantly related to subsequent defection from the Popular Front in the Chamber of Deputies.

A Refinement of the Causal Analysis

The analysis of the Popular Front has thus far resulted in the development of two opinion dimensions, right-wing-ideology and Popular Front reform-policy, that place the Popular Front deputies in a broad ideological continuum at locations which, we have been able to show, are related to the subsequent voting behavior of the deputies as measured by the PF1 and PF3 vote factors. But the results are nonetheless incomplete. We have argued that the defectors singled out by the PF1 factors are of crucial importance for the decline of the Popular Front, and yet our path models accounted for only 31–35 percent of their variance, which leaves much unknown about this type of voting behavior and its ideological sources. Moreover, the tendency for the Radicals to have been more supportive of the right-wing-ideology items does not help us determine their ideological position with great precision; for instance, the advocacy of a right-wing governing coalition appears as an item in the right-wing-ideology factor—does this mean that a significant number of Radicals actually expressed this opinion?

At this point it is essential to make the investigation more specific. Larmour, it will be recalled, added specificity to the question of the role of the Radicals' ideology or belief system by presenting the following hypothesis. In his view, it was not the Popular Front social and economic reforms that the Radicals were resisting, especially since by the time of the "pause" in the spring of 1937, if not before, the Radicals felt that the government's posture in these areas was virtually identical with their own. Rather, he asserts, what led to the eventual defection of much of the Radical party was a fear of their "Communist bedfellows" that grew with the persistent demonstrations and labor unrest, the Communist advocacy of involvement in the Spanish Civil War, and the dwindling likelihood of a real danger to the Republic from the extreme Right in this period.

To test this hypothesis we must change our methodology somewhat. Up to this point we have looked for dimensions in the opinions data themselves, interpreted them, and then tested their correspondence with the vote dimensions. This has been valuable for assessing the relationship between the most important ideological cleavages and the most important voting cleavages that the separate analyses of the two types of data concerning the deputies revealed.

But now we must determine with much greater precision (1) the ideological dimensions that *best* account for the critical PF1 and PF1* vote defections and (2) whether these dimensions bear any close relationship to the general ideological dimensions of the Chamber and the Popular Front. The way this is done is as follows. The first step is to select just those opinions that seem most likely to explain the PF1 factors (PF1 and PF1*). However, many opinions may correlate with these vote dimensions due to their correlation with the PF3 vote factors, which, it will be remembered, correlate moderately well with the PF1 factors. We therefore took partial correlations of all opinion variables with the PF1 factors, controlling for the corresponding PF3 factors. Those variables with partial correlations above a certain cutting point were retained and submitted to principal-components analysis. The significant factors that were produced were then regressed on the corresponding PF1 factors.

Given Larmour's interpretation of the Radicals' role in the Popular Front's decline, what empirical results should we find? First of all, we know that there was a large set of reforms—those loading on the Popular Front reform-policy dimension—that were supported by the Socialists and the Communists but about which the other Popular Front parties were less enthusiastic. One would suppose that such a factor would again emerge in the analysis of the selected opinions. But Larmour argues that concern among the Radicals for the government's actions and intentions in the social and economic spheres was never a serious influence on their loyalty to the coalition and, if anything, became less important later on in the post-Blum period. The influence of this factor in explaining the PF1 vote factors should therefore be very limited in both periods. More important, we should expect to find a second factor, one which contains the expression of worry over the Communists. This factor should be somewhat independent of concern for the Popular Front reformist tendencies and, moreover, should be a very powerful predictor of PF1 and PF1*. This is the crux of this hypothesis. Let us now turn to the empirical results.

The Blum Period

Table 7 presents the obliquely rotated loadings of the first three factors from the principal-components analysis of those opinion variables that had partial correlations of .20 or greater with PF1.[8] Examination of those variables loading highly on the first factor reveals that they consist of three issue areas. The first is relief for the disadvantaged. It includes items dealing with the expressed need to

Table 7   Factors of Opinion Variables with Partial Correlations with PF1 above .2 (Controlling for PF3), Oblique Rotated Solution

Variable	Factor Pattern Matrix		
	First Factor: Popular Front Reform Policy*	Second Factor: Anti-Popular Front	Third Factor
835 Benefits to workers	-.747	.076	-.124
836 Public works program	-.867	-.215	-.073
851 Increase welfare	-.757	-.035	-.134
867 Control credit, Bank of France	-.808	-.132	-.113
868 Fight "Wall of Money"	-.701	-.103	-.104
869 End paramilitary leagues	-.846	-.203	-.078
870 Nationalize war industries	-.889	-.176	-.013
878 Fight fascism (domestic)	-.796	-.159	-.105
872 Make France militarily prepared	.526	.083	-.528
877 Against Popular Front	-.312	-.866	.072
866 Balance budget, cut spending	-.017	-.605	-.138
923 Against communism	-.035	-.835	.111
929 Laval decrees justified	-.166	-.630	.058
945 Less state intervention	.041	-.576	.419
865 Defend franc, no devaluation	-.344	.110	-.974

	Factor Correlation Matrix	
	First Factor	Second Factor
Second Factor	-.629	
Third Factor	-.374	.471

improve the pay and benefits of workers, to institute large public works programs, and to increase welfare. Second, there is a concern over private economic power, as indicated by the perceived need to assert more control over credit and the Bank of France, to fight the power and influence of big business and financial circles, and to nationalize the private manufacture of arms. The third type of issue is political, and concerns the threat from the antirepublican extreme Right. In this category are two items, advocacy of the dissolution of the right-wing paramilitary leagues and the need to fight fascism.

Finally, loading much less strongly is the expression of the need to keep France militarily prepared to defend itself—this last opinion with a coefficient opposite in sign to the rest to indicate nonsupport rather than support from the Marxist wing of the Popular Front. This factor seems remarkably similar to the Popular Front reform-policy dimension in terms of subject matter, a similarity borne out by the correlation between the two factors, which is .901. Because of this similarity we shall label the factor the Popular Front reform-policy* dimension. Thus the first anticipated result is found: a factor representing the nonsupport by moderates of many core issues of the Popular Front program—its opposition to the threat from the extreme Right, its antimilitarism, and its welfarist, somewhat anticapitalist reform posture—does emerge from among the opinion variables correlated with PF1. However, we already know that many of these opinions were not supported by a considerable portion of the non-Marxist Left (see fig. 18) and therefore that this factor can only have a moderate statistical relationship with PF1, which selects out a rather small group of defectors.

Much more germane to the specific import of the Larmour thesis is the second factor. Basically, there are five opinions that have sizeable loadings on this factor. One is the variable that formed part of the right-wing-ideology dimension: the urging of a policy of balanced budgets and strict economies on expenditures. The next two are new:[9] one is an expression of concern over the degree of "étatisme," or government intervention into the life of the country, and the other, even more conservative, is the expression of the view that the Laval decree-laws instituting the policy of salary and pension cuts that was part and parcel of the policy of deflation, were actually justified. Finally, there is, as we had speculated, the articulation of opposition to the Communist danger or, in a few cases, to the Popular Front *because it carried that danger.*[10]

This seems in all likelihood to be the factor that represents the sort of political opposition to the whole idea of a Popular Front including both Socialists and Communists that, in Larmour's view, was the real motivation for Radical defection. The presence of this factor demonstrates that there was undoubtedly in the Popular Front a group of deputies who did not accept the most fundamental premises of the Popular Front experiment—that the whole system of strictly balanced budgets, deflation, and laissez-faire was wrong and that only a coalition of the entire Left could save France and the Republic. Moreover, while this factor is correlated with the Popular Front reform-policy* dimension (r = .629), it is nonetheless a separate dimension with a considerable degree of independence from the mere nonadvocacy of the economic, social, and political sentiments of the Popular Front that were included in Popular Front reform-policy*. Thus, while the Radicals were generally considered left-wing and seemed to like to consider themselves so, there was clearly a section of their party that rejected not just specific extreme measures of the Marxist parties, such as control or nationalization of the Bank of France, but instead the very idea of coalition with Communists to alter the traditional ways of dealing or not dealing with the nation's problems. We shall refer to this factor as the "anti–Popular Front" dimension.

The presence of the anti-communism, anti-Popular Front, and balanced-budget items in the anti–Popular Front factor suggests that it may be regarded as a refinement of the right-wing-ideology dimension in much the same manner as the first factor, Popular Front reform-policy*, proved to be a refinement of Popular Front reform-policy. Supportive of this interpretation is the moderately strong correlation of -.588 between the anti-Popular Front and right-wing-ideology dimensions. Thus the change in research strategy that we adopted in this section has not radically altered the types of ideological dimensions that emerge from the Popular Front deputies' electoral statements. Instead, the ideological dimensions that characterize the Popular Front in general are to a large extent the same as the ideological dimensions that seem most likely to account for those voting defections that we interpreted as being critical to the Popular Front's unity (the PF1 factor). Essentially, then, what we have achieved with this change in strategy is a more precise determination of what it is about the right-wing-ideology and Popular Front reform-policy dimensions that appears to have led to subsequent vote defections of importance as measured by PF1. How significant this increase in specification is will be indicated by the degree to which our ability to statistically account for PF1 is improved by using these new opinion factors as independent variables.

An examination of the scatterplot of the deputies' scores on the anti–Popular Front and Popular Front reform-policy* dimensions makes clear the manner in which they are interrelated (fig. 21). In the scatterplot, the Communists and the Socialists are located at the negative end of the first or Popular Front reform-policy* axis, indicating basic support for the opinions on that factor, while the three other Popular Front parties are located at the positive end of the axis. However, of this group of essentially non-Marxist deputies there is a small subset of deputies that is also located at the positive end of the second or anti–Popular Front axis, indicating support for the opinions that load on it. Although some of the members of the USR and GI parties can be found there, the bulk of the deputies are Radicals. We already have good reason to believe that Popular Front reform-policy* by itself will have a moderate degree of relationship with PF1: like PF3 it separates most of the non-Marxist Left from the Marxists, and like PF3 it should correlate well with PF1. In addition, it is closely related to the Popular Front reform-policy dimension which did relate moderately well with PF1. But the really interesting question is, to what extent is the small group of deputies extreme on the

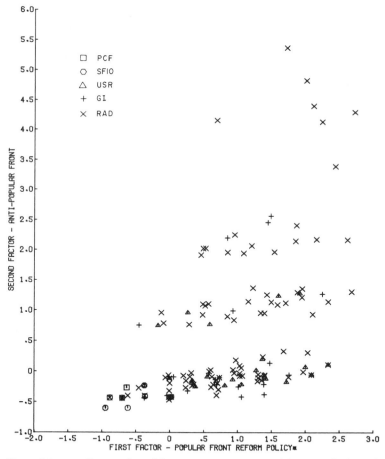

Figure 21.   Scatterplot of deputy scores on rotated factors of selected opinion variables, Popular Front deputies

anti–Popular Front dimension the same as the small group of PF1 defectors? In other words, how well does the anti–Popular Front dimension account for PF1? To test this proposition we regressed PF1 on the anti–Popular Front and Popular Front reform-policy* dimensions. The findings from this regression are presented in Figure 22.

The Larmour hypothesis essentially depends on there being a strong influence on PF1 that goes beyond the mere opposition to or nonmentioning of a number of the more extreme Popular Front proposals (the Popular Front reform-policy* dimension); it depends, in other words, on the anti–Popular Front dimension entering the regression in a substantial way. The path model of figure 22 confirms this expectation to a very considerable degree. Quite clearly, the more fundamental opposition to the Popular Front idea that is represented by the anti–Popular Front dimension is a very strong predictor of the key voting defections that have concerned us in the Blum period, considerably more so than the Popular Front reform-policy* dimension. This is, of course, a reflection of the greater power right-wing ideology had over Popular Front reform-policy in accounting for PF1, which was noted in the last section. What we have achieved in pursuing this matter, however, is the specification of what it is about these factors that led to their respective relationships with the PF1 vote factor. This conclusion is supported by the larger raw correlations that the new factors—Popular Front reform-policy* and anti-Popular Front—have with PF1[11] and the considerably larger amount of the variance of PF1—51.6 percent as compared with 35 percent—that they jointly account for. Thus the development of the anti–Popular Front and Popular Front reform-policy* dimensions has not only clarified the interpretation by drastically reducing the number of variables loading on the original ideology dimensions but it has also greatly improved our ability to account for the critically important PF1 vote defections.

In conclusion, the change in research design that we introduced in this section has significantly advanced our understanding of the

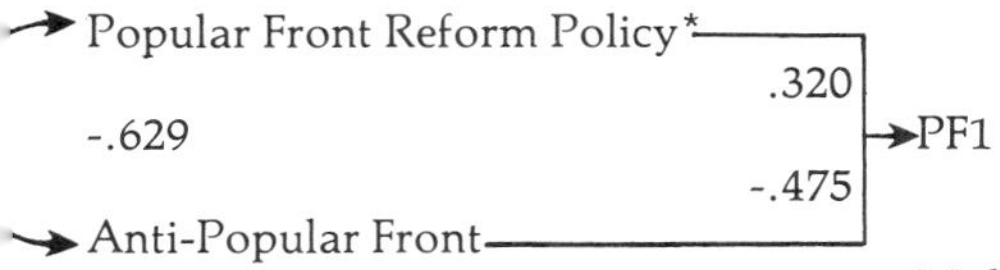

Popular Front Reform Policy*
-.629   .320
                                             PF1
Anti-Popular Front   -.475

Multiple Correlation .719
Percentage of Variance
Explained 51.6%

Figure 22.   Path model accounting for PF1 vote factor with Popular Front reform-policy* and anti-Popular Front ideology dimensions

Popular Front under Blum. Previously we found that there are two general ideological dimensions that characterize the Popular Front and that both can be used to account for subsequent vote defections in the Chamber. One of these dimensions, Popular Front reform-policy, consisted of reform proposals in the Popular Front program that appeared in the electoral statements of the non-Marxist deputies much less often than in the statements of the Communist and Socialist deputies. Unfortunately, the large number of items in this factor made it less than evident which particular proposals were most associated with the propensity of moderates to defect on the very important PF1 roll calls. By the introduction of the requirement of a correlation with PF1, however, we have been able to isolate a cluster of eight such items. Three of these represent a lack of enthusiasm on the part of some moderates for welfare proposals and assistance for the poor and the working classes, another three represent a reluctance to join in the Popular Front attack on the power and influence of the financial and industrial leaders, and a final pair reveal a tendency not to be concerned with the threat to the regime from the extreme Right. This dimension proved to be a moderately powerful predictor of the PF1 vote defections.

The second general ideological dimension, right-wing-ideology, which consisted mainly of opinions advocated in opposition to the Popular Front, is the major left-right ideological dimension in the Chamber. It generally allocated to the deputies of the non-Marxist Left an ideological position between that of the right-wing opposition and the Marxist parties, but again the refinement of this factor enabled us to specify which of its items most strongly predict subsequent vote defections of consequence for the Popular Front. The analysis demonstrated that there was a smaller subsection of the group of moderate Popular Front deputies with less than total support of key items in the Popular Front program—deputies who had in addition a subsidiary set of beliefs of a much more compromising nature for the success of the Popular Front experiment. The two key beliefs were: (1) the support of a policy of strictly balanced budgets and expenditure cutbacks, and (2) the fear of the Communist influence in the Popular Front. The first belief negated the whole theory of deficit spending or "pump-priming" that marked the Popular Front's economic departure from traditional thinking. As Colton noted, "The one unifying economic theme behind the experiment was the need to combat the depression by increasing the purchasing power of the masses and restoring consumer demand."[12] The second belief was one that Larmour feels sustained the Radical party's defections even after the Blum government (and its successors) had abandoned most of what was innovative in the field of social and economic policy. This set of beliefs proved to be even more potent in accounting for the highly significant PF1 roll-call defections.

The Post-Blum Period

The next step is to see if these hypotheses are substantiated in the case of the post-Blum roll-call factors. One would naturally expect that as the gap between the time the electoral statements were written and the time the roll-call votes were taken increases, the degree of correlation between the factors derived from the two will diminish. This indeed proves to be the case, and for the initial selection of opinion variables to be analyzed we were obliged to use a lower cutting point of .15 as the minimum partial correlation between an opinion and the PF1* factor that justified inclusion. Even with this lower threshold, the number of opinions that entered into the principal-components analysis dropped from fifteen to ten. When these were analyzed, two factors with eigenvalues greater than one were produced, accounting for 42.3 percent of the variance. The loadings on these two factors are given in table 8.

Table 8   Factors of Opinion Variables with Partial Correlations with PF1* above .15 (Controlling for PF3*), Oblique Rotated Solution

Variable	Factor Pattern Matrix	
	First Factor: Popular Front Political Policy	Second Factor: Anti-Popular Front*
867 Control credit, Bank of France	.579	.235
833 Fight unemployment	.576	-.184
853 Defend secular state	.709	.071
874 Support League of Nations	.708	-.162
878 Fight fascism (domestic)	.742	.065
866 Balance budget, cut spending	-.084	-.697
923 Against Communism	-.154	-.727
937 Increase industrial tariffs	.153	-.409
936 Maintain order, end violence	.038	-.486
877 Against Popular Front	.013	-.614
Correlation between the factors:	.162	

In a statistical sense the first factor bears a strong similarity to the first or Popular Front reform-policy* dimension produced to account for PF1: they correlate at -.822. However, the subject matter appears to have shifted in the direction indicated by the Larmour hypothesis. Thus the strong presence of opinions concerning social and economic reforms urged by the Marxist parties seems to have declined in importance; only concern for control over or nationalization of the Bank of France and concern over unemployment are present with loadings in the .5 range. The three opinion variables with very high loadings (in the .7 range) are all distinctly political and consist of support for secularism and the separation of church and state, for a foreign policy based on the League of Nations, and for the need to fight the fascist threat. We shall therefore refer to this factor as the "Popular Front political-policy" dimension. The second factor also resembles its predecessor statistically with a correlation of .746, but here the overlap of subject matter is also good. The three principal opinion variables loading on it are: (1) a fear of communism, (2) an associated opposition to the Popular Front, and (3) the need for a balanced budget and expenditure economies. (Two other opinions, the need to maintain order and, inexplicably, the need to protect industry through higher tariffs, also load weakly on this factor). Because of this basic similarity of subject matter, this factor will be designated the "anti–Popular Front*" dimension.

The similarity between the ideological factors that emerge for the Blum and post-Blum periods should come as no surprise since the opinion variables they contain were selected to best account for PF1 and PF1* respectively, dimensions of voting in these two periods that were found in chapter 4 to be highly correlated. Thus the two dimensions that emerge from the present analysis, Popular Front political-policy and anti-Popular Front*, can also be considered as refinements of the general dimensions of Popular Front ideology that the principal-components analysis of the electoral statements data produced.[13] Moreover the changes that do occur in the post-Blum period, such as the shift in subject matter of the first factor from that of its counterpart for the Blum period, are in directions that one would anticipate: namely, a decline in restlessness over the coalition's social and economic "extremism" on the part of its more moderate members as the pace of reform slackened in the post-Blum period. This basic similarity does not necessarily verify the hypothesis of the continued or increased importance of the fear of communism or support of deflation opinions in leading to critical Popular Front defections in this era, however. This hypothesis requires the path model of figure 23 to be tested.

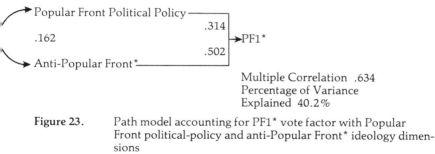

Multiple Correlation .634
Percentage of Variance
Explained 40.2%

Figure 23.   Path model accounting for PF1* vote factor with Popular
Front political-policy and anti-Popular Front* ideology dimensions

As figure 23 shows, the path model accounting for PF1* does give
results consistent with the hypothesis: the path from anti–Popular
Front* to PF1* has a coefficient of .502, which is considerably larger
than the .314 coefficient between Popular Front political-policy and
PF1*. The findings, then, do point to a continued tendency for the
Popular Front defectors on the PF1-type roll calls to be deputies who
doubted not so much the political or socioeconomic reform policies as
the more fundamental issues of: (1) whether a coalition with Communists was desirable or safe, and (2) whether the abandonment of
traditional economic practices was wise. Larmour's hypothesis of the
continuing importance of anti-communism in the Radicals' alienation
from the coalition is supported, and we see evidence of the declining
importance of the social and economic reforms in this period as well.

The Submerged Part of the Iceberg

To assess more graphically the manner in which the ideology dimensions account for the PF1 voting dimension, we present in figure 24 the
scatterplot of PF1 by the Popular Front reform-policy* and anti–
Popular Front factors, the latter two linearly combined using weights
derived from the regression equation predicting PF1. Given the
subjectivity of the opinions data and the ample scope for all kinds of
bias and error, the fit seems remarkably good; virtually all of the
deputies that defected on the PF1 factor also had extreme scores on the
combined ideology variable. The error that does enter into the plot is of
the opposite kind, for clearly many deputies had scores deviant from
the norm set by the PCF and SFIO parties on the combined ideology
variable yet remained loyal in their voting. A very similar pattern
emerges when PF1* is plotted against a linear combination of the two
ideology dimensions that account for it, Popular Front political-policy
and anti–Popular Front*.

This is a highly intriguing pattern for it suggests a possible interpreta-

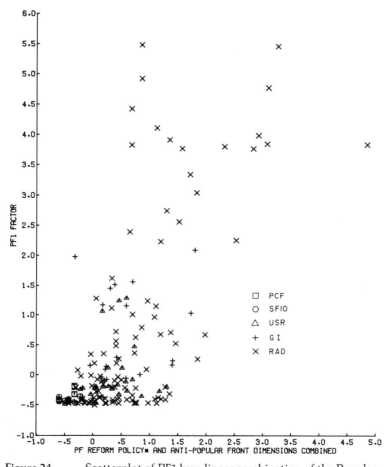

Figure 24.   Scatterplot of PF1 by a linear combination of the Popular
Front reform-policy* and anti-Popular Front dimensions

tion of the error or unexplained variance from the regressions. It may be
that this error is not error in the normal sense of simply reflecting the
inadequacy of the independent variables but is rather a reflection of the
inconsistency between the basically undisciplined nature of the electoral statements (for the non-Marxist deputies) and the more disciplined situation of being obliged to sustain one's coalition in power.
The category of deputies who deviated on opinions but not on votes
may in effect be the submerged part of the iceberg, that group of
mainly Radical deputies who were unwilling to openly defy the
coalition by defecting on the roll-call votes but who were quite uneasy

about some aspects of the coalition and ultimately put pressure on Blum to give up under the Senate attacks of June 1937 and April 1938.

If this hypothesis is valid, we are presented with a problem. Since we have been arguing that the bulk of the non-Marxist deputies were substantially divergent from the Marxist deputies in ideology or beliefs, how can we explain why some of the moderate deputies were willing to go against the pressures to preserve bloc solidarity and to express their dissidence openly in the roll-call votes while the others were not? Inspection of the scatterplot might suggest that, with respect to our opinions data, the division of the non-Marxist deputies into voting defectors and nondefectors is basically random. Viewed in this manner, the interpretation of our findings would be that: (a) the strength of the relationship between PF1 and PF1* and the ideology dimensions comes entirely from the solidarity in opinion and voting of the Marxist deputies and the nonsolidarity in both of these areas of the defecting deputies; but that (b) within the three non-Marxist parties the deputies who did not deviate on the PF1 factors are just as distant ideologically from the Marxists as those who did and that therefore we have no way of explaining the distinction.

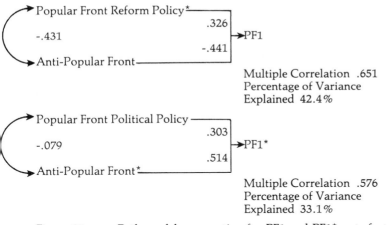

Popular Front Reform Policy*
−.431   .326 →PF1
Anti-Popular Front   −.441

Multiple Correlation .651
Percentage of Variance
Explained 42.4%

Popular Front Political Policy
−.079   .303 →PF1*
Anti-Popular Front* .514

Multiple Correlation .576
Percentage of Variance
Explained 33.1%

Figure 25.   Path models accounting for PF1 and PF1* vote factors, non-Marxist deputies only

This interpretation can readily be tested by performing the regression of the PF1 factors on the same ideology dimensions for the non-Marxist deputies alone. The results of this regression are presented in figure 25 in path analytic form. The most significant finding in these path models is that, despite the seeming weight the consistency in ideology and roll-call voting of the Marxist deputies gave to the previous regressions, the relationship of the ideology factors to the PF1 factors is only slightly less strong for the non-Marxists. Undeniably, almost all of the non-Marxist deputies deviate to some extent from the Marxists' ideological position, but there is nevertheless a distinction between the ideological positions of these non-Marxists and those of the deputies who ultimately did defect in key roll-call votes. Put another way, while only a small part of the non-Marxist deputies actually defected in the roll-call votes, there existed a body of them that occupied, roughly speaking, a middle position between these defectors and the Communists and Socialists, a position not so far ideologically from these parties to lead them to actually oppose the Popular Front governments in the roll-call voting, but perhaps far enough to refuse to support a constitutional struggle with the Senate over its right to end the Blum governments. Non-quantitative sources have emphasized the importance of this subterranean force; our data for the first time point to the size and intensity of this body of opinion in a demonstrative way.

Anti-Communism as a Cause of Popular Front Dissidence

There is one final matter that needs to be cleared up. The development of the ideology dimensions in this section has enabled us to account to a very respectable degree for the type of critical voting defections measured by PF1 and PF1* and to suggest that the actual extent of the defections from the Popular Front may have been understated in the roll-call situation. But we have not in all this specified exactly the nature and degree of relationship between these findings and the interpretation of Larmour. In fact the relationship is indirect at best, for all that we have been able to show is that anti-communism loads highly on the anti–Popular Front dimensions which in turn are strongly related to the PF1 factors. It must be emphasized, however, that the loadings used to combine linearly the opinion variables to form the anti–Popular Front dimensions were selected to maximize the degree of common variance among these variables; they do not reflect how well each individual opinion variable predicts the PF1 factors. Thus, by attempting to find structure in the opinion variables, a direct test of the Larmour hypothesis has been avoided. To arrive at some indication of the importance of the anticommunism variable relative to the other variables loading highly on the anti–Popular Front factors with respect to the express purpose of accounting for PF1 and PF1*—a more direct test of the Larmour thesis—a multiple regression of the appropriate opinion variables themselves on the PF1 factors is necessary.

Table 9 presents both the simple correlation coefficients and the standardized multiple regression coefficients (beta weights) derived from these regressions. Clearly, both sets of coefficients point to the same conclusion: the anti-communism item and the anti–Popular Front opinion that followed from it in some cases dominate the others in their explanatory power over PF1 and PF1*. The multiple correlation coefficients show that performing these regressions adds nothing to the overall explanatory power of these opinion variables since they are virtually identical with the simple correlations between the anti–Popular Front dimensions and the PF1 factors. However, the regressions do show that what makes the anti–Popular Front dimensions such powerful predictors are the high loadings of the anticommunism

Table 9	Explaining the PF1 Factors with the Opinion Variables That Load Highly on the Anti-Popular Front Dimensions

Dependent Variable: PF1		
Independent Variables	Simple Correlation Coefficient	Standardized Multiple Regression Coefficient
866 Balance budget, less spending	.386	.164
929 Laval decrees justified	.245	.094
945 Less state intervention	.240	.110
877 Against Popular Front	.490	.320
923 Fear of communism	.511	.277
Multiple Correlation	.641	
Correlation of Anti-Popular Front factor with PF1	-.674	
Dependent Variable: PF1*		
866 Balance budget, less spending	-.369	-.163
936 Maintain order, end violence	-.189	-.093
937 Increase industrial tariffs	-.176	-.057
877 Against Popular Front	-.393	-.229
923 Fear of communism	-.472	-.290
Multiple Correlation	.561	
Correlation of Anti-Popular Front* factor with PF1*	.553	

and anti–Popular Front variables on them, thus adding considerable weight to the Larmour hypothesis.

Equally important in the evaluation of the Larmour hypothesis, however, is the fact that, while anticommunism is a very powerful predictor of the PF1 factors, it does not constitute a completely independent attitude but is closely related to the advocacy of a deflationary economic strategy. Moreover the anticommunism and anti–Popular Front variables have very high correlations of -.761 and -.636, respectively, with Popular Front reform-policy*, a dimension which itself is a significant predictor of the PF1 vote defections. Thus the argument put forward by Larmour that anticommunism was the sole source of Radical defection from the Popular Front seems somewhat overstated. In fairness, Larmour does argue that anticommunism became increasingly important after the Popular Front came to power, not in the electoral campaign of 1936 when the electoral statements were written, in which case our data may represent too early a time-point to assess the true weight of this variable. This explanation seems quite plausible and may explain why the post-Blum path model is noticeably less powerful as a predictor of PF1* than the Blum path model is as a predictor of PF1. However the important point is that, among those who do mention anticommunism in 1936, this mentioning is associated with other attitudes unfavorable to the Popular Front (deflation, nonadvocacy of key aspects of the Popular Front reform program, and so on), and that these other attitudes are themselves associated with defection on the PF1 roll calls. Anticommunism was a very important part of the story of the disintegration of the Popular Front, but it by no means stands alone in this regard.

The Popular Front: Summary and Conclusions

In the first section our findings pointed to the existence of two basic ideological dimensions among the deputies elected to the Chamber in 1936. The dimension we labelled right-wing-ideology measured the degree of support for a number of right-wing political positions; the Marxist-ideology dimension, on the other hand, assessed the support for items most commonly mentioned by the Communists and Socialists. This latter factor was tainted, however, by the possibility that it partially represented a presumably false distinction between those deputies whose personal statements were so scanty that their party platforms had to be used as supplements and those deputies who provided adequate personal statements. Fortunately for the analysis, right-wing-ideology proved to be by far the major Left-Right ideological dimension, as was indicated by its high degree of association with the left-right alignment of deputies on the bloc-loyalty vote factors. The chief distinction between bloc loyalty and the two ideology dimensions—the lack of a large gap between the Popular Front and right-wing deputies on ideology—had a suggestive implication, however. The existence of a continuous rather than dichotomous ideological spectrum of deputies, plus the close relationship of this spectrum to the predominant dimension of roll-call voting, indicated that an ideological basis for serious difficulties for the Popular Front governments may have actually preexisted their tenure of power. The key issue is, how closely related to the Popular Front vote defections are these dimensions of ideological disagreement?

The focussing of attention on the Popular Front in order to attempt to explain the vote defections within the coalition turned out to have an important advantage in controlling for the possible biases in the Marxist-ideology dimension. Of course one solution to this problem would have been to simply discard all opinion variables that appeared only or chiefly in the lengthy Marxist party statements as being only minor items included in those sources for reasons of comprehensiveness. Only a very few items actually had a clear-cut distribution of responses of this kind, however, and an analytic method of separating out variables to the extent that they approached this pattern was clearly preferable. Principal-components analysis of the Popular Front opinions variables achieved this objective by dividing Marxist-ideology into two component factors, one of which reflected the coding bias and the other of which aligned the Popular Front deputies according to their support for the coalition's reform program, regardless of how they were coded. This latter dimension was labelled Popular Front reform-policy.

By deriving the Popular Front reform-policy and right-wing-ideology dimensions and regressing the PF3 vote factors on them, we were able to show of the Radical party in particular that it was not only measurably more right-wing than the Socialist and Communist parties on the most central of the Popular Front's policies, but that it also tended to support items of the counterideology of the Right more than did the rest of the Popular Front. This reinforced our interpretation of a serious lack of ideological unity within the Popular Front that the previous analysis had uncovered.

Concerning the critical PF1 vote factors, it was found that, unlike the PF3 factors, the vote defections the PF1 factors measured can more substantially be accounted for by the right-wing-ideology dimension than by the Popular Front reform-policy dimension, indicating an even greater ideological distance from the Popular Front position on the part of the PF1 defectors. It was evident, however, that ideology factors more specific in their content and better able to account for the PF1 vote factors were needed if we were to adequately understand the nature and causes of this important type of dissidence within the Popular Front.

To achieve this goal, we changed our research strategy somewhat. Instead of relying on the general ideological dimensions to account for the subsequent dimensions of roll-call voting, we decided to derive new ideological dimensions that optimally differentiate the most important of the Popular Front dissidents—those who were prepared to go into opposition to the coalition on key roll calls in the Chamber. There is no necessity that dimensions so defined resemble the general ideological dimensions that characterize the Popular Front. For one thing, the PF1 vote factors probably underestimate the true extent of the dissidence in the Popular Front because of the sanctions against openly violating the coalition's solidarity. What a development of ideological dimensions that best account for PF1 and PF1*, controlling for PF3 and PF3* respectively, will do, therefore, is to identify the ideological correlates of only the most blatant dissension in the coalition. But if it should prove to be the case that the sources of these defections (a) attracted many more moderate deputies than actually defected on these key roll calls and (b) are closely related to the major ideological dimensions of the Popular Front, we would have strong evidence that the Popular Front suffered from the beginning from a serious ideological disunity centering on these particular issues that undermined its experiment in government.

The empirical findings that flowed from this line of inquiry fulfilled both these expectations. The principal-components analyses of opinion variables best accounting for the PF1 factors produced dimensions that not only allow us to specify more precisely what kinds of beliefs led to significant vote defections but can also be interpreted as refinements of the general ideological dimensions of the Popular Front. For instance, there emerged anti–Popular Front dimensions for both the Blum and post-Blum periods that contained as their principal ingredients: (a) a rejection of the philosophy of deficit spending and an advocacy of the former policies of deflation, and (b) a fear of communism and rejection of a Popular Front coalition susceptible to communist influence. These dimensions can be considered refinements of right-wing-ideology in the sense that the latter dimension also contained these items. The interpretative value of the anti–Popular

Front dimensions is, however, that the more basic right-wing political opinions in the right-wing-ideology dimension—support for a right-wing government, a desire to strengthen the executive's power over the legislature, a failure to mention the need to defend the republican regime—turned out to be absent from them, indicating that the PF1 defectors were motivated more by an economic conservatism and an anti-communism than by a more sweeping political rightism. This interpretation is reinforced by the higher correlations of the anti–Popular Front dimensions with the PF1 factors than was true of right-wing-ideology.

For the Blum period, the other factor produced by the principal-components analysis of the selected opinion variables was a refinement of Popular Front reform-policy which we labelled Popular Front reform-policy*. It, too, entailed an increase in specification of the sources of dissension by indicating more exactly what it was about the Popular Front reform program that is associated with key vote defections. Three areas in particular stood out: lack of support for welfare and assistance measures for workers and the poor; absence of concern over the power and influence of big business and finance; and a failure to show concern over the threat from the extreme Right. This last element indicates that the interpretation of the Radicals as socially and economically conservative but politically leftist must be tempered somewhat. Clearly, they differed sharply from the Right in not supporting constitutional changes in favor of a stronger executive and in solidly supporting the defense of republican liberties and institutions. However, much of the moderate wing of the Popular Front and in particular the PF1 defectors, most of whom were Radicals, evidently did not take to heart the central political motivation for the coalition of the Left, the "fascist" threat to those institutions and liberties.[14] Moreover, in the post-Blum period, when the Popular Front's social and economic reform program had declined in salience, the refinement of Popular Front reform-policy that was produced to best account for PF1* took on a decidedly political tone and was accordingly named Popular Front political-policy. It also pointed to a lack of unity within the Left in political matters. It would seem that the moderate wing of the Popular Front was in reality not all that more left-wing on political issues than on social or economic ones and in both areas occupied an ideological position as close to the right-wing opposition as to the Marxist Left.

In general, then, we did find that the ideology dimensions that optimally account for the critical vote defections measured by PF1 and PF1* are correlated with, and can be regarded as refinements of, the principal dimensions of ideological cleavage that characterize the Popular Front deputies' electoral statements. This suggests that it is the *key* ideological divisions among the Popular Front deputies, divisions that predated the assumption of power by the coalition, that account for the subsequent dissension within and decline of the experiment. This conclusion is borne out by the multiple regression (path) analysis which indicated that about one-half of the variance is accounted for in the regression of PF1 on the Popular Front reform-policy* and anti–Popular Front dimensions and 40 percent of the variance in regressing PF1* on the Popular Front political-policy and anti–Popular Front* dimensions. It seems clear that much of the unexplained variance is due to the fact that the vote defectors were only the most extreme subset of a larger group of Popular Front deputies who had positions deviant from the Marxists on these ideology dimensions but who for the most part held fast in their voting, presumably out of fear of being seen to openly damage the coalition. Covert pressure from these deputies, which has been suggested as the prime cause of Blum's resignations in the face of Senate opposition, is a very real possibility in view of these findings.

Finally, the primacy of the anti–Popular Front dimensions in accounting for the PF1 factors could not in itself be taken as confirmation of the Larmour hypothesis, which concentrates on the importance of the fear of communism in the alienation of the Radicals from the Popular Front, because these factors contain the "balanced budget" item, among others, as well as the anticommunism item. To ascertain which of these items best predict the PF1 factors, we regressed them on the individual component items of the anti-Popular Front factors. It was found that the anticommunism variable and the closely associated anti–Popular Front variable were by far the dominant predictors of PF1 and PF1*, affirming the importance Larmour had attributed to this belief in the Radicals' loss of allegiance to the Popular Front.

While anticommunism is highly important in explaining the vote defections measured by the PF1 factors, it did not prove to have the exclusivity that Larmour claimed for it, for Popular Front reform-policy*, which contained a number of the Popular Front key reform proposals, did make a significant contribution in accounting for PF1, and so did Popular Front political-policy with respect to PF1*. It might be countered that the electoral statements of 1936 represent too early a time-point to gauge the full impact of the anticommunism theme. This is probably true and may explain our decreased ability to account for PF1*, but it remains the case that, where anticommunism was voiced in the electoral statements, it was highly related to other opinions that themselves contribute to accounting for PF1 in particular. The interpretation our findings seem to point to is one that bears in mind that anticommunism, while probably the single best predictor of the critical PF1 defections, formed part of a syndrome which also included the advocacy of more traditional economic practices and, moreover, is highly associated with the nonsupport of key reforms of the Popular Front program, as measured by the Popular Front reform-policy* dimension, a dimension which itself is related to the PF1 defections.

In sum, we found in the data analysis of this chapter that most of the moderates in the Popular Front were quite deviant from the Marxist deputies in their degree of support for the reform program and that this deviance is associated with defections on the critical PF1 vote factors. There was, moreover, a subgroup of these deputies who also rejected the most basic tenets of the Popular Front experiment— an alliance of the *entire* Left, deficit spending, government intervention into the economy and society—and they were even more responsible for the cracks in the solid front of the Popular Front coalition than our roll-call analysis revealed. The conclusion that the vote defections measured by the PF1 factors were not merely the result of Popular Front policy failures in the financial and economic spheres, but rather reflected ideological divisions within the French Left that coexisted with and eventually undercut the Popular Front movement, seems undeniable.

In our historical synopsis of the period we introduced the necessity of further study of the Popular Front by posing an unresolved dilemma: does the Popular Front experiment constitute a disproof of the thesis that the inability of the Left to form viable governments in twentieth-century France is attributable to ideological fragmentation or was it merely a more complex and sophisticated exemplification of that rule? Translated into more concrete terms, did the Popular Front disintegrate because of the failure of certain of its policies or because fundamental ideological cleavages that divided the Left prior to 1936 still existed behind the camouflage of the Popular Front movement? The roll-call analysis enabled us to pinpoint the center of internal Popular Front disintegration, but the consideration of the subject matters of the roll calls that provoked critical dissidence could not resolve this question. There were clear indications of policy failure leading to defections—the financial emergency and devaluation roll calls—but the fact that these same dissident deputies also defected on aspects of labor and agricultural legislation seemed to indicate that the financial difficulties may have only aggravated cleavages that had already existed on grounds of ideology or political belief. This conclusion was reinforced by the failure of the dissidents to increase in numbers over time or for the dissidence to be noticeably affected by changes in Popular Front prime ministers or governments.

The analysis of this chapter was undertaken to cast some light on this matter, and we believe that it has achieved this end. Our data seem to point quite unequivocally to the conclusion that to a very considerable extent the Popular Front was fated to have difficulties even before it took office. Although the parties involved had accepted the coalition and its program, large numbers of non-Marxist deputies did not wholeheartedly assent to the reforms being proposed and many expressed concern over either the threat of communism generally or, more specifically, the threat represented by the Communist presence in the coalition. These kinds of ideological dissidence within the Popular Front proved to be strongly related to subsequent voting defections of a critical nature for the coalition. It is clear that not only would Blum have had difficulty in making the Popular Front program work but also that any deviations from it made necessary by circumstances would have to have been made in a more moderate direction if they were to carry the support of the non-Marxist wing of the coalition. The implications of these findings and conclusions for our overall interpretation of the Popular Front, its fate, and its place in French politics and history will be considered in the next and final chapter.

Chapter Six

The Popular Front
and the Nature of Politics
in the Third Republic

In this study a considerable array of data has been
presented to illuminate aspects of the Popular Front experience. The
Popular Front was not, however, an isolated occurrence in French
political history; rather it constituted, as we have noted, a key episode
in the decline of the Third Republic. In interpreting this evidence,
therefore, it is necessary to bear in mind that it should be consistent
with a more general theoretical framework that can account for the
nature and functioning of this regime. The purpose of this chapter is to
develop just such a framework.

Theoretical Perspectives on French Politics

Let us begin this task by reviewing some of the attempts that have
been made to account for the nature of politics in French parliamentary regimes. The basic thrust of the social-scientific literature on the
Third and Fourth Republics has, of course, been highly critical of the
stability and effectiveness of these regimes. In a nation where popular
revolution came early, how have social scientists sought to explain the
failure of Frenchmen to develop a more workable democratic
formula?

Frequently the blame for this failure has been placed squarely on certain deficiencies in the political culture of Frenchmen, deficiencies which are held to have serious implications at the level of political institutions. The most pervasive version of this viewpoint emphasizes the importance of the two "opposing conceptions of life" that have divided French society and politics since the Revolution. These conceptions go under a variety of labels, but probably the most colorful are Nordlinger's epithets, "the France of hierarchical order" and "the France of idealistic egalitarianism."[1] As Nordlinger correctly points out, proponents of this interpretation of the source of the instability of French parliamentary politics trace the power of this cleavage to its ubiquity: "what makes the mutual antagonism so intense and pervasive is the solid congruence of these two conceptions of government with their accompanying attitudes towards religion, the family, social equality, the relationship of man to society, resulting in two remarkably resilient cultural edifices supporting the two conflicting views of the ideal political system."[2] In the political arena these two uncompromising "cultural edifices," often referred to simply as the authoritarian and republican traditions, are held to have prevented a consensus emerging on a set of "mixed" political institutions capable of both effective leadership and democratic responsiveness. As Wahl puts it, "the real vice lies in the continued availability to Frenchmen of two unreformed myths about how political decisions may be made and two unreformed sets of political institutions that give pseudo-reality to these myths"[3]—the highly centralized and hierarchical state bureaucracy and the excessively egalitarian and unruly parliamentary apparatus. The result has been a historical oscillation between authoritarian regimes headed by a single, supreme authority-figure (Napoléon, Louis-Napoléon, Pétain, and perhaps de Gaulle) and weak, ineffectual parliamentary regimes such as the Third and Fourth Republics.

A second line of argumentation elaborates on this latter aspect, the institutional deficiencies of French parliamentary democracy. Shirer makes mention of two such defects which frequently appear in the literature: the weakness of the party system and the weakness of the executive arm of government.[4] Parties in France were small, poorly organized, and rarely disciplined. This was especially true of the Radical party, a perennial participant in government. Indeed the Radicals did not even make the effort to acquire a mass membership, nor did they exert centralized leadership. Their local committees were in name and fact autonomous, and the deputies they sent to Paris tended to represent the parochial interests of those committees to the detriment of the national interest. Moreover the Chamber of Deputies, unlike the British House of Commons, never gave up power to the cabinet. Instead cabinets existed "at the mercy of whimsical ever-changing parliamentary majorities."[5] Cabinets, formally possessing the power of dissolution, in practice could never appeal to the electorate except during the regular quadrennial legislative elections. By then, "the confusion wrought by five or six successive governments was so great—the lines separating the parties so indistinct—that no considered judgment by the people was possible."[6]

Crozier has attempted to link these perspectives on French politics by striking at their common cultural roots.[7] According to his theory, two traits stand out in the way Frenchmen view authority. First, face-to-face dependence relationships are perceived as difficult to bear; second, authority is still viewed in absolute terms. In the bureaucratic setting, the solution to this apparent contradiction lies in the widespread use of impersonal rules and centralization. The absolutist view of authority which precludes bargaining, as well as the strong sense of egalitarianism and the consequent desire to avoid being subject to another man's whims—the two fundamental orientations—can thereby be satisfied. Unfortunately, the managing of these two orientations toward authority cannot be so neatly achieved in the parliamentary arena. Effective political action requires an ability to organize, cooperate with, and ultimately accept leadership; democracy requires that the role of the leader not be imbued with absolute authority. French parliamentary politics, reflecting a political style that rejects both principles, has never achieved a "juste milieu" conducive to government that is both effective and democratic:

> The "political class," just like the bureaucratic strata, has become an isolated group, extremely egalitarian, rebellious against any kind of authority, unable to build stable leadership and to engage in constructive collective action. Its main failure has been its inability to understand that it cannot deny the government the right to act independently, coupled with its refusal to assume its own share of responsibility.[8]

In Crozier's analysis, the fundamental problem in both the bureaucratic and parliamentary settings is that of change. The rigidity of the structure and the inability of the leadership to interfere with subordinate strata—conditions that result from the heavy insistence on rules in French bureaucracies—make change possible only through crises. Since routine is the predominant form of bureaucratic activity, this rule-bound rigidity is not, however, overly harmful; it is only in the Chamber of Deputies, whose function ought to be change or reform, that tremendous weakness becomes manifest—hence the theme of institutional deficiencies. Crises, which must arise because the political system is impervious to change, have inevitably found governments unable to act. It is only when the force of circumstances becomes overpowering that parliament will yield to the government (or a strong man) for as long as is necessary to handle the crisis. The parliamentary norm, however, is impotence.

There would seem to be no necessity to construe this thesis as a *total* refutation of the "two traditions" thesis which has so often functioned as an explanation of French political history since the Revolution.[9] It could be that one tendency in French society, that traditionally identified with the right wing, has emphasized the absolutist or hierarchical aspects of the French authority-pattern, while the other, associated with the left wing, has leaned towards the egalitarian component. Yet the Crozier approach has been interpreted as an alternative explanation of the course of French politics in the nineteenth and twentieth centuries, one which obviates the need for viewing French society as segmented into "opposing conceptions of life." Nordlinger, for instance, sees the Crozier thesis as having one powerful advantage over the picture of French politics painted as a conflict of incompatible political traditions and perspectives: it better accords with Nordlinger's belief that parliamentary politics in the Third Republic was based on "excessively pragmatic bargaining techniques rather than on a clash of ideologies."[10]

The issue has not been allowed to come to rest with this observation, however. Instead this very point has been seized upon by Lijphart in an attempt to show that there is no fundamental incompatibility between these two perspectives provided that both are viewed in terms of his model of "consociational democracy."[11] It is possible, Lijphart argues, for a highly segmented society, such as a society sharply divided over two opposing political traditions, to achieve democratic stability if the leaders of each tradition or segment are prepared to foresake ideological politicking in favor of interelite bargaining and cooperation in order to stabilize the existing system and make it work. Examples of political systems functioning under this sort of "cartel of elites" are the Netherlands, Belgium, Switzerland, and Austria (since the Second World War). The consociational democratic solution to sharp societal and political cleavages is most likely to be embraced by elites and masses alike in times of external threat, and the *Union sacrée* that guided France through the First World War comes to mind in this context. But what is equally crucial is the strong organization of the segments of society, for such solidarity affords elites the flexibility to negotiate and compromise with one another. This, of course, is exactly what was lacking in France because the French style of authority precluded the strong organization of segments or the subordination of nonelites to elite decision-making. Thus any tendency by elites towards pragmatism and compromise was not accompanied by an ability to organize themselves or their followers into cohesive political organizations guided by strong leaders.[12] Excessive individualism therefore remained the hallmark of French legislative politics, and a stability of coalitions and governments that would sustain authoritative decision-making was generally absent.

We seem to be faced with a diverse and fascinating array of alternative interpretations of French politics and political history, most of which borrow heavily from one another. The question is, do any of these general theories fit the particular facts of the Popular Front as we know them?

The theory that appears at first glance to apply most readily to the Popular Front experience is Lijphart's consociational democracy thesis. Despite Lijphart's negative overall evaluation of the suitability of French parliamentary regimes, could one not interpret the Popular Front as a sort of consociational solution forced on the fragmented political system by the apparently serious threat to the regime from the extreme Right as well as by the challenge posed by the severity and longevity of the Depression? Granted that the Popular Front was not a "grand coalition" of all significant political forces, nevertheless it controlled nearly two-thirds of the Chamber of Deputies and, unlike previous governing coalitions, maintained enough internal voting cohesion to rapidly enact the principal provisions of its program of reform. Thus the inability to develop cohesive political formations that was the French parliamentary system's key weakness, in Lijphart's view, was considerably overcome through the Popular Front. Why, then, did this consociation of political parties fall apart? According to Lijphart, a consociational government will run into difficulties when the problems facing it are too severe and thus not susceptible to resolution by means of compromise measures the various components of the government coalition would be willing to accept.[13] On this basis, one could attribute the disintegration of the Popular Front to the failure of the agreed-upon program of stimulat-ing the economy by providing more spending power for the working classes. We have also noted that the flexibility afforded Blum to institute new policies once the original ones either failed or met resistance was very limited. Thus the consociational democracy theory is both general and consistent with a number of circumstances specific to the Popular Front and its failure. In addition it can account for the decline of the Third Republic by taking the position that once problems of such severity arise that even a consociational solution can not resolve them, the decline of a regime founded on a sharply divided polity is inevitable.

We have seen that this interpretation, although consistent with the rough outlines of the Popular Front and the Third Republic as we have described them to this point, flounders on the outcome of the data analysis of the last three chapters. There is scant evidence in the roll-call votes for the hypothesis that disillusionment and disintegration within the Popular Front had its sources in the failure of the coalition's program of reform; rather, the voting defections that the Popular Front experienced were found to have their source in ideological differences that existed before the coalition came to power. It is clear that the ultimate failure of policies adopted by the Popular Front in order to remedy the economic situation was not the cause of the disintegration of the coalition.

This finding forces our attention back to the ideological fragmentation that has so generally been assumed to explain the instability of French politics. And indeed, when the data were analyzed over the entire Chamber, strong indications appeared that the characterization of French political life as divided into two hostile camps has empirical support. Not only did there emerge a sharp cleavage between the Left and the Right in the roll-call voting—a hardly surprising finding—but there was also a definite Left/Right alignment of the Chamber on the ideology dimensions as well. While these latter dimensions produced a continuous rather than dichotomous grouping of deputies, it was nonetheless evident that there was very little crossing over of the line separating the two camps. In short, the fundamental division of Left and Right was clearly evidenced in the Popular Front legislature.

What is just as clear, however, is that this left/right division had little to do with the fate of the Popular Front experiment. Instead, a different ideological cleavage, the Marxist/non-Marxist distinction that figured so large in our discussion (in chapter 2) of French politics between the world wars, was very evident in the ideology dimensions and, more important, strongly related to subsequent vote defections. Our conclusion concerning these findings was that the sources of Popular Front division and disintegration can be seen in terms of this latter cleavage. This raises an interpretive dilemma that is absolutely critical, for it means that the results of the data analysis cannot readily be subsumed under the more general interpretation of French politics outlined above. How, then, are the data findings of this study to be interpreted?

It is our contention that the resolution of this question is to be found in a consideration of the historical development of the Third Republic, starting from its founding in the 1870s. In particular, it is necessary to grapple with the fundamental fact of this history, which is that, despite the deficiencies and weaknesses in French political culture and the regime's institutions and practices, the Third Republic's record is not one of uniform failure. Instead, as we noted in chapter 1, there is in the political history of the Third Republic a readily identifiable period of reasonable success in handling the issues of the day that preceded the period of undoubted decline. The key to untangling the failure of the Popular Front lies in understanding what caused this shift in the regime's fortunes. Once this foundation has been laid, the findings of the data analysis and the contributions both of Crozier's observations on French political culture and of the "two traditions" approach will fall readily into place. In addition, it will be possible to explain how the politics of the Third Republic, which in the Popular Front era seem to have been characterized by ideological divisions, could be interpreted as "excessively pragmatic." Finally, having established this point, we shall show that the consociational democracy approach need not be interpreted as inconsistent with an ideology-based explanation of the fate of the Popular Front and in fact can be made to accord reasonably well with the understanding of the Popular Front that has been reached in this study.

The Historical Framework of the Popular Front

We shall begin this task of interpretation and synthesis by examining the nature of political conflict in the Third Republic prior to the Popular Front. This discussion will of necessity be brief and not fully documented; it has, however, the compensatory advantage of following very closely a line of interpretation that has been established by many distinguished students of French political history. As we indicated, the findings of the present study render an interpretation of the Popular Front that fits very neatly into this larger framework and thereby supports its validity.

In the early decades of the Third Republic, the major forms of political conflict consisted of certain challenges to the regime itself, two of which stand out as of central importance. Interestingly, both had their origins in events that occurred outside of France's frontiers around the time of the creation of the Republic: the unifications of Italy and Germany and the revival of ultramontanism in the Catholic church.

The source of the church-state conflict that was to be waged off and on in France for thirty-five years was the particularly reactionary decisions that emerged from the Vatican Council of 1870. Influenced undoubtedly by the conquest of its territories by the newly created Italian state, the church was led not only to enunciate the doctrine of papal infallibility but, more important, to condemn the basic liberal democratic principles that inspired the Third Republic. As Thomson put it:

> The renunciation and condemnation by the papacy of all forces of Liberalism, Republicanism, and tolerance in the modern world and the alliance of so many Catholics with monarchy, pre-determined a clash between clericals and anti-clericals during the Third Republic.[14]

The problem posed by the unification of Germany involved the need for a large military establishment (especially after the 1870 defeat of France by Germany) coupled with the fear of Bonapartism that a strong army engendered among republicans. Oddly enough, the first trouble was stirred up by the supposedly republican General Boulanger, whose initial fame had come from his work in transforming the professional army into a "democratic," conscription-based force. But the discredit the regime suffered as a result of the Wilson scandal,[15] the discontent stemming from the depression of the 1880s, and the revanchist enthusiasm directed towards Boulanger, all gave Boulanger the desire and support to move forcefully onto the political scene. Fortunately for the regime, the intended coup d'etat never came off, but the republican government fully appreciated that it had been incapacitated in its moment of greatest danger principally by the fear that the army could not be counted upon to defend the regime against the popular hero.

The Boulanger affair, by revealing the threat presented by the army, marked the beginning of the much-noted switch in allegiances of Right and Left, with the Right becoming nationalistic and even jingoistic and the Left, previously the more ardent defender of the *patrie*, coming to oppose militaristic ideas and men. This reversal reached its culmination in the famous Dreyfus affair. The importance of the Dreyfus affair in the history of the Third Republic lies in the crystallizing effect it had among proponents and opponents of the regime. Ideologically, it caused the Right to concentrate its sympathies on the army in contradistinction to the "sordid" and "unruly" parliamentary regime. In Rémond's words:

> Rightist writers magnified the grandeurs and virtues of military institutions. They began to see in it the instrument of national salvation. Whoever dared to shake the foundation of its discipline was guilty of a true sacrilege.[16]

Among the Left, the gradual revelation that the army and its supporters regarded the matter of Dreyfus's actual guilt or innocence as secondary to that of the army's prestige, plus the army's purge of Jewish and Protestant officers, raised the whole question of individual rights and justice in a democracy. Politically, the affair induced the two main centers of opposition to the regime, the church and the army, to throw in their lot together and risk all on this one battlefield, thus enabling the entire Left to rally around a common objective, the defense of the Republic. The ensuing conflict reached its height in the late 1890s when two right-wing coups were attempted, but the regime's counterattack—separation of church and state, severing of relations with the Vatican, creation of a secular school system, and a purging of antirepublican elements in the officer corps—was for the most part brought to a successful conclusion by 1905.

The essential characteristic of pre–World War I France that produced these crises and *affaires* was the division of the society on the question of the type of regime that should govern the nation. In this struggle the Right had important bases of power:

> The conservatives remained masters of the army, navy, diplomatic service, the judiciary, and many public administrations. . . . The world of finance, business, and a large fraction of the liberal professions were naturally dominated by them. Above all . . . they controlled a majority of the newspapers and possessed the support of the Church.[17]

But the fact that the challenges of this era all came from enemies outside the republican fold determined that the regime and its defenders would have the final victory. For one thing, it meant that the issue was always one on which the entire Left, that is, the entire republican camp, could unite; for another, the Left was almost always able to dominate the government and thereby command the resources needed for victory. In Thomson's words: "The first generation of the regime, between 1870 and 1905, was spent in liquidating the past, and the chief unifying force amongst the parties seeking to make it more democratic was common hostility to the 'enemies of the Republic.'"[18]

If the society was divided politically on the question of the legitimacy of the regime, it does not necessarily follow that social consensus was absent. Indeed, Hoffmann has argued that certain characteristics of the French style of authority elaborated by Crozier (the mixture of an absolutist, centralizing authority with an extreme rebelliousness and individualism; the "atomism" or inability to develop a rich associational life in French society) together with the traits of economic Malthusianism discussed earlier were ingredients of a type of consensual socioeconomic system, the "stalemate society." The stalemate society consisted of:

> a very broad consensus on a form of "equilibrium" which accepted social mobility and evolution toward more industrialized order, but only within sharp limits and along well-defined channels. Economic change was welcome only if new factors (such as techniques) were fitted into preexisting frameworks, so that the traditional way of life would be affected very slowly. As John Clapham has put it, "there was industrialization without industrial revolution."[19]

The role of the state, from which society both needed and feared authoritative leadership, was sharply circumscribed by the ultimate necessity of preserving the socioeconomic equilibrium:

> What the stalemate society needed was state protection, not domination; it wanted an instrument, not a master. Economic intervention was justified only when it operated to preserve the economic equilibrium, either through legislation (especially in tariffs and taxes) or through piecemeal administrative intervention. Otherwise the state's function was an ideological one.[20]

Hoffmann traces the source of this consensus on stalemate to the historical struggle between bourgeoisie and aristocracy.[21] Ultimately, of course, the bourgeoisie was victorious, and this assured that continued industrial development would remain an economic objective. However, the long and intense resistance of the aristocracy meant both that a broad-based social trust could not develop ("hence . . . the bitter equalitarian suspiciousness which pervaded French society")[22] and that nonentrepreneurial aristocratic values penetrated the attitudes of the bourgeoisie and even of the workers. Consequently, when the bourgeoisie did emerge victorious, its principal goal was to preserve its hard-won position: "The basic motivation of business was social rather than economic: to insure the continuity of the family and its predominance rather than to produce the greatest amount of goods."[23]

Thus, there existed in pre–World War I France a curious disjuncture between the political and the social and economic worlds. Socially and economically, the bourgeoisie shared a consensus on the desirability of the status quo with the peasantry, whose basic economic aspirations had been largely met with the land redistribution of the Revolution. This consensus was motivated both by the felt need to defend their positions from above and below and by the realization that the lack of a general social trust meant that there could be no agreement on any one direction for change. But politically, the defense of these "conservative" interests entailed the adoption and vigorous pursuit of a left-wing political ideology—republicanism— which alone would guarantee a state whose activities would be appropriate to the stalemate consensus and the style of authority that underlay it. As Hoffmann notes: "The ideological formula of the regime included the Extreme Left but kept out the counterrevolutionary Extreme Right, whereas the social formula—the preservation of the stalemate society—entailed just the opposite."[24]

As long as the challenges to the regime remained political or doctrinal, the Left could present a unified front of defense of republicanism, for no element of the Left wanted a monarchist or Bonapartist restoration. But what would happen when the battleground shifted to take account both of the Left's political successes and of the long-term impossibility of social and economic stalemate in an era of increasingly rapid industrialization? This in essence was the challenge of the interwar period. On the one hand, the Right by the 1920s came to be represented more by big business and financial interests than by church or army and, concurrently, its ideology changed. No longer concerned with the issue of the legitimacy of the republican regime, it came to occupy what might by and large be considered to be a standard, modern, right-wing position. According to Rémond, "Within the framework of republican institutions this Right wanted to follow a conservative policy."[25] On the other hand, a significant part of the Left became associated with the advancement of the growing working class which had been excluded from the stalemate consensus and the benefits of industrial growth. With the moderate Left (the Radicals) having exhausted its meager enthusiasm for social and economic reform by the early 1900s, it was inevitable that the unity of the political Left in the face of the antirepublican challenges of the nineteenth century could only with difficulty be maintained once the matter of socioeconomic reform became, as it did in all industrialized twentieth-century societies, the central issue. As Hoffmann observes:

> . . . most French parties had not been created around the issue of
> economic and social balance or around foreign affairs, since these

had been pillars of French consensus. Consequently, when these became the major political issues, the parties proved incapable of agreeing on coherent measures and unable to get their own members to agree.[26]

As we have seen, the political history of France in the interwar period can largely be written in terms of this dilemma. Because the economy was no longer taking care of itself, economic noninterventionism could not be maintained. In the 1920s the key problems were financial—inflation, flights of capital, Treasury bankruptcy—which the right-wing financial community exploited to influence governmental policy to suit its interests. In the 1930s the issue became economic catastrophe. In each case, the inability of the ruling Left to cope with the situation can be attributed to the fact that the fundamental political cleavage was no longer between the parties of the old Left and Right that had shared the prewar socioeconomic consensus but between them and the rising mass parties of the extreme Left that in the interwar period became the true representatives of change in the social and economic spheres. As Hoffmann perceptively points out, the early response to the Depression, the policy of deflation, which the Radicals shared with the Right, reflected this division of opinion on the virtues of maintaining the economic status quo:

> The policy of balanced budgets and cuts in wages and salaries was an attempt at preserving the stalemate society which, one feared, would be upset both by monetary manipulations and by an extension of the role of the state in economic affairs. . . . Freezing the stalemate society at a low level of economic activity was thought preferable to experimentation which might upset both the social hierarchy and the well-established relation of society to the state.[27]

But the destruction of the stalemate and the upsetting of the social hierarchy that disadvantaged their constituents was precisely the aim of the Socialists and Communists. Since the Radicals represented a rural and small-town constituency, however, they were not in a position to share or appreciate this point of view, as Goguel has pointed out.[28]

The Marxist parties had neither the representation in parliament nor the willingness to govern by themselves, but together the Radicals and the Right, both of which wished to preserve the stalemate consensus, did. Why, then, did not the political configuration—the bases of coalitions and governments—become restructured to reflect the new sources of consensus and cleavage? The answer seems to be quite simply that the weight of history and tradition would not allow such flexibility. As Goguel points out: "the leaders of the left-wing parties, for electoral reasons and because of faithfulness to their prewar practices, never resigned themselves to take account of the gap between the nature of their political alliances and their governmental programmes."[29] Instead, the Radicals continued to be regarded as they regarded themselves: as being on the Left. Hence the repeated failures of Radicals and Socialists to cooperate in government, the repeated falling-out of left-wing electoral alliances with consequent losses of power to the right-wing "minority" in 1926, 1934 (and 1938), and the widespread confusion that seemed at times to dominate the working of the parliamentary game. Perhaps the essence of the dilemma was most accurately, if somewhat cynically, expressed by a right-wing candidate campaigning in the 1932 elections:

> The Radicals say they are attached to the principles of private property, individual freedom, and the idea of the nation [*patrie*]. So they are. But they are unable to separate themselves from the Socialists of the SFIO who want to destroy property, individual freedom, and the idea of the nation. Does that make sense to anybody?[30]

Given what would seem to be an insurmountable impasse, how was it possible to bridge the gap and unify the entire Left, Marxist and non-Marxist, under the banner of the Popular Front? Larmour, whose study of the Radical party in the 1930s is the most extensive and authoritative in the literature, puts the Radicals' willingness to join the movement down to three (noneconomic) motivations: "pride, fear, and ignorance: pride enough to be annoyed at insults [from the Right], fear of the Leagues—or, as they were called, fascism—and ignorance of the Communist party."[31] Viewed within the context of our discussion of the political history of the Third Republic, it is evident that all three reasons can be subsumed under the Radicals' time-honored reflex—defense of the Republic: "For the first time since the Dreyfus era the entire left wing consolidated its strength with the declared purpose of defending the republic against its enemies both at home and abroad."[32] Yet, according to Larmour, the shallowness of the Radicals' motivations, their joining the coalition on the basis of an "instinctive reflex"[33] rather than careful consideration of the program of the Popular Front and of the aims of its Communist members, made possible their almost immediate defection from the movement once it had achieved power.[34] What in particular provoked this early disaffection from the Popular Front? As we have noted, Larmour finds no evidence for attributing the Radicals' disaffection to either the social or economic reforms of the government or to their party's loss of votes and seats in the 1936 elections. Instead, what disillusioned the Radicals, in particular the more conservative ones, was the outbreak of the sit-down strikes in May and June of 1936 and the subsequent labor unrest, largely in protest over the government's policy of nonintervention in Spain, that lasted throughout the Popular Front years. Just as they had joined the coalition out of fear of the increasing disorder caused by the right-wing leagues in the early 1930s, so the Radicals turned from the Popular Front for the same reasons:

> The relation of the Spanish question to the strikes considerably strengthened the conservatives within the party, and made even the left-wingers uneasy. It permitted the accumulated anxieties over the foreign situation and the fear of disorder at home to be focussed on a single scapegoat: the Communist party.[35]

At this juncture the logic in the train of thought we have been following breaks down. To demonstrate why this is the case, let us briefly summarize the essential points entailed by the preceding line of argumentation concerning the nature of the pre–World War I Third Republic. First, it is hypothesized that there existed in France a broad consensus on social and economic stalemate that permitted politics to be waged at a "doctrinal" level between pro- and antirepublicans and, as a consequence, that the party alignments became in large measure constructed around this fundamental political cleavage. In the post-war era, when the contested area switched from the legitimacy of the regime to the appropriate scope of economic intervention, the party system remained frozen in its prewar configuration with the result that the Left, theoretically the majority, was frequently in disarray. Just as the situation looked its worst, however, an apparent right-wing assault on the Republic (the February 6, 1934, riots) led the entire Left to rally behind the prewar theme of "defense of the Republic." That, in Larmour's argument, disaffection among the Radicals was the result once the Popular Front had gained power and the principal threat to order came no longer from the extreme Right but from the extreme Left in the form of factory occupations, strikes, and demonstrations, seems reasonable. But to go one step further and accept the thesis that this was the sole cause of the Radicals' disaffection requires that we completely downplay the importance of the social and economic rift between the Marxist and the non-Marxist Left, a rift which we had argued to be the critical factor in French politics in the interwar period.

It is at this point that the data analysis of this study contributes most to the historical and theoretical analysis of the Third Republic. First, it confirms Larmour's point that the opposition of the more moderate Popular Front deputies came very early in the Blum experiment and therefore was not for the most part the result of disappointment at the failure of the Popular Front economic program. This does not necessarily invalidate Sauvy's argument that, but for the forty-hour week, the Popular Front would have succeeded. On the contrary, one could reasonably argue that, if the Blum experiment's economic policies had revived the economy and avoided the financial and currency crises that ultimately destroyed it, the Radicals, including the Senate Radicals, would have found it politically impossible to bring down the government, whatever their feelings may have been. However, our findings do show that the moderates in the Popular Front certainly did not wait until the economic failure was clear before demonstrating their opposition. Second, the data analysis demonstrated that the internal Popular Front opposition was motivated by fundamental ideological or belief differences between Marxists and non-Marxists that included as a very strong element the fear-of-communism theme emphasized by Larmour. Third, with reference to Larmour's argument that the opposition was not to the Blum government per se but to the whole Popular Front movement, the continuity of opposition between the Blum and post-Blum periods tends to confirm this as well. And fourth, the analysis of the electoral statements has enabled us indirectly to demonstrate that the small number of Popular Front dissenters that the roll-call analysis unveiled were merely the more extreme section of a much larger group of non-Marxist Popular Front deputies who were noticeably more moderate ideologically than the Communists and the Socialists, even in the elections of 1936. This finding is particularly significant because of the well-known strictures against showing open dissidence in the roll-call voting.

There is one critical area, however, in which our findings do not accord with the Larmour thesis. To begin with, the examination of the subject matters of the PF1 and PF1* roll calls revealed that one source of dissidence was specific aspects of the government's social and economic reforms—in particular certain aspects of its agricultural and labor relations bills. Moreover the principal-components analysis of the Popular Front deputies' electoral opinions showed that a very important component of ideological cleavage within the coalition centered on the matter of the Popular Front program, with most weight going to its social and economic reform proposals (the Popular Front reform-policy dimension). When we attempted to get a more precise assessment of the ideological cleavages that explained most adequately the PF1 factor, which is the appropriate dependent variable since the Blum period was by far the most important period of social and economic reform, we again found a key factor to be aspects of the Popular Front reform package, most of these aspects being proposals for social and economic reform (the Popular Front reform-policy* dimension). Finally, we found that the other key factor from this latter analysis, the anti–Popular Front factor, contained in addition to the anticommunism and anti–Popular Front items certain opinions of an economic nature, the general drift of which was a desire for a return to the deflationary policies of the pre–Popular Front era. In other words, not only did key vote defections have an issue-specificity which suggests that beliefs mattered, but the non-advocacy of many of the Popular Front social and economic reforms among the non-Marxist deputies was strongly related to these vote defections; in addition, anticommunism was not an isolated issue but formed part of a syndrome of attitudes which included the espousal of a conservative economic strategy. The question of what to do or not do with the socioeconomic status quo was clearly at the source of Popular Front disunity.

This is not meant to minimize the importance of the fear-of-communism theme which Larmour is correct to emphasize in accounting for the Radicals' defection from the Popular Front. Given his thesis that anticommunism became increasingly important after the Popular Front assumed power, it is quite possible that the electoral statements data underestimate its later significance in accounting for the disintegration of the coalition. Even in our data, anti-communism is the single most powerful predictor of the PF1 factors. But what seems to us critical is that anticommunism, where it did appear in the electoral statements, did not stand alone but was highly associated with the desire to pursue economic policies consistent with the preservation of the stalemate society and highly correlated as well with nonsupport of key reforms of the Popular Front program, especially social and economic ones, a nonsupport which itself fairly strongly accounted for the vote defections of the PF1 factor. It seems likely that if anticommunism did become more popular among Radicals after the 1936 elections, it did so among deputies who were most deviant from the Marxist parties on these other issues as well.

Our conclusion is that the hypothesized cleavage in interwar French politics between the bourgeois "have" parties and working-class "have-not" parties clearly emerged within the Popular Front with serious consequences for its success. Although the older Left/Right cleavage that dominated pre-1914 politics had been largely supplanted as the critical dividing line in French politics with respect to the central issue of the day, socioeconomic reform, it had not lost all relevance; party alignments and consequently legislative voting behavior continued to respect the Left/Right distinction, and the ideological spectrum of the Chamber of Deputies showed a bifurcation into Left and Right. Indeed, the persistence of the older cleavage as the basis for coalition behavior past the time of its political saliency is, under our interpretation, the very problem. The Popular Front experiment, the most promising opportunity to break the deadlock created by the incompatibility of the new social and economic issues of the day with the prewar mold of French political party alignments, must definitely be considered as an exemplification rather than an exception to this interpretation of politics in the French Third Republic.

Theoretical Perspectives on French Politics Revisited

In the introductory chapter of this study, it was suggested that the investigation of the Popular Front experiment constitutes a good test case of the ability of certain general interpretations that have been applied to French politics to account for both the early successes and the ultimate failure of the Third Republic. One such theory that the findings of the data analysis apparently fail to support is Lijphart's model of consociational democracy as applied to France. Lijphart interpreted the French case as having the pragmatic political style but not the organizational strength to foster a consociational solution to France's political divisions. In the Popular Front era, at least, it is clear that the very opposite was the case: ideological divisions ultimately undermined the considerable parliamentary cohesiveness that had been established within the ruling Left.

This raises the question of how it has been possible for students of French politics to interpret elite behavior as both pragmatic and ideological. It seems plausible that the pragmatic quality of French political life could be a consequence of the isolation of the political class from the larger issues and interests of the nation and its own internal rebelliousness towards authority or leadership that Crozier analyzes so well. In such a vacuum it is not difficult to see that politics would revolve around pork-barrel concerns, the "erratic, short-sighted, self-centered interests" so bitterly condemned by Luethy.[36] When events occur which make the "parochial viewpoint" no longer the central concern, when indeed it appears that the political system itself is under attack, a different type of politics is summoned up: the politics of republican defense. Hence one finds mobilized in the mid-1930s the classic ideological cleavage in French society between Left and Right, equality and hierarchy, republicanism and authoritarianism. Unfortunately, there were problems. First of all, the parliamentary Right was not antirepublican; second, it is difficult to see what the Left had in common except republicanism, and that ideal united them only on Moscow's orders. Thus the cleavage that the political system reflected and articulated through the division of political affiliations into pro- and anti–Popular Front was not a salient cleavage; it had in fact been resolved and buried a generation before. What appeared, therefore, as the source of dissension and disintegration was a newer cleavage which represented a critical division of society on the question of the preservation of the stalemate society, a fundamental matter of belief or ideology. The Popular Front attempted to overcome this division by proposing on the one hand significant reforms and on the other hand a rejection of "structural" changes or the violation of "bourgeois legality." The analysis of the data at our disposal indicates that the Popular Front failed in this objective.

Our contention is that there was ideological fragmentation precisely because the structure of French politics was no longer congruent with its chief ideological cleavage and hence was not able to reflect and articulate the competing demands created by that cleavage. This implies that a politics of bargaining and compromise among elites in intensely divided political systems may be possible only if the political segments they represent accurately reflect the main societal cleavages of the time. When leaders form coalitions on the basis of political divisions that are no longer significant, to the detriment of those that are, behavior based on political ideology or belief can be anticipated from the rank and file.

It is highly significant that this conclusion corresponds closely to an observation made by Lijphart that there must be an adequate articulation of the interests of the various segments in order for a cartel of elites to be able to deal with these issues in a de-ideologized atmosphere. As he notes with reference to the linguistic problem in Belgium, "the religious and class issues have been effectively articulated by the political parties and have by and large been resolved, but the linguistic issue has not been clearly articulated and remains intractable."[37] Analogously, it is because the Radical leaders looked leftward to what they felt were their natural allies to form a coalition dealing not just with the perceived fascist threat to the regime but also with social and economic matters about which there were fundamental differences of

belief that political behavior on the basis of those beliefs was provoked among the rank and file. These differences, not respected by the
leadership, had to be manifested in the attitudes and behavior of a
supposedly pragmatic political class, behavior which doomed the
Popular Front experiment. Thus, when the Lijphart interpretation of
French politics is refined to allow for ideological conflict to emerge in
a situation of incongruence between the political structures and the
issues that must be resolved in the political arena, this theory provides
an explanation of the Popular Front and the Third Republic consistent
with the findings of our data analysis.

If this reinterpretation of Lijphart is justified, it means that we have
reached the point where, finally, the contributions of all the theorists
mentioned above fall into place. The division between the authoritarian and republican camps appeared in the early decades of the
Republic over the question of the legitimacy of the new regime;
accordingly, ideology played a fundamental role in the behavior of
political actors. Repeatedly the regime itself was challenged, and each
time its supporters survived the attack. Moreover, they successfully
counterattacked with the secularization of the school system, the
separation of church and state, and the purging of the army. Paralysis
was not the overriding characteristic of the regime in these matters.

With these "doctrinal" victories, politics could take on a pragmatic
quality which assumed that serious intervention into the social and
economic life of the nation was undesirable, and legislators indulged
in their favorite activity of destroying any attempt at authoritative
leadership by the executive. It is at this point that Crozier's analysis of
the French style of authority is most powerful as an explanatory tool.
When financial and economic crises raised the issue of how to restore
satisfactory performance in these areas, however, an all-encompassing
consensus on the desirability of stalemate could no longer serve as the
chief principle of (in)action. Instead there appeared a sharp cleavage
between the defenders of the stalemate society and the Marxist
advocates of fundamental socioeconomic change. Because this cleavage was never fully accepted as a new basis for political alignments,
ineffectiveness in dealing with these crises and unauthenticity in
translating electoral majorities into governmental majorities became
characteristic of national politics in the interwar period. This is the
theme of institutional deficiencies and governmental impotence.

Inability to form cohesive organizations and rebelliousness towards
authority were very much in evidence in Third Republic politics
throughout, and perhaps Lijphart is correct in asserting that this
prevented a true consociation of the entire political spectrum in times

of crisis. However, the formation of a diverse but majoritarian coalition in the Chamber was possible, and the self-imposition of an impressive voting discipline by the Popular Front for over two years indicates that the much-touted individualism of the political class was not an all-powerful behavioral motivation. But the resolution at an elite level of diverse standpoints on issues that sharply divide polities presupposes the formation of political groupings that reflect these issues. If leaders see opponents as allies and allies as opponents, it is not surprising to find that their followers show tendencies to behave otherwise. Lijphart is surely correct in asserting that the most divisive cleavages must be recognized and reflected in the structure of political groupings; only then is cooperation possible among the leaders of the various groupings in order to resolve potential or actual conflict.

The leaders of what was considered the moderate Left were faced with a difficult dilemma in those years. Ideologically their parties stood between the conservative Right and the Marxist Left, as the analysis of the electoral statements showed. With the Marxists they shared a sense of threat to the Republic itself from the extreme Right, but they were closer to the moderate Right in their social and economic conservatism.[38] Choosing for historical reasons to ally with the Marxist Left, they ran the risk of a lukewarm commitment to the Popular Front program of reform on the part of their followers. This lack of commitment did not prevent the enactment of these reforms, and their success in reinvigorating the economy would have quelled any serious dissidence; but in the face of setbacks and disappointments, disintegration on ideological grounds was an inevitable consequence.

Other Factors Affecting the Popular Front Experiment

There is a danger in making as strong an argument as we have for the Third Republic's "fatal flaw" being an incongruence between the newer interwar problems and issues and the rigid prewar party system, the danger being that the failure of the Popular Front will be put down too simplistically to problems of "structure." We shall briefly discuss two other considerations beyond the political system's influence or control to show the necessity of tempering conclusions that lay all the responsibility on the political system.

The first such consideration is the matter of the prevailing state of economic knowledge. We have several times pointed to the difficulties caused by the Radicals' favoring of left-wing alliances and right-wing economics. This caused much governmental instability at times, yet it is nevertheless the case that the Radicals did face reality to the extent of supporting right-wing governments long enough for them to effectively impose what they believed to be the correct remedy for the economic difficulties: the policy of deflation. This policy failed in its objectives but not because of any problems in the structure of party politics. The same may be said of the failure of Popular Front economics. As we commented earlier, while it is not justified to explain the disaffection of the Radicals and other moderates from the Popular Front in terms of the failure of the economic strategy, it is a reasonable speculation that had the forty-hour week not been allowed to kill the gradual upswing in the economy consequent upon the devaluation of the franc, it would have been difficult for the Senate or anyone else to deny the Popular Front its right to govern. Certainly the actual occasion of Blum's defeat—the request for emergency powers to deal with a financial and currency crisis—would not have occurred. If we wish to explain the successive adoption of the wrong economic policies, we must look outside the realm of politics:

> In France it is not too much to say that intellectuals not only were poor in economics but also that they were bored with it. Therefore the government was allowed to take its cue from leading bankers and other "experts" who, even had they wished, could not rise above the deplorably bad teaching in economics offered by France's law faculties, which at the time had a monopoly of university economics.[39]

As Hoffmann has pointed out, "the same experts often served Laval and Blum."[40]

A second outside influence was the international situation. In numerous accounts of the Popular Front era, much has been made of this factor in accounting for the Popular Front's difficulties. This emphasis would seem to be somewhat unwarranted since the conduct of foreign affairs was not a matter that defeated governments in the late 1930s nor was it a matter of widely differing policy positions: both the Popular Front and the Right were basically pacifist in 1936–37. There are, nevertheless, two aspects of the international situation that did have a bearing on the Popular Front experience. First of all, the increasing danger from Nazi Germany put pressure on the Popular Front, which had officially adopted a policy of disarmament, to launch a massive rearmament program. This added expenditure significantly contributed to the Treasury deficits, deficits which (rightly or wrongly) destroyed business confidence, provoked flights of capital abroad, and launched attacks on the franc that damaged

Popular Front governments severely on more than one occasion. Moreover, the very question of whether to appease or prepare to resist was ultimately to divide the parties of the Popular Front, setting Communists against Radicals and splitting the Socialists into two irreconcilable factions.[41] Second, the Spanish Civil War was itself a highly divisive issue and the Popular Front policy, initiated by Blum, of disallowing aid to the beleaguered Spanish Republic motivated much of the subsequent labor unrest that, in Larmour's view, so alienated the Radicals from their Communist allies.

While these extraneous factors must be brought into the analysis of the failure of the Popular Front, it is nevertheless vital to realize that their significance derives largely from the way they impinged on the structural incongruence of French party politics. Consider the failure of economic policy. France was not the only country to lack a sure-fire economic recovery plan. What doomed her efforts more than those of the United States, for example, was the lack of flexibility or room for experimentation that was a hallmark of the Roosevelt administrations. Blum was allowed to get away with certain policy changes, the devaluation being the most notable example, but the fundamental rift between the Marxist and non-Marxist parties on economics not only led to Popular Front defections (on the devaluation question as well as on others) but also meant that certain policies such as nationalization or exchange controls to prevent exportation of capital could not even be tried. By the same token, disastrous policies such as the forty-hour week could not be touched by the Radicals because of opposition from the Marxist parties.

Much the same can be concluded of the rearmament issue. The cost of rearming France's military forces would not have become a serious drain on government finances and a threat to business confidence had it not been for the failure of the Popular Front economic policies to revive the economy and thereby generate adequate tax income to support rearmament. The impact of this issue on the Popular Front should therefore be linked with that of the economic failures, as discussed above. Moreover, the division of the Popular Front parties into appeasers and resisters, while critical to the eventual collapse of France in 1940, did not take on serious proportions until well after the fate of the Popular Front experiment had been decided. For instance, the bifurcation of the SFIO, a party of inveterate pacifists, on this question gained damaging force after the Anschluss of 1938, when Blum suddenly became convinced "that only the firm and determined will of an antifascist coalition of powers could thwart further Nazi expansion."[42] His short-lived second government, which took office immediately after the Austrian annexation, was dedicated to rearming France with this goal in mind. By this time, however, Blum regarded the Popular Front idea as outdated by these events: his (unsuccessful) first choice had been to form a government of "national union" to meet the Nazi challenge to national security.[43]

The Spanish Civil War is a much more thorny issue. Clearly Blum's policy of nonintervention divided the Popular Front from the beginning, although not along the Marxist/non-Marxist dividing line, as has sometimes been supposed. As Brower points out in his study of the Communist party in the Popular Front era, "Blum received the support of most of the Socialists, and probably the great majority of all Frenchmen. Within the Delegation of the Left the Communists were in complete isolation on the Spanish question."[44] Thus while nonintervention constituted a *crise de conscience* for Blum and some of his close associates, the parties participating in Popular Front governments were in basic support of this policy. The Communist response did create problems, of course, but it, too, must be kept in perspective. According to Brower, "Their propaganda campaigns were in large measure a form of compensation for the acceptance of policies they disliked. For the sake of the unity of the Popular Front, they accepted what in fact was a subordinate position in the coalition."[45] Larmour is undoubtedly correct in asserting that the Communist-inspired labor unrest evoked or activated a fear of communism among the Radicals. These strikes and demonstrations against nonintervention, while quite disruptive at times, did not represent the whole story of the Communists' influence on the working class, however: "On the more important issue of social calm and increased production, the Communists were most often on the side of the government."[46] Finally and most significantly, it must be remembered that the data analysis clearly indicated that where the anticommunism theme was present in the electoral statements, it was closely tied to the advocacy of a deflationary economic policy and the nonsupport of key aspects of the Popular Front reform program; it did not stand alone as a cause of Radical defection, as Larmour asserted. Thus, to the extent that the labor unrest did threaten the Radicals and other moderates, it was able to achieve this result only because the Marxist and non-Marxist parties were split on the question of the preservation of the stalemate society which excluded the working class from the benefits of industrialism. This, we believe, accounts for the finding of a close association of anticommunism with the opposition to Popular Front aims in the social and economic spheres.

The conclusion, then, is that while the Popular Front was severely hampered by its adoption of harmful economic policies and divided by foreign events such as the Spanish Civil War, it was the internal division that existed from the very beginning between the non-Marxists, whose basic social and economic goals were conservative, and the Marxists, whose aims were not, that denied the Blum government the flexibility it needed to cope with an unprecedented situation. This division prevented the government from imposing more extreme measures to combat the adverse reactions of the business and financial community and caused dissension and eventually complete alienation of the moderates from the Popular Front.[47]

Summary and Conclusions

We began this investigation by noting a theme which frequently crops up in the literature on French politics and which, if taken to extremes, seems to deny the utility of the sort of explanatory enterprise in which we have been engaged. This is the theme that French parliamentary democracy has been weak and prone to collapse because of faults in its political-cultural base. One version of the theme asserts that French politics owes its instability and ineffectiveness to the division of the nation into two fundamentally irreconcilable political orientations, republicanism and authoritarianism. A second version looks instead to the combination of opposing orientations toward authority within individual Frenchmen. The essential point in this perspective is that the coexistence of a highly egalitarian, rebellious, antiauthority attitude with a felt need for absolutist authority from above precluded a "mixed" approach to political leadership that would have allowed for strong party organization, stable coalitions, and, in another version, a consociational democratic solution to political cleavages. In national politics this authority style resulted in a system of government where the executive was "at the mercy of whimsical, ever-changing parliamentary majorities"[48] and, hence, was denied the right to govern; or one where a (conservative) prime minister had to be invested with *pleins pouvoirs* to act without parliamentary interference or obstructionism. These approaches, while providing a valuable background to this study, were not found by themselves to adequately account for the decline of the Third Republic or a critical episode in it, the Popular Front experiment.

The political-cultural approach to the regime's political inadequacies finds a parallel in the economic-cultural explanation of the failure of the economy to pull out of the Depression. Extended into a conspiracy theory in which the conservative industrial-financial oligarchy sabotaged the Popular Front, this thesis failed to account for the fact that the economy did respond for a time to the favorable economic conditions created by the September 1936 devaluation of the franc. But in its more restrained form, in which it is argued both that business leaders were ill-disposed to the Popular Front and its program of social and economic reform and that they lacked a psychology appropriate to dynamic economic growth and expansion, this thesis, too, seemed to provide an essential background to our study.

How exactly, one may wonder, are the political and economic cultural backgrounds related to the more specific foreground of the statistical analysis of the Popular Front legislature? The key that we have adopted for this purpose is the idea of congruence between the structure of political alignments and the nature of issue or ideological cleavages that must be confronted and managed by the political system. In pre–World War I France there was a consensus on minimizing social and economic change—what Hoffmann refers to as a "stalemate society"—and this allowed politics to be wrapped up in the question of the regime's legitimacy. The structure of politics was accordingly established around this issue and the republican side, the Left, emerged victorious in spite of political-cultural weaknesses that supposedly prevented effective political action. The more frequent instability, ineffectiveness, and loss of support for the regime in the interwar years was, following this reasoning, a consequence of the fact that the socioeconomic consensus was not shared by all relevant political forces and that the economy was no longer taking care of itself adequately without state interference. An attempt in the form of the Popular Front was made to paper over the fundamental cleavage between the non-Marxist supporters of the stalemate society and the Marxist forces of change in order to defend the regime itself and remedy the ailing economy, but this attempt failed and ultimately so did the regime.

There are several factors that must be considered in explaining this failure. The economic Malthusianism of business and industry must have made the task of stimulating economic expansion a particularly difficult one. Similarly, the conservatism of business and financial circles, their commitment to the socioeconomic "stalemate," automatically put them at odds with the Popular Front government led by opponents of the prevailing social and economic system and committed to an economic experiment with deficit spending. Policy failures of the Popular Front unquestionably hurt: the forty-hour week has been convincingly demonstrated to have been the cause of the downward turn in the economy towards the end of the Blum experiment, and the roll-call analysis pointed to circumstances associated with the failure of economic policy—the devaluation and emergency financial powers roll-calls—as involved with the disintegration of the coalition. But much more significant are the strong indications in the data analysis undertaken in this study that the fundamental ideological cleavage that divided supporters and opponents of the stalemate society was not overcome by the Popular Front movement and that this failure was very closely related to the movement's disintegration. If one accepts that a solid Popular Front was necessary to allow the flexibility needed to cope with an unprecedented economic problem for which no proven remedies were available, the internal rift within the Popular Front that made such flexibility impossible must loom very large in any account of the Popular Front's failure.

The Third Republic thus becomes a regime for which one must entertain a mixed evaluation. It was built on a political and economic cultural base of certain weaknesses, to be sure, but the construction was such that the issues and challenges it faced were met adequately for the first forty or so years of its history. As long as these problems and challenges accorded with this base, the regime could and did respond effectively and successfully. But the construction proved to be too rigid; it could not adapt to the new problems of the interwar years. Its failure was not an ignominious one, however; the Popular Front was a magnificent attempt to overcome existing divisions and to adapt practice and policy to the new situation. Had not a few contingencies occurred, such as the sit-down strikes forcing the enactment of a forty-hour week, it might have succeeded. But in the end luck did not save it from the consequences of the failure to adequately resolve the structural incongruities between the party system and the challenges of the twentieth-century world.

Appendix A

An Introduction to the Statistical Techniques Used in This Study

This study attempts to explore the Popular Front experiment with the aid of fairly advanced and powerful multivariate statistical techniques. Because it seems undesirable to assume total familiarity with these techniques, a brief "intuitive" introduction to them is presented in this appendix. It is, of course, quite impossible in such a short space to develop the topics of regression, correlation, principal-components analysis, and Guttman scaling in a fashion that will be totally comprehensible to the statistically uninitiated. For those whose statistical background is somewhat less than strong but who would like to follow more closely the line of argumentation presented in chapters 3–5, however, it is hoped that the explanation of these techniques presented here will provide the necessary stepping-stone. To this end, we have avoided detailed mathematical derivations of the techniques in favor of an approach that combines verbal reasoning with geometric illustration.

In the latter part of this appendix, attention becomes increasingly shifted from the techniques themselves to their relative roles in the analysis of legislatures, especially legislative roll-call votes. That discussion is an abbreviated version of an argument developed more thoroughly and in greater detail in two recent articles by the author.[1] Those readers particularly interested in the question of the choice and application of statistical techniques to the legislative context are referred to these articles for a fuller articulation of the author's point of view.

165

Fundamental Notions of Variability

The basic starting point in the quantitative analysis of data is the idea of "variability" and its statistical measure, "variance." To "explain" in the sense used here means nothing more than to account for the different amounts or degrees of a concept or property that different people or things ("cases") have. This assumes that different cases do exemplify different amounts of the concept, or in other words that the concept has variability and hence is quite literally a "variable." Variance is a statistical concept used to summarize the variability in a given variable. The variance of a variable is calculated by taking the value each individual case has on that variable, subtracting the mean or average value of the variable from it, squaring that difference, summing the squared differences over all the cases and dividing by the total number of cases, i.e.,

$$\sigma^2 = \sum \frac{(X_i - \overline{X})^2}{N} \tag{1}$$

where $\overline{X}$ = mean of variable X
               X_i = the value of X for an individual case "i"
               Σ = the summation sign
               N = the number of cases

To statistically explain is therefore to "account for" the variance in the dependent variable by means of one or more independent variables. Since it rarely happens that the variance in the dependent variable can be totally accounted for, we will frequently note the percentage of the total variance that the independent variables do account for. Naturally the aim is almost always to maximize this percentage.

The concept of variance, because it is derived from squared differences, is always written as if it had been squared, i.e., σ^2 in notational form. This implies the existence of another concept naming the square root of variance, i.e., σ. This is referred to as the "standard deviation" of a variable. It can be shown that subtracting the mean of a variable from each of its cases and dividing the result by the standard deviation of the variable produces a "standardized" form of the variable. No matter what the variability of the original variable was, this standardized form always has a mean of 0 and a standard deviation of 1. That the mean becomes 0 can be grasped intuitively if one realizes that the mean of a variable is its "center-point"; consequently all the deviations from it, both positive and negative, should cancel out and produce a sum of 0. By subtracting the mean from each individual value we indicate that we intend to deal only with the deviations from the mean, and since we must sum them up to get their mean, the result is zero. The property of always having a standard deviation of 1 is somewhat more difficult, but the essential point is that no matter how much variability a variable has, if one divides it by a concept reflecting this variability such as its standard deviation, this variability is cancelled out or standardized to a set value, in this case 1.

The Vector Geometric Interpretation of Statistics

Perhaps the best way (although not the most common) to describe the statistical procedures in question without going into lengthy mathematical derivations is through vector geometry.[2] The basic idea behind using vector geometry is that any variable can be represented in a multidimensional space by a point, or the vector (straight line) joining that point to the origin (zero point) of the space; the two are completely equivalent. This geometric representation of a variable is achieved by letting the cases be represented by the axes spanning the space and plotting the "variable vectors," as we shall term them, from these axes. For instance, suppose the variable is education measured in years and individual A has had 20 years of it while individual B has had only 10. (For simplicity's sake we assume only two cases, although the discussion that follows can readily be expanded to incorporate any number of cases without violating the basic principles that we are about to delineate.) If we let each individual be represented by an axis in figure 26, we can easily plot education by finding the one point that has a value of 20 on axis A and 10 on axis B and labeling it "E" for education. The straight line joining E to the origin is then the variable vector E.

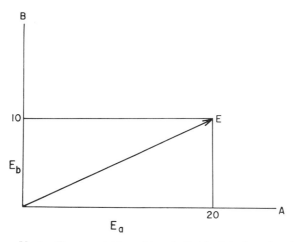

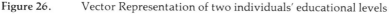

Figure 26.   Vector Representation of two individuals' educational levels

The length of the variable vector E can be derived using the Pythagorean theorem, which states that the square of the length of the hypoteneuse, or longest side of a right-angled triangle, is equal to the sum of the squares of the other two sides. In our example, if we take the triangle formed by sides E, E_a, and E_b, the squared length of E is equal to the sum of the squares of the values on education of individuals A and B, or

$$E^2 = E_a^2 + E_b^2 \qquad (2)$$

This turns out to be a relationship of critical importance for the geometric development of statistics, one that makes the geometric approach so valuable as a way to introduce the subject. With a small amount of mathematical manipulation, we shall present the first of several reasons why this is the case.

Suppose that, instead of dealing with variables in their raw form, we perform the following transformations on them. First, we subtract from each individual's score on a variable the mean of that variable, so that we are dealing only with deviations from the mean; second, we divide each of these new scores by the square root of the total number of cases. In notational form we have effected the following transformation:

$$\text{new X or X}^* = \frac{X_i - \overline{X}}{\sqrt{N}} \qquad (3)$$

For individuals A and B, their new values on education would be

$$A^* = \frac{E_a - \overline{E}}{\sqrt{N}} \text{ and } B^* = \frac{E_b - \overline{E}}{\sqrt{N}}$$

Then, according to the Pythagorean theorem, the length of the vector E is given by

$$E^2 = \frac{(E_a - \overline{E})^2}{N} + \frac{(E_b - \overline{E})^2}{N} \qquad (4)$$

The crucial point to grasp is that this equation (4) for the square of the length of E is equivalent to the formula for·calculating its variance (1), the only difference being that we have written out the terms for each case where formerly we gave the general form. Thus the squared length of a vector representing a variable in this form is equal to the variance of the variable; and the length therefore equals its standard deviation. Moreover, the contributions of individuals A and B to the squared length or variance of E are given by their *squared* deviations from the mean, not just by the deviations themselves. This explains why we took the squared deviations from the mean as the basis for the definition of variance instead of the more obvious absolute values of the deviations, a procedure which may have puzzled the reader earlier.

Regression

Having developed the concepts of variance and standard deviation and their geometric interpretations, we can move quite readily into a consideration of multiple regression. The object of multiple regression is to account for as much variance in a dependent variable as possible using an appropriately weighted summation of two or more independent variables. The algebraic form that this takes is

$$\hat{Y} = a + b_1 X_1 + b_2 X_2 + \ldots + b_n X_n \qquad (5)$$

where $\hat{Y}$ = predicted value of the dependent variable Y

a = a constant
$b_1 \ldots n$ = the weights given to the X variables in accounting for Y

The error, e^2, which we wish to minimize, is given by the difference between the actual and predicted values of Y, squared and summed over all cases, i.e.,

$$\Sigma (Y - \hat{Y})^2.$$

The objective of minimizing the sum of the *squared* errors is why regression is often referred to as a "least squares" fit of the independent variable(s) to the dependent variable. By converting into geometric form the problem of deriving a means of always arriving at optional values of a and of the b's for predicting Y, we can show why the error, like variance, is composed of squared differences.

Suppose that we take as an example a three-dimensional space that is spanned by three perpendicular axes which represent individuals A, B, and C and that contains three variables, X_1, X_2, and Y, represented as vectors in this space (fig. 27). Let us further suppose that the variables have undergone the transformation of (3) and thus that their squared lengths are equal to their variances. We take X_1 and X_2 to be the independent variables which we wish to use to explain as much of the variance of the dependent variable, Y, as possible. With elementary geometry it can be shown that the vectors X_1 and X_2 form a two-dimensional plane in this space such as that sketched in figure 27 and that all points (vectors) in this plane are linear combinations of X_1 and X_2, i.e., can be expressed in the form "$b_1X_1 + b_2X_2$." The similarity of this mathematical expression to the right-hand side of equation 5 indicates that what we are really looking for in multiple regression is a vector that is in the X_1 - X_2 plane (i.e., is a linear combination of X_1 and X_2) and that accounts for as much of the squared length of Y as possible.

From the previous discussion of the Pythagorean theorem, we know that we can account for the squared length of Y by forming a right-angled triangle with Y as the hypotenuse. Since we wish to account for the variance of Y with a linear combination of X_1 and X_2, one side of this triangle will have to be a vector lying in the X_1 - X_2 plane. The vector in this plane best able to account for the variance of Y will be the one that forms the longest possible side of the right-angled triangle. It is intuitively evident that this means choosing the point in the X_1 - X_2 plane closest to Y and that this is achieved by dropping a perpendicular line "e" from Y to the plane at point $\hat{Y}$. The $\hat{Y}$ vector is therefore the best estimate of Y that can be gotten from X_1 and X_2.

From the Pythagorean theorem, the ratio of the squared length (variance) of $\hat{Y}$ to that of Y is the proportion of the latter's variance that can be attributed to $\hat{Y}$ (i.e., X_1 and X_2); it is this proportion that we mentioned earlier as something that we would like to be as high as possible. The other side of the triangle, the perpendicular e, is the error, that proportion of the variance that cannot be explained by X_1 and X_2. Its relative contribution to the variance of Y is also given by the ratio of its squared length, e^2, to the squared length of Y. Since e represents the distance between $\hat{Y}$ and Y, i.e., $(\hat{Y} - Y)$, it follows

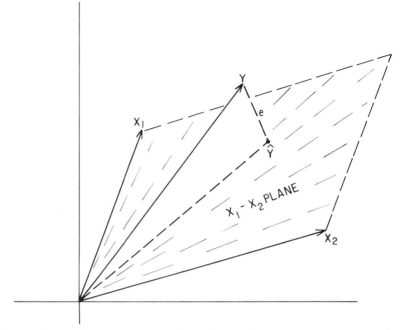

Figure 27.   Graphic representation of the multiple regression of vector Y on vectors X_1 and X_2

that minimizing e^2 is equivalent to minimizing the sum of the squared deviations of $\hat{Y}$ from Y, as noted earlier.

What one achieves from multiple regression, then, are values of a and the b's that produce the one vector $\hat{Y}$ that maximally accounts for the variance of Y. The constant, a, is that point where the X_1 - X_2 plane cuts the Y axis. Since we have subtracted the original means from all three variables to give them means of zero, this junction of Y with the X_1 - X_2 plane takes place at the origin, making $a = 0$ in our example. Concerning the b's, although they are the weights attached to the independent variables, their magnitudes are not necessarily indicative of the relative importance of the two X's in accounting for Y. Much still depends on the units used in measuring the X variables. For instance, if X_1 were "income," the value of b_1 would depend on whether income was measured in cents or in dollars. The problem of differences arising over what units a variable is measured in can be overcome, however. Since the difference between income measured in dollars and income measured in cents is that the latter's variance is much greater than the former's, standardization can control this by giving both measures of income a standard deviation and variance of 1. When variables are standardized, the intercept a will equal 0, and the magnitudes of the b's, sometimes referred to as "beta weights," will reflect the relative contribution of each predictor variable in accounting for the variance of the dependent variable Y, independent of the other X variables (and of the original variances of the variables). It is these beta weights that are used in path analysis to calculate the relative importance of different "paths" to the dependent variable.

Correlation

We observed in the last section that the object of multiple regression is, in geometric terms, to maximize the squared length of the vector $\hat{Y}$ and to minimize the squared length of the vector e (the error) in the right-angled triangle formed to account for the dependent variable Y. We also indicated that the contribution of $\hat{Y}$ in accounting for Y's variance is given by the ratio of the squared length of $\hat{Y}$ to that of Y. If we take the square root of this ratio, we end up with what is termed the *simple* correlation coefficient between $\hat{Y}$ and Y. Since the vector $\hat{Y}$ is the optional linear combination of X_1 and X_2 for accounting for Y, this is equivalent to the *multiple* correlation coefficient of X_1 and X_2 with Y ("multiple" because it is a correlation of more than one X with Y). The (simple) correlation between two variables, then, is that coefficient which, when squared, yields the proportion of the variance of the dependent variable accounted for by the independent variable, or in the more correct noncausal terms, the proportion of the variances of the two variables that is shared or common to both. As such it reflects the strength of the relationship between the variables.

If we standardize the variables we are dealing with, this interpretation of the correlation coefficient can be made even simpler. Standardization, it will be remembered, gives a variable or vector a mean of 0 and a variance and

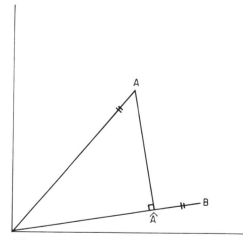

Figure 28.   The projection of vector *A* on vector *B*.

standard deviation of 1. This means that its (squared) length in vector space is equal to 1. In figure 28 we have pictured two such vectors, A and B. Following the practice in multiple regression, we begin the assessment of the degree of relationship between these two variable vectors by dropping a perpendicular from one to the other, for instance, from A to B at point Â, although it could be the other way around with no change in result. The ratio of the squared length of Â to that of A is of course the proportion of the variance of A accounted for or shared by B, and its square root, Â/A, is the correlation coefficient between A and B. Since the vector A has length 1, however, this ratio is in fact equal simply to the length of Â. Thus when we use standardized variables, the correlation coefficient between two variable vectors is equal to the length of what is termed the "projection" (Â in our example) of one vector upon the other. Naturally the closer the two variable vectors are, the longer will be this projection and hence the greater will be their correlation coefficient. This finding is crucial to understanding of principal-components or factor analysis, to which we now turn.

Principal-Components Analysis

Consider that we have a large number of variable vectors, say fifty, in a multidimensional space. The maximum number of dimensions that this space would need to hold these fifty vectors is fifty. That this is so can be appreciated if we note that there is no fundamental difference between an axis and a vector; hence the fifty vectors could in fact be identical with the fifty axes or dimensions that span the space, if they were all at right angles with each other. The significance of their being at right angles lies in the fact that a vector at a right angle to another has no projection on it and thus is uncorrelated or "independent" of it. However this is only one possibility, and not at all the most likely. In fact it is almost always the case that there will be some degree of intercorrelation among most or all of the fifty variables. If several variables are fairly highly intercorrelated, it means that a considerable proportion of their variance is shared, in other words that the variance of some variables could be accounted for to some extent at least by others. Naturally if this degree of redundancy in some of the fifty variables were high, we would not need fifty dimensions to account for their variance. Instead we could for all practical purposes eliminate those dimensions that had been included to account for variables that turn out to be highly correlated or dependent on others and in this manner reduce the dimensionality of the space. This is roughly the approach of factor analysis, or more correctly "principal-components analysis," which is the type we use in this study.

   The fundamental logic of principal-components analysis is this. We know that our fifty variables can be located as vectors in a fifty-dimensional space. What we wish to discover is whether there is enough dependency (inter-correlation) among these fifty variable vectors to allow a space of fewer dimensions to account for most of their variance. If we could do this in a space of three dimensions, for example, we would be in a position to postulate that the fifty variables we started with really have three underlying dimensions, which we would then try to identify in substantive terms. These three dimensions, being much fewer in number than the original fifty variable vectors yet accounting for, we would hope, most of their variance, would then be vastly more suitable for subsequent analysis and interpretation.

Principal-components analysis is a statistical procedure for discovering axes known as "factors" which can account for as much of the variance of the original variable vectors as possible. An impression of how it works can be given by means of an illustration. Suppose that we have in a vector space a cluster of variable vectors as indicated in figure 29. (In subsequent analysis, these vectors will be plotted as points, a representation that is both simpler and perfectly equivalent.) This cluster of variables could be in more than two dimensions, although we are more or less constrained to picture it in two dimensions. The preceding discussion of correlation analysis led to the finding that the correlation coefficient between two variable vectors is equal to the projection of the one upon the other and, consequently, that the closer two vectors are, the more highly correlated they become. Moreover, from the way we defined correlation, we know that the square of the correlation coefficient is equal to the amount of variance the two variable vectors have in common. In simple terms, what principal-components analysis would do in our example would be to find a factor or axis that is located as close to as many of the variable vectors in the cluster as possible and hence that shares a maximum amount of their variance. This factor is then said to account for that amount of the variance of the variable vectors.

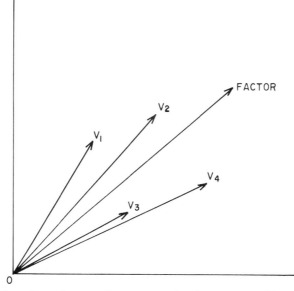

Figure 29.   Locating a factor to best account for the variance of four variable vectors

The output from this analysis would therefore contain two pieces of information. First, it would list the projections of each variable vector on the factor. These of course are equivalent to the correlations of each variable with the factor and in factor analysis terminology are known as "factor loadings." Second, it would give the "eigenvalue" or total amount of variance accounted for by the factor. Since the amount of variance of each variable vector explained by the factor is given by the square of the correlation coefficient between them, the eigenvalue is equivalent to the sum of the squared loadings or correlations of the vectors with the factor. In our illustration (fig. 29) there are four variable vectors; the total variance to be explained is therefore 4 (i.e., the variables are in standardized form and each has a variance equal to 1). If the factor in question has an eigenvalue of 3, this would mean that it accounts for three-quarters, or 75 percent, of the total variance. In cases where there is more than one factor, for each factor produced there is a corresponding set of factor loadings and an eigenvalue associated with it.

Principal-components factoring finds factors or axes that account for maximum amounts of variance in the variable vectors. If we had a situation where the variable vectors formed two distinct clusters that could be represented essentially in a two-dimensional space, as pictured in figure 30, the first factor found would be located as it is, since in that position it is as close as possible to both clusters. The second factor would then be located at a right angle to it so as to be independent or uncorrelated with it. The point of making the second factor independent of the first is that by so doing we rule out the possibility of the two having any shared variance. The variance explained by the second factor must then be variance left over or unaccounted for by the first factor. If we were dealing with more than two dimensions, a third factor independent of the first two and accounting for as much of the variance still unaccounted for would be found, and so forth, until all the variance was accounted for. Since the total number of factors so produced would equal the number of variables in most cases, we obviously need a cutting point. The usual standard is that factors with eigenvalues of less than 1 are ignored since they account for less variance than one single variable and hence defeat the point of factor analysis. With a few exceptions that are justified theoretically, this standard is followed in this study.

It is evident that the location of the two factors in figure 30 is not theoretically the most meaningful. Since the idea of a factor is that it be a new variable summarizing the common elements of a number of original variables and since the location of the original variables clearly indicates that they constitute two distinct types of whatever we are dealing with, it would be more satisfactory if we had one factor that represented each type. This is achieved in factor analysis by the "rotation" of the two factors so that each passes through one of the variable clusters. This rotation is permissible because once the vector space that is adequate to account for enough variance in the variable vectors has been defined (according to the maximizing principle of principal components mentioned above), it makes no difference mathematically where in this space we locate the factors or axes that span it.

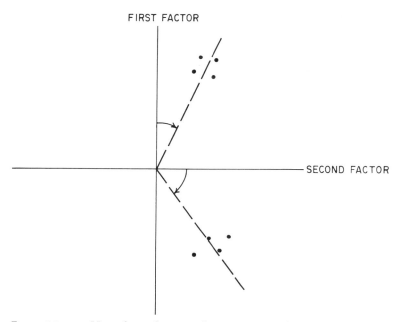

Figure 30.   Hypothetical principal-components solution to account for
eight variables in two clusters

In fact there need no longer be any requirement that the factors be independent of or "orthogonal" to each other, and if this stipulation is waived the
rotation is known as an "oblique" rotation. (We have indicated the oblique
rotated factors in figure 30 by dotted lines.) In the factor analyses performed
in this study, we always opted for oblique rotation with the objective of
placing factors through clusters of variables to best summarize the type of
voting behavior or political attitudes that these clusters represent. This is not
the only method used by factor analysis; for our purposes, however, it
proved to make the most sense.

If oblique rotation is employed, the output from the procedure consists of:
(1) the new or rotated factor loadings (the "pattern matrix"), (2) the correlations between the rotated factors, and (3) the "structure matrix." The
distinction between the pattern and the structure matrix is that the former
gives the projections of the variables on each factor independent of their
projections on other factors, while the latter lists the overall correlations of
each variable with each factor, including indirect influences by means of other
correlated factors. It is the pattern matrix that we use to assess the relative
contribution of each variable to each factor, since we wish to have this
information in a form independent of their mutual correlations with other
factors. By guessing at what the variables with the highest loadings on a given
factor have in common, one can make hypotheses concerning what each

factor represents in substantive or theoretical terms. Having considered only the direct contributions of each variable to each factor by concentrating on the pattern matrix, we may then utilize the factor correlations to assess the degree to which the different factors, and thus the subsets of variables that make them up, are associated.

It is usually the case in factor analysis that the pattern matrix plus the factor correlations suffice for the analyst to make his interpretation of the factoring. Because we are dealing with data on a legislature, however, we are aided in this sometimes difficult task by one further type of finding. Since a factor is in reality a new variable that summarizes the behavior of a number of original variables, each of the individuals or cases that had values on the original variables can have values on the factors formed from them. These values are known as "factor scores" and are calculated from the factor loadings and the values each case had on the original variables that make up the factor. Because we have means of identifying our legislators in political terms, namely their party affiliations, by plotting the factor scores of the legislators produced by factor analyzing their roll-call votes, for example, we can readily see how a given factor divides the parties and we can render an interpretation with the assistance of this information. For instance, suppose we found a factor that loaded roll-call votes of so many different subject matters that one common, substantive basis for the factor could not be found. Interpretation from these data would be impossible, but if we plotted the factor scores and found that the factor sharply divided the Communists, for example, from the rest of the legislature, we would have the common element needed to facilitate the interpretation of the factor. Thus we would note that there were a number of roll-calls of diverse subject matters that elicited support (opposition) from the Communists but, generally speaking, from no one else, and from there a closer and probably more fruitful look at which roll-calls did this would be warranted. In general, we shall interpret factors, first, by the way they divide the legislators and only then, if appropriate, by the nature of the variables that loaded on them.

The Issue of Data Measurement

The statistical techniques that have been discussed up to this point are all based on an assumption that frequently plagues the social scientist, namely, that the level of measurement of the data is "interval." In simple terms what this means is that the intervals between integer numbers that are assigned to different values of each variable are equal. For instance, in the roll-call data, we have coded a negative vote as –1, an abstention as 0, and an affirmative vote as +1, where "affirmative" means in support of the Popular Front. Consequently, our findings from the factor analyses of these roll calls are strictly speaking only valid if the interval between 0 and –1 is equal to the interval between 0 and +1. We believe that this is the case for the following reasons. First, in terms of the objective facts of parliamentary arithmetic, an abstention is equivalent to exactly one-half of a vote for the other side. Thus if a party or coalition has decided to vote for a measure and one of its members disagrees, an abstention on his part would deny one vote to his coalition but add nothing to the other side, while a vote against the measure would both cost his coalition one vote and add one vote to the oppositon's total, thereby doubling the effect of a mere abstention. Mathematically this implies that the intervals are equal. Second, it seems reasonable to assume that if the facts of parliamentary arithmetic are such as have just been described, the subjective meaning to the legislator would be the same. In other words we make the assumption that since an abstention is a half-way house, arithmetically speaking, between voting "for" and "against," legislators will perceive it as such and act accordingly.

Guttman Scaling

There is a well-known technique for deriving "dimensions" composed of a number of original variables which does not make the assumption of intervality and has been extensively used in roll-call analysis, namely, cumulative, or Guttman, scaling. What Guttman scaling tries to do is to arrange a set of items (usually questions) in a scale based on their "extremeness" or difficulty in being answered affirmatively. For instance, if each person in a sample of the white population of the United States was asked if he or she would object to his or her daughter marrying a black, one may presume that a considerable proportion would answer affirmatively. If asked if they would mind a black family moving into their community, a smaller subset of this group would probably answer "yes." However, to the question of whether they minded that blacks were allowed to travel in the same buses as whites, only a very few of the most prejudiced respondents would answer that they did. The idea, then, is that the questions become arranged in order of increasing extremeness, that is, the respondent has to be more and more prejudiced to continue answering affirmatively with each successive question, thereby yielding a cumulative pattern. The questions are said to form a scale to the extent to which those answering affirmatively to the most extreme or difficult questions also do so to the less difficult questions, but not vice versa.

Duncan MacRae has made a useful adaptation of this principle for the purposes of roll-call analysis.[3] He notes that Guttman scaling expects the sort of relationship depicted in table 10 for two variables to be said to scale. In the table we have indicated with X's the cells where respondents may validly be located. The critical criterion for Guttman scaling is that there be few or no respondents answering affirmatively the more difficult question but failing to do so on the easier question. In other words, the principle of Guttman scaling is that in relationships between any two variables in the scale, there must be one cell, in this example cell "b," that is empty or nearly so. MacRae has noted that there is a measure of association for four-fold contingency tables, Yule's Q, that achieves a value of plus or minus 1 when the scaling criterion is exactly met and that approaches unity as the relationship approaches it. Therefore, to find all the Guttman scales that may exist in a set of roll-call votes, one simply has to compute a matrix of Yule's Q's of every roll call by every other roll call and, by visual inspection, to select groups of roll calls that all have very high Yule's Q values with one another. In this manner several different Guttman scales can be discovered in a single set of roll-call votes and can be labeled the dimensions of voting behavior in the legislature under study.

Table 10   Ideal Relationship between Two Questions That Are Considered to Scale

| | | Easier Question | | | |
		Yes		No	
More Difficult Question	Yes	a	X	b	
	No	c	X	d	X

NOTE: X's indicate where respondents may be located.

Since the technique is based on Yule's Q, a statistic designed for dichotomous variables, this method avoids the problem of having to assume, without proof, that one's data are interval. However there are disadvantages to more than offset this. Since the roll calls are coded dichotomously, abstentions, which we regard as a valid type of behavior, are ignored.[4] Also, the measurement tends to be imprecise. The cutting-point, that value of Yule's Q considered high enough to indicate scaleability, can only be arbitrarily chosen, and different cutting-points will often produce different scales. Moreover, legislators whose vote patterns deviated too greatly from a scale pattern would presumably have to be weeded out and excluded from that scale. Similarly, roll calls that did not fit in any of the scales would be ignored in the analysis. Finally, the scales produced are ordinal rather than interval in level of measurement, and the use of regression and correlation techniques on them would be suspect.[5]

For all these reasons the use of Guttman scaling has been curtailed in this study. Nevertheless some interesting questions do arise concerning it. Since scaling is based on a completely different principle from factor analysis, will the scales produced resemble in any way the factors resulting from a factor analysis of the same data? Under what conditions could this happen, and, if it does not happen in every instance, which reflects the greater reality, factoring or scaling? Or would they both reflect equally valid aspects of the reality, related in some way but nonetheless distinct? We explore these questions at certain points in the roll-call analyses of chapters 3 and 4, where it turns out that Guttman scaling does supplement the interpretation of the data derived from the factor analytic technique.

Appendix B

The Roll-Call Sample

The ninety-three roll calls analyzed in this study constitute, with one qualification, a simple random sample of the approximately six hundred roll-call votes held in the French Chamber of Deputies in the June 1936–December 1938 period. The qualification is that a roll call had to have 7 percent or more dissidence, that is, no more than 93 percent of the deputies voting the same way, in order to be included in the sample. Listed below are several pieces of information on these roll-calls, starting with their *Journal Officiel* numbers and the numbers assigned to them in this study, which follow the code: 001-037 = 1936, 101-137 = 1937, 201-219 = 1938. In addition, brief descriptions of the subject matter of each roll call are given to aid the reader in interpreting the data findings of chapters 3 and 4. These subject matters were determined on the basis of a study of the debates that culminated in each of the roll-call votes, and they generally involved many more complexities and nuances than these very short descriptions indicate. Finally, the outcome of each roll-call vote is noted following its description. For the purposes of statistical analysis, these outcomes were recoded so that the Popular Front government's position was always indicated as +1, votes against this position as –1, and abstentions as 0. Deputies listed as "absent," "on vacation," and so forth on a given roll call were treated as missing data for that roll call.

179

Number	Journal Officiel Number	Date	Description
1	4	June 11, 1936	Paid vacations bill. Opposition to bill over its possible application to agriculture. Defeated 452–108.
2	16	June 18, 1936	Election inquiry. Demand for an inquiry into the election of a Communist deputy. Defeated 226–190.
3	19	June 19, 1936	Bill setting limit on Treasury bonds in circulation. Rightist deputy objected that government's policies were inflationary and would lead to a devaluation. Defeated 392–148.
4	21	June 23, 1936	Confidence vote on government's foreign policy. Adopted 382–198.
5	23	June 23, 1936	Election inquiry. Supported the election of the right-wing candidate. Adopted 207–110.
6	35	July 3, 1936	Wheat office bill. Government wanted to bypass discussion of several counterbills and start discussion of its bill immediately. Adopted 375–215.
7	43	July 3, 1936	Wheat office bill. Article 8: Wheat office council to control importing of wheat and purchasing of surplus domestic wheat. Adopted 353–153.
8	46	July 9, 1936	Creation of committee to investigate reform of the state. Left objected as they did not feel reform was needed since the Popular Front had a majority. Adopted 383–210.
9	62	July 21, 1936	Bill to organize (bring under state control) the coal market. Adopted 409–149.
10	64	July 23, 1936	Election inquiry. Right tried to delay the vote, accused Left of wanting a witch-hunt. Defeated 352–206.
11	72	July 28, 1936	Retirement bill. Attempt to get certain courts exempted from cabinet's proposed right to set compulsory retirement ages in the administration and the military. Defeated 493–60.
12	88	July 31, 1936	Confidence vote on government's foreign policy. Adopted 385–199.
13	91	August 1, 1936	Wheat Office. Senate amendment to article 9, supported by government, sharply delimiting grain imports. Right-wing wanted no imports under any circumstances. Adopted 311–259.
14	96	August 4, 1936	Illegal price rises. A right-wing deputy who felt this bill infringed on "commercial liberty" wanted it sent back to committee. Defeated 372–198.

Number	Journal Officiel Number	Date	Description
15	99	August 6, 1936	School-age bill. Some right-wing deputies felt that because of teachers' pacifism more money should not be spent on them. Defeated 409–159.
16	105	August 7, 1936	Wheat Office. Attempt to squash the whole bill. Defeated 398–73.
17	107	August 7, 1936	Wheat Office. The bill provided that the Central Council would be appointed for its first year by the minister, thereafter by professional associations. Amendment was an attempt to have it appointed by professional associations from the beginning. Defeated 368–176.
18	109	August 7, 1936	Wheat Office. Amendment to prevent grain dealers from having to obtain Wheat Office's authorization to conduct business. Defeated 378–188.
19	116	August 7, 1936	Wheat Office. Amendment to prevent senators and deputies from holding offices in the Wheat Office. Defeated 385–40.
20	125	August 12, 1936	Wheat Office. Amendment to prevent grain merchants whose previous activities would have been in violation of the bill from being excluded from doing business; an example of "retroactive punishment." Defeated 387–157.
21	136	September 28, 1936	Loi monétaire. Article 1. Suspended old exchange rate of the franc and Bank of France's obligation to assure convertibility of gold. Adopted 348–220.
22	137	September 28, 1936	Loi monétaire. Amendment to give Parliament, not the Cabinet, the right to set new franc value. Defeated 348–220.
23	140	September 28, 1936	Loi monétaire. Amendment to assure that financial deals made before devaluation would be payable in old francs, not devalued ones. Defeated 347–232.
24	148	October 1, 1936	Loi monétaire. Entire bill. Adopted 354–217.
25	153	November 13, 1936	A resolution which asked the government to introduce without delay a bill giving people right to defend themselves against defamation of character. Adopted 380–187.
26	154	November 26, 1936	Fiscal reform. Amendment to assure that new sales tax could never be greater than old taxes it was meant to replace. Defeated 382–191.

Number	*Journal Officiel* Number	Date	Description
27	161	November 27, 1936	Fiscal reform. Amendment to get tax exemptions for social and sports activities, to encourage benevolence among business leaders for their workers. Defeated 376–202.
28	166	November 27, 1936	Fiscal reform. Aim of bill was to lighten tax load on hard-pressed sectors of society, simplify methods of calculating taxes, end fiscal fraud through tighter controls, tax rich more. Adopted 385–190.
29	167	December 1, 1936	Labor conflicts bill. An attempt to stop the bill before it had been debated in general. Defeated 525–49.
30	176	December 1, 1936	Labor conflicts. An amendment to have labor and employer representatives from other organizations besides the CGT and CGPF on the proposed National Labor Commission. Defeated 359–217.
31	195	December 8, 1936	Modification of press law. Amendment to have more serious crimes of incitement sent to *cours d'assizes* where they would get jury trials. Defeated 387–197.
32	214	December 22, 1936	Amnesty for political crimes. Amendment to prevent amnesty for use of illegal means to achieve work stoppages, higher wages. Defeated 404–193.
33	218	December 23, 1936	Labor conflicts. A counterbill which would have prevented government from having extensive powers of intervention into labor disputes. Defeated 361–238.
34	235	December 30, 1936	1937 budget. During devaluation many commodity suppliers had existing contracts set aside so that they could get higher prices. Government wanted these contracts honored, if they were legitimate business deals. If not, a 100% levy was to be placed on speculative profits. Amendment was to eliminate these provisions. Defeated 434–151.
35	237	December 30, 1936	1937 budget. Entire bill. Adopted 494–67.
36	239	December 31, 1936	Slight modification of rules concerning composition of legislative bureau. Defeated 467–80.
37	245	December 31, 1936	1937 budget. Senate rejected roll call 34, government rewrote clause to reduce levy on profit-taking during the devaluation from 100% to 50%, but excluded exemption for

Number	*Journal Officiel* Number	Date	Description
			legitimate business deals as opposed to speculation. This amendment was to reinsert this exemption. Adopted 283–267.
101	256	January 19, 1937	Political amnesty bill. Amendment to extend amnesty to crimes committed by property developers (*lotisseurs*). Defeated 362–235.
102	262	January 21, 1937	Amnesty bill. An addition to provide that nationalized citizens who lost their citizenship because of political activities would regain it. Adopted 299–245.
103	271	February 4, 1937	Employment Office bill. Article 3. Abolished private agencies and established a national one for the food industry. Adopted 393–183.
104	284	February 12, 1937	Business (*Fonds du commerce*) bill. Amendment was a Communist attempt to strip sellers of their rights if buyers have become too poor to repay. Defeated 488–83.
105	288	February 11, 1937	Business (*Fonds du commerce*) bill. Adopted 511–52.
106	293	February 18, 1937	Attempt to move up the date for discussion of objections to the government's price rise for wheat, which was deemed too low in light of the devaluation of the franc. Defeated 230–342.
107	300	February 22, 1937	Collective price agreements in agriculture. Amendment to have price controls only on those products approved not only by the minister but also by Parliament. Defeated 229–300.
108	301	February 25, 1937	Collective price agreement in agriculture. Article 8. Minister's authority to extend an agreement accepted by half the agricultural producers in a given region to the whole region. Adopted 364–205.
109	307	February 26, 1937	Confidence motion in particular on the government's objectives of "economic renewal and social reform." Adopted 361–209.
110	319	March 11, 1937	Price rises bill. Amendment to have farm production excluded. Defeated 299–255.
111	329	March 12, 1937	Price rises bill. Article 5. To set up a special court, without appeal, for violation of the bill. Adopted 329–251.
112	336	March 18, 1937	Organization of ministry of public health. Amendment to provide that reorganization of the ministry would not result in reduction of certain social benefits. Adopted 297–290.

Number	*Journal Officiel* Number	Date	Description
113	337	March 18, 1937	Family allowances for tenant farmers. Amendment so that farm owners would be considered as employers and required to contribute to the plan. Adopted 394–177.
114	342	March 23, 1937	Right-wing deputy's attempt to have a special parliamentary committee set up to investigate the Clichy incident. Defeated 322–261.
115	350	March 25, 1937	Hotel prices bill. Attempt to suppress article 2, which would give special commissions the right to set hotel rates. Defeated 261–322.
116	355	March 25, 1937	Adjournment of the Chamber of Deputies until April 27. Right wing wanted it to reconvene earlier. Adopted 362–223.
117	370	May 20, 1937	Farm property bill. Amendment to make tenant-farmer's improvements on the property reimbursable upon his departure only if they were authorized by the owner, and to require compensation to farmer if the property has depreciated. Defeated 354–236.
118	376	May 21, 1937	Farm property. Amendment to limit right of tenant farmer to first refusal if the farmer intends to sell his land, especially if he is selling it within the family. Adopted 307–281 (against the government).
119	381	May 25, 1937	To close discussion on election inquiry. Right had fought it because winner was a cousin of Blum. Adopted 327–207.
120	395	June 15, 1937	Tariff bill. Amendment to assure that agricultural products would have same tariff rates as other products. Defeated 331–261.
121	397	June 15, 1937	Motion to delay session. Right wanted more time to consider the government's bill asking for financial emergency powers. Defeated 358–230.
122	400	June 15, 1937	Bill giving government financial emergency powers. Adopted 346–247.
123	404	June 19, 1937	Government asked for repassage of its original emergency financial powers bill, as against the bill the Senate passed, which had serious limitations on the government's freedom of action. Adopted 346–248.
124	419	November 19, 1937	Confidence motion on general program of government. Adopted 399–160.
125	422	November 25, 1937	Amendment to bill providing more benefits for civil servants, invalids, war veterans, civil servants with families. Defeated 363–231.

Num-ber	*Journal Officiel* Num-ber	Date	Description
126	425	November 25, 1937	Bill to help civil servants, invalids, war veterans. Adopted 521–4.
127	426	November 30, 1937	Attempt to send back to committee a bill simplifying budget voting procedure. Opponents of the bill feared loss of parliamentary prerogatives. Defeated 406–164.
128	436	December 4, 1937	Budget (1938) of Ministry of Interior. Adopted 451–78.
129	438	December 9, 1937	Government proposal to put off discussion of budget of Ministry of Foreign Affairs till minister could be present. Adopted 383–96.
130	441	December 16, 1937	Amendment to 1938 Budget to eliminate the right of communes to a surtax on mineral water, carbonic acid produced in their communes because this would have favored certain communes. Adopted (against government) 318–288.
131	454	December 23, 1937	Bill to re-open 1937 World Fair. Adopted 338–250.
132	455	December 28, 1937	1937 budget expenditures. Amendment to stop government from cancelling 4 million francs in educational expenditures for which it claimed there was no need. Defeated 384–214.
133	466	December 29, 1937	Bill on rents. Amendment to a provision that would have rolled back certain rents that had been allowed to rise. Opponents to provision felt that would have been retroactive legislation. Adopted (against government) 287–281.
134	474	December 30, 1937	1938 budget. Article 2, series B. To give government the right to check bank accounts or demand that taxpayers provide details on all accounts. Adopted 387–208.
135	481	December 30, 1937	1938 budget. Adopted 535–45.
136	484	December 30, 1937	Bill on rents. Communist amendment to set allowable rent rises on prewar buildings at a rate lower than the government had proposed. Defeated 525–73.
137	488	December 31, 1937	1938 budget. Repassed in basically the original form after Senate had changed many provisions. Adopted 539–42.
201	511	February 1, 1938	Electoral reform. Elimination of an article supported by a right-wing deputy favorable to the introduction of proportional representation and reducing the number of deputies. Defeated 444–118.

Number	Journal Officiel Number	Date	Description
202	512	February 1, 1938	Electoral reform. Elimination of article supported by Communists that would have forbade high government or civil service officials from holding positions in private corporations. Adopted 399–88.
203	538	February 18, 1938	Conciliation and arbitration law. Amendment to increase representation of employers and labor on the proposed Supreme Court of Arbitration. Defeated 375–209.
204	541	February 18, 1938	Conciliation and arbitration law. Amendment to disallow arbiters from adding to provisions of an existing labor contract. Defeated 380–203.
205	542	February 18, 1938	Conciliation and arbitration bill. Adopted 400–177.
206	544	February 24, 1938	Collective work contracts. Amendment to prevent government's proposed right to intervene into disputes from applying to agriculture. Defeated 346–195.
207	550	February 28, 1938	Conciliation and arbitration bill. Amendment to exclude from the bill the demarcation of the employers' "rights" over hiring and firing and to make this a subject of arbitration. Defeated 384–199.
208	553	February 28, 1938	Conciliation and arbitration bill. Amendment to suppress provision that union's representative on arbitration committee would have right to examine all documents submitted in a dispute. It was feared that this would infringe upon management's right to manage. Defeated 378–213.
209	557	February 28, 1938	Conciliation and arbitration bill. Amendment to give other organizations besides CGT and CGPF a voice in selection of labor and employers' representatives on Supreme Court of Arbitration. Defeated 349–250.
210	565	March 2, 1938	Conciliation and arbitration bill. Amendment to suppress the provision that if a separate bill for agriculture was not passed by April 15, an administration decree would be issued to cover the extension of conciliation and arbitration procedures to agriculture. Defeated 318–234.
211	571	March 3, 1938	Conciliation and arbitration bill. Amendment to have hiring regulated by common law, not by this law or by arbitration. Defeated 329–236.

Number	*Journal Officiel* Number	Date	Description
212	582	March 3, 1938	Conciliation and arbitration bill. Adopted 455–130.
213	584	March 22, 1938	War measures bill. Government questioned on whether arms meant for the French military were being sent to Spain. Defeated 388–63.
214	586	March 22, 1938	Agreement with Bank of France. Allowed for more advances to Treasury from the Bank. Adopted 343–243.
215	590	March 24, 1938	War measures bill. Amendment to allow military to limit by its own discretion its obligation to answer all questions posed by parliamentary committees to their own discretion. Defeated 385–177.
216	594	March 25, 1938	Agreement with Bank of France. Repassed after Senate modifications. Adopted 347–247.
217	598	April 12, 1938	Emergency financial powers bill. Right-wing deputy proposed that all government decrees be submitted to parliamentary committees for comment before issuance. Defeated 429–97.
218	612	October 4, 1938	Government request to put off a Communist interpellation on its foreign policy; made a matter of confidence. Adopted 535–75.
219	614	December 9, 1939	Confidence vote. Reformation of a Center-Right majority, end of the Popular Front coalition. Adopted 315–241.

Appendix C

The Coding of the
Electoral Statements of the
Deputies Elected
to the Chamber in 1936

The information used to derive the ideological dimensions of the 1936 Chamber came from a coding of the electoral statements or "professions de foi" of the victorious candidates in the 1936 legislative elections. These statements were compiled after each election and published in a single volume by the Chamber of Deputies. The fact that this was by 1936 a time-honored procedure suggests that a certain amount of standardization in the way the electoral statements were prepared took place. At the very least, it made the task of collecting this data much easier than it would be in most nations.

The basic idea in the coding was that any position, recommendation, goal, or other idea expressed by more than a couple of deputies was made a variable, and all deputies mentioning that idea were coded 1 on that variable. Deputies not mentioning the idea were automatically coded 0. Occasionally, it was possible to maintain an opposite position on a variable, and mentions that fit this category were coded -1. All instances of a -1 category are indicated in the variable descriptions that follow.

Because we are dealing for the most part with dichotomous or dummy variables, it is particularly important for statistical reasons to ensure that all variables analyzed have a reasonable minimum of variance. For the trichotomously-coded roll-call votes, we imposed a minimum standard of 7 percent dissidence for inclusion in the statistical analysis. In the case of these dichotomous variables, we felt obliged to use a slightly tougher 10 percent dissidence standard. The consequence is that, while over ninety variables were originally coded, only the seventy-nine listed below found their way into either the analysis of the entire Chamber's or the Popular Front's ideological makeup.

Finally, it must be noted that the coding of electoral statements was not always a matter of recording the individual candidate's personal views. Specifically, the Communist and Socialist parties both issued party platforms, and in many cases their candidates did little more in their own statements than to refer the reader to the party statement. In such instances, it was necessary to code the appropriate party statement in place of or as a supplement to the candidate's statement. This creates, of course, a possible bias or inaccuracy in the coding process. This problem is dealt with in considerable detail and ultimately resolved in the first half of chapter 5.

Variable Number	Description
830	Cleaner, more honest politics; less financial ties and involvements; end to scandals.
831	Amnesty for political offenses, crimes of "opinion."
832	Electoral reform—proportional representation, vote for women.
833	Fight unemployment.
834	Stronger government, executive; use of executive's right of dissolution; restore authority of the state.
835	Improve conditions, situation of workers; better wages; minimum wage; forty-hour week; paid vacations; etc.
836	Support for a public works program.
837	Eliminate foreign, immigrant labor.
838	Defend "parliamentary initiative in matters of expenditures." End it = -1.
839	Defend, extend the law on unions; unionize more workers and industries.
840	Need for more protective tariffs for agriculture.
841	Increase agricultural prices.
842	Establish a Wheat Office, other agricultural offices.
843	Defend private property; extend ownership of private property to all. Abolish private property = -1.
845	Financial aid for farmers; loans, cheaper credit ("*crédit agricole*"), moratorium on debts; farm subsidies.
846	Electrify, build better roads, assure water

Variable Number	Description
	supplies for countryside.
849	Defend republican institutions.
851	Increase social insurance; workers' pensions; unemployment benefits; workmen's compensation; more social legislation.
852	Extend social legislation, family allowances to agricultural workers.
853	Defend the secularity of the state; secular or neutral education.
854	More funds for education; extend school-leaving age.
855	Rent control; moratorium on collection of unpaid rents, especially farm rents.
856	Taxes too high for average man, small man; "fiscal *détente.*"
857	Support, consult, give greater powers to the National Economic Council.
858	Lower taxes for *commerçants* (small retailers), artisans; protect them from department store chains.
859	Progressive (income) tax; increase tax rates for higher income-brackets.
860	End deflation; increase purchasing power of people.
861	Higher taxes for industry; industrial profits too high. Better deal for industry $= -1$.
863	Less waste, cut costs of civil service.
864	Control or nationalize key industries, de facto monopolies; more state monopolies. Fewer nationalized industries, essential nationalizations only $= -1$. Nationalize everything $= 2$.
865	Defend the franc; no devaluation.
866	Balanced budget; less expenditures; a policy of more economies in government spending.
867	Nationalize or control credit, Bank of France, other banks.
868	Fight "Wall of Money," industrial oligarchy, cartels, abuses of capitalism.
869	Against paramilitary leagues.
870	End the private manufacture or sale of armaments.
872	Make France militarily prepared to defend itself; need a strong France; increase military allocations. Decrease military spending $= -1$.
873	Support Soviet alliance. End it $= -1$.
874	Support League of Nations, collective security.

Variable Number	Description
875	Support work for (joint) international disarmament.
876	Establish a French Soviet Republic.
877	Against Popular Front; fight Popular Front.
878	Fight fascist threat, reaction, right-wing revolution.
879	Reconcile all Frenchmen; work for internal unity.
880	Reveal financial backers of the press; legislate against defamation of character by the press.
908	Protect the saver, bond-holder (*"petit rentier"*).
909	Support collective-work contracts to guarantee social legislation, salaries.
910	Improve public health laws; protect public health.
911	Support for Popular Front, *Rassemblement populaire*, united Left.
912	Reestablish equilibrium between production and consumption.
913	Provide, guarantee jobs for all; right to work.
914	Fight fiscal fraud.
915	Lower costs of transportation, utilities, espcially for farmers.
916	Protect farmers against natural disasters.
917	End speculation, *"mévente"* of agricultural products, large gap between retail and whole-sale prices, middlemen.
919	End, humanize the (deflationary) decree-laws; end measures against the most hard-hit categories; end salary or pension cuts of war veterans, railway or civil service employees, retired people; increase allowances for large families.
920	Disallow government employees from joining private companies.
921	Modify inheritance laws.
922	Support system of alliances, ententes—Britain, *Petite Entente*; establish more alliances.
923	Against communism, Communist Revolution, collectivism.
924	End tax on farm property, end it if land is farmed by the owner; end all agricultural taxes.
926	Purge armed forces of all fascist or royalist elements.
927	Limit powers of Senate; abolish the Senate.

Variable Number	Description
928	End slums; construct more housing for workers.
929	The Laval decree-laws (enforcing deflation) were justified; should be strengthened.
931	Protect the family, have a policy in support of the family (*politique familiale*); institute a family vote; tax breaks for families; extend rights of family, especially over children's education.
932	Support a *union républicaine, union nationale, concentration républicaine.*
935	Freedom of thought, conscience.
936	End violence, restore order, support a republic of order.
937	Increase tariffs on manufactured goods.
940	Organize, consult agriculture, peasantry.
942	Fiscal justice; a fair tax system.
943	End political differences, separate interests, quarrels, parties, rivalries in government.
945	Reduce government involvement in the economy; less regulation of business; less "*étatisme*."
946	Organize, increase credit to commerce and industry.
947	Establish a less inquisitorial tax system.
948	Defend peasant property from trusts.
949	Fight speculation, flight of capital.
950	Moral regeneration, redressment of society.

Notes

Chapter 1

1. These interpretations will be discussed and evaluated in chapter 6.

2. H. Luethy, *France against Herself* (New York: Praeger, 1955), p. 40.

3. H. Eckstein, *Division and Cohesion in Democracy: A Study of Norway* (Princeton, N.J.: Princeton University Press, 1966), p. 228.

4. J. Ollé-Laprune, *La Stabilité des Ministres sous la Troisième République, 1879–1940* (Paris: Plichon et Durand-Auzias, 1962), p. 297. (All quotations from sources in French are the author's translations.)

5. Ibid., p. 246.

6. André Siegfried, *De la Troisième République à la Quatrième République* (Paris: Éditions Bernard Grasset, 1956), p. 46. This theme will be taken up more thoroughly in chapter 6.

7. Eckstein, *Division and Cohesion in Democracy*, p. 229.

8. William R. Sharp, *The Government of the French Republic* (New York: Van Nostrand, 1938), p. 301.

9. Luethy, *France against Herself*, p. 43–44, for instance.

10. David Thomson, *Democracy in France Since 1870*, 4th ed. (London: Oxford University Press, 1964), pp. 171–72.

11. François Goguel, "The Historical Background of Contemporary French Politics," *Yale French Studies* 15 (Winter 1954–55): 35.

12. Alfred Sauvy, *Histoire Économique de la France Entre les Deux Guerres*, 2 vols. (Paris: Fayard, 1965–67).

13. See Georges Dupeux, "Léon Blum et la Majorité Parlementaire," in *Léon Blum, Chef du Gouvernment, 1936–1937,* Cahiers de la Fondation Nationale des Sciences Politiques, no. 155 (Paris, 1967).

14. Peter J. Larmour, *The French Radical Party in the 1930's* (Stanford Calif.: Stanford University Press, 1964), p. 226.

15. France, Chambre des Députés, *Rapport fait au nom de la commission chargée de réunir et de publier les programmes et engagements aux élections législatives des 26 avril et 3 mai 1936* (Paris: Imprimerie de la Chambre des Députés, 1936).

Chapter 2

1. Larmour, *The French Radical Party,* p. 63.

2. The elections of 1919 and 1924 were conducted under a different system which, nevertheless, rewarded interparty cooperation. See P. Campbell, *French Electoral Systems and Elections since 1789,* 2d ed. (London: Faber and Faber, 1965), pp. 90–101, for details.

3. M. Wolfe, "French Interwar Stagnation Revisited," in *From the Ancien Regime to the Popular Front,* ed. C. K. Warner (New York: Columbia University Press, 1969), p. 163.

4. Jean Jeanneney, "La Politique Économique de Léon Blum," in *Léon Blum, Chef du Gouvernement, 1936–1937,* p. 210.

5. Wolfe, "French Interwar Stagnation Revisited," p. 162.

6. Larmour, *French Radical Party,* p. 71.

7. Wolfe, "French Interwar Stagnation Revisited," p. 175.

8. D. Brower, *The New Jacobins: The French Communist Party and the Popular Front* (Ithaca, N.Y.: Cornell University Press, 1968), p. 91. The Communists still hoped for a mass movement independent of the parties, but without Socialist and Radical support this hope remained a vain one.

9. Larmour, *The French Radical Party,* p. 173.

10. Brower, *The New Jacobins,* p. 139.

11. Ibid., p. 117.

12. J. Colton, *Léon Blum: Humanist in Politics* (New York: Knopf, 1966), p. 111.

13. Brower, *The New Jacobins,* p. 120.

14. According to Brower, this was a disappointment to the Communists, who wanted a Radical government because of the Radical party's role in bringing about the Franco-Soviet Pact. Brower, *The New Jacobins,* p. 138.

15. A. Prost, "Les Grèves de juin 1936: essai d'interprétation," in *Léon Blum, Chef du Gouvernement, 1936–1937,* pp. 78–79.

16. Colton, *Léon Blum,* pp. 161–62.

17. Ibid., p. 166.

18. Ibid., p. 174.

19. Ibid., p. 185.

20. Ibid., p. 189.

21. N. Greene, *Crisis and Decline: The French Socialist Party in the Popular Front Era* (Ithaca, N.Y.: Cornell University Press, 1969), p. 74.

22. Colton, *Léon Blum,* p. 193.

23. Greene, *Crisis and Decline,* p. 106.

24. Brower, *The New Jacobins,* p. 199.

25. Colton, *Léon Blum*, p. 297.

26. Barrington Moore, *The Social Origins of Democracy and Dictatorship: Lord and Peasant in the Making of the Modern World* (Boston, Mass.: Beacon Press, 1966), pp. 40–45.

27. Jesse R. Pitts, "Continuity and Change in Bourgeois France," in Stanley Hoffmann et al., *In Search of France* (New York: Harper and Row, 1963), p. 248.

28. Ibid., p. 247.

29. Ibid., p. 253.

30. J. E. Sawyer, "The Entrepreneur and the Social Order," in *Men in Business*, ed. W. Miller (Cambridge, Mass.: Harvard University Press, 1952), p. 18.

31. Ibid., p. 17.

32. Charles Bettelheim, *Bilan de l'Économie Française, 1919–1946* (Paris: Presses Universitaires de France, 1947), pp. 150–69.

33. Ibid., p. 176.

34. David S. Landes, "French Business and the Businessman: A Social and Cultural Analysis," in *Modern France: Problems of the Third and Fourth Republics*, ed. Edward M. Earle (New York: Russell and Russell, 1964), p. 339.

35. Larmour, *The French Radical Party*, p. 131.

36. Thomson, *Democracy in France*, pp. 70–71.

37. Colton, *Léon Blum*, p. 179.

38. Ibid., p. 181.

39. Val Lorwin, *The French Labor Movement* (Cambridge, Mass.: Harvard University Press, 1954), p. 80.

40. Henry W. Ehrmann, "The Blum Experiment and the Fall of France," *Foreign Affairs* 20 (1941–42): 156–57.

41. Georges Dupeux, "L'Échec du Premier Gouvernement Léon Blum," *Revue d'Histoire Moderne et Contemporaine* 10 (1963): 41.

42. M. Wolfe, *The French Franc Between the Wars, 1919–1939* (New York: Columbia University Press, 1951), p. 171.

43. Prost, "Les Grèves de juin 1936," p. 86.

44. Lorwin, *French Labor Movement*, p. 80.

45. Charles P. Kindleberger, *Economic Growth in France and Britain, 1851–1950* (New York: Simon and Schuster, 1964), p. 205.

46. Jeanneney, "La Politique Économique," p. 228.

47. Sauvy, *Histoire Économique*, 2:297–307.

48. J. C. Asselin, "La Semaine de 40 heures, le chômage et l'emploi," *Le Mouvement Social*, 54 (January–March, 1966): 184–204.

49. Joel Colton, "Politics and Economics in the 1930's: The Balance Sheet of the 'Blum New Deal,'" in *From the Ancien Regime to the Popular Front*, ed. C. K. Warner (New York: Columbia University Press, 1969), p. 196.

50. Sauvy, *Histoire Économique*, 2:465.

51. Wolfe, *The French Franc*, p. 171.

52. Larmour, *The French Radical Party*, p. 258.

53. Ibid., p. 208.

54. Ibid., p. 209.

55. Ibid., p. 213.

56. Ibid., p. 218.

57. Sauvy, *Histoire Économique*, 2:465.

58. Larmour, *The French Radical Party*, p. 250.

Chapter 3

1. The sample is a simple random sample with the one qualification that roll calls with less than 7 percent dissidence (that is, more than 93 percent voting one way) were excluded as not suitable for analysis. Sufficient dissidence (in statistical terms, variance) must be present since that is what is statistically analyzed; the 7 percent cutting-point was arbitrarily chosen but appears to be reasonable in this regard.

2. In addition, roll-call votes may be misleading because of informal sanctions against openly going against one's side. This possibility is considered in some detail in chapter 5.

3. Further development of the methodology adopted in this study may also be found in P. Warwick, "A Re-Evaluation of Alternate Methodologies in Legislative Voting Analysis," *Social Science Research* 4 (September 1975), and idem, "The Definition and Measurement of Similarity Among Legislative Roll-Call Votes," *Social Science Research* 4 (December 1975).

4. Analysts will sometimes differentiate principal-components analysis from factor analysis proper. It is commonplace in the empirical literature, however, to refer to principal components as "factors," and we will adopt this practice simply for ease of expression. It should not be forgotten that the "factors" referred to in this study are, strictly speaking, principal components.

5. The abbreviations for party names used in figure 2 and subsequent figures are as given in the discussion which follows.

6. Although we have this data for all the deputies, the analyses reported in this and the next chapter were performed on the sample of 294 deputies for which we coded electoral statements. The sampling design is discussed in chapter 5, at which point its rationale will be clearer. The important point to note here is that we used the sample for reasons of continuity with chapter 5 only; all findings reported here are equivalent to those derived when the entire population of deputies was subjected to the same analysis.

7. Duncan MacRae, *Issues and Parties in Legislative Voting: Methods of Statistical Analysis* (New York: Harper and Row, 1970), pp. 257–59.

8. The small numbers of Socialist and Communist deputies in figure 3 and subsequent figures is a consequence of our sampling design, as discussed in chapter 5. The basic rationale was that since these parties displayed high degrees of uniformity in voting and in their electoral statements, only small samples were needed. In the statistical analysis, appropriate weights were applied to restore these parties to their correct strengths.

9. The sole exception is roll-call 36, which is located at the negative end of the second factor in figures 4 and 5 because it shows the moderate rather than the extreme Right in opposition to the Popular Front.

Chapter 4

1. Because of the short time in office of the second Blum government (less than one month) we feel free to refer to roll calls dated after the fall of Blum's first and more important government as the "post-Blum" roll calls.

2. This scatterplot is a bit misleading in that it shows the PCF to be once again the party most cohesive with the Popular Front, a finding belied by the cohesion trend lines. This discrepancy was caused by the fact that this unrotated first factor was not optimally placed to measure bloc loyalty. The oblique rotation we applied shifted the location of the factor slightly to produce an alignment of the parties on it that correctly reflected the cohesion trend lines.

Chapter 5

1. We use the term "ideology" to indicate expressions of political belief found in the electoral statements, whether these are specific policy proposals or opinions of a more abstract or philosophic nature, such as expressions of anti-communism.

2. The second factor is the first victim of this type of coding bias: it loads opinions mentioned only in the Communist party statement. Here the bias can be controlled by simply excluding this factor from the interpretation. Unfortunately, the coding bias in the first factor is not so easily handled, as will become evident.

3. The comparison is between this figure and the corresponding scattergrams for the Blum and post-Blum bloc-loyalty factors, presented in figures 3 and 12.

4. A loading of .50 or greater was considered high enough to warrant inclusion as a significant ingredient in the interpretation of this factor.

5. This opinion was, however, also supported by the Communists, who felt that a devaluation would hurt the working class the most. See above, p. 105.

6. Antoine Prost and Christien Rosenzveig, "La Chambre des Députés (1881–1885). Analyse factorielle des scrutins," *Revue française de Science politique* 21 (February 1971): 31.

7. The second factor loaded opinions listed only in the Communist party statement and will therefore not be interpreted in detail. The third factor resembled the right-wing-ideology factor but with weaker loadings; we will stick with the latter factor because of its greater interpretability and because it relates this type of Popular Front disunity to the right wing's ideological position more clearly.

8. Of these three factors, only the first two will be interpreted. The third factor is both very weak in terms of explained variance and, moreover, was found to have no significant relationship with the PF1 vote factor beyond that effected by the first two factors.

9. These items did not appear in principal-components analysis of the Chamber that produced the right-wing-ideology factor because they had insufficient dissidence over the whole Chamber to justify inclusion.

10. In coding the data, it was found that whenever opposition to the Popular Front was mentioned by deputies belonging to Popular Front parties, it was in conjunction with a fear of communism.

11. The refinement of Popular Front reform-policy into Popular Front reform-policy* results in an increase in the correlation with PF1 from .492 to .617. Similarly, the development of Anti-Popular Front from elements of right-wing-ideology results in an increase in the absolute value of the correlation with PF1 from .562 to -.674.

12. Colton, *Léon Blum: Humanist in Politics*, p. 161.

13. Correlations bear out this point: right-wing-ideology correlates -.607 with Anti-Popular Front* and Popular Front reform-policy correlates -.880 with Popular Front political-policy.

14. This may reflect the fact that the threat from right-wing extremism had subsided somewhat by 1936. The extent of this should not be exaggerated, however; Blum himself was assaulted by a rightist mob early in 1936.

Chapter 6

1. E. Nordlinger, "Democratic Stability and Instability: The Case of France," *World Politics* 18 (October 1965): 128.

2. Ibid., p. 129.

3. N. Wahl, "The French Political System," in *Patterns of Government*, ed. S. H. Beer and A. B. Ulam (New York: Random House, 1962), p. 279.

4. William L. Shirer, *The Collapse of the Third Republic* (New York: Simon and Schuster, 1969), pp. 96–100.

5. Ibid., p. 99.

6. Ibid., p. 100.

7. M. Crozier, *The Bureaucratic Phenomenon* (Chicago: University of Chicago Press, 1964).

8. Ibid., pp. 256–57.

9. This is especially evident in ibid., chapter 10, where Crozier appears to acknowledge in the contrast between private enterprise and the civil service the existence of the two traditions.

10. E. Nordlinger, "Democratic Stability and Instability: The Case of France," p. 130.

11. Arendt Lijphart, "Consociational Democracy," *World Politics* 21 (January 1969), pp. 222–24.

12. The Communist and Socialist parties were exceptions to this generalization, but presumably they represented segments of the polity too fundamentally inimical to the preservation of the existing regime to be available as permanent partners in government.

13. Lijphart, "Consociational Democracy," p. 218.

14. Thomson, *Democracy in France*, p. 139.

15. President Grévy's son-in-law, Daniel Wilson, was discovered to be selling decorations and honors from his residence in the presidential palace. This was one of many scandals, of which the most famous were the Panama and Stavisky affairs, which periodically revealed corruption in high places and did much over the years to bring discredit to the Republic.

16. Réné Rémond, *The Right Wing in France*, trans. J. M. Maux (Philadelphia: University of Pennsylvania Press, 1966), pp. 210–11.

17. Ibid., p. 204.

18. Thomson, *Democracy in France*, pp. 112–13.

19. Stanley Hoffmann, "Paradoxes of the French Political Community," in Hoffmann et al., *In Search of France*, p. 4.

20. Ibid., p. 15.

21. A more complete discussion of this point was given in chapter 2.

22. Ibid., p. 8.

23. Ibid., p. 4.

24. Ibid., p. 17.

25. R. Rémond, *The Right Wing in France*, p. 267.

26. Hoffmann, "French Political Community," p. 25.

27. Ibid., p. 22.

28. François Goguel, *La Politique des Partis sous la Troisième République* (Paris: Éditions du Seuil, 1946), pp. 325–27.

29. Ibid., p. 327.

30. Maurice Le Corbeiller, *Rapport fait au nom de la commission chargée de réunir et de publier les programmes et engagements électoraux des candidats aux élections législatives des 1er et 8 mai 1932* (Paris: Imprimerie de la Chambre des Députés, 1932), p. 1093, cited by Herbert Tint, *The Decline of French Patriotism, 1870–1940* (London: Weidenfeld and Nicholson, 1964), p. 190.

31. Larmour, *French Radical Party*, p. 172.

32. Gordon Wright, *France in Modern Times: 1760 to the Present* (Chicago: Rand McNally, 1960), p. 477.

33. Larmour, *French Radical Party*, p. 176.

34. Larmour even considers the history of the *first* Blum government under the rubric "The Decline of the Popular Front."

35. Ibid., p. 215.

36. Luethy, *France against Herself*, p. 44.

37. Lijphart, "Consociational Democracy," p. 221.

38. A more pronounced gap between the moderate and extreme Left in this area was prevented from appearing in our electoral statements data because the Marxists renounced their more extreme demands in favor of the moderate reform proposals of the Popular Front program in this election.

39. Wolfe, "French Interwar," p. 166.

40. Hoffmann, "French Political Community," p. 26.

41. The Communists supported rearmament and resistance to Nazism until the 1939 pact between Stalin and Hitler obliged them to return to their pre-1935 doctrine of "revolutionary defeatism." The Radicals were basically defeatist all along.

42. Greene, *Crisis and Decline*, p. 199.

43. Ibid., pp. 198–99.

44. Brower, *The New Jacobins*, p. 170.

45. Ibid., p. 238.

46. Ibid., p. 240.

47. Brower, it would appear, concurs with this conclusion: "The disillusionment which crept like a blight over the Popular Front, in parliament and among the workers, had only a very little to do with Communist agitation. The pernicious effects of the Depression distorted and undermined all the reforming efforts of the government. The coalition was plagued by the differences of opinion separating Socialists and Radicals. The timidity of the Radical party in economic and social matters weakened the Popular Front from the start" (*The New Jacobins*, p. 235).

48. Shirer, *The Collapse of the Third Republic*, p. 100.

Appendix A

1. Warwick, "A Re-evaluation of Alternate Methodologies" and "The Definition and Measurement of Similarity."

2. A more extensive development of the geometric interpretation of multi-

variate statistics is given in Wonnacott and Wonnacott, *Econometrics* (New York, Wiley, 1970), chap. 15.

3. D. MacRae, *Issues and Parties in Legislative Voting*, chaps. 2 and 3.

4. Although to the best of our knowledge a dichotomous coding scheme is always used, we have pointed out elsewhere that it is possible to scale trichotomous roll calls. See Warwick, "A Re-Evaluation of Alternate Methodologies," p. 251.

5. There are other weaknesses in Guttman scaling of roll calls as well. These are discussed in Warwick, "A Re-evaluation of Alternate Methodologies."

Selected Bibliography

Books

Almond, G. and Verba, S. *The Civic Culture: Political Attitudes and Democracy in Five Nations.* Boston: Little, Brown, 1965.

Azéma, Jean-Pierre, and Winock, Michel. *La Troisième République (1870–1940).* Paris: Calmann-Levy, 1970.

Bardonnet, D. *Évolution de la Structure du Parti Radical.* Paris: Montchrestien, 1960.

Beau de Loménie, E. *La Mort de la Troisième République.* Paris: Éditions du Conquistador, 1951.

———. *Les Responsabilités des Dynasties Bourgeoises.* Paris: Éditions Denoel, 1963.

Bettleheim, Charles. *Bilan de l'Économie Française, 1919–1946.* Paris: Presses Universitaires de France, 1947.

Bloch, Marc. *Strange Defeat.* Translated by G. Hopkins. London: Oxford University Press, 1949.

Bodin, L., and Touchard, J. *Front Populaire 1936.* Paris, 1961.

Bonnefous, E. *Histoire Politique de la Troisième République.* 6 vols. Paris: Presses Universitaires de France, 1965.

Brogan, D. W. *The Development of Modern France, 1870–1939*. 2d ed. London: Hamish Hamilton, 1967.

Brower, D. *The New Jacobins: The French Communist Party and the Popular Front*. Ithaca, N.Y.: Cornell University Press, 1968.

Campbell, P. *French Electoral Systems and Elections Since 1789*. 2d ed. London: Faber and Faber, 1965.

Chapman, G. *The Dreyfus Case: A Reassessment*. London: Rupert Hart-Davis, 1955.

Cobban, A. *A History of Modern France*. Vol. 3: *1871–1962*. Harmondsworth: Penguin, 1965.

Colton, Joel. *Léon Blum: Humanist in Politics*. New York: Alfred A. Knopf, 1966.

Cot, Pierre. *Triumph of Treason*. Chicago and New York: Ziff-Davis, 1944.

Crozier, Michel. *The Bureaucratic Phenomenon*. Chicago: University of Chicago Press, 1964.

Dalby, L. E. *Leon Blum: Evolution of a Socialist*. New York: Yoseloff, 1963.

Debu-Bridel, J. *L'Agonie de la Troisième République, 1929–1939*. Paris, 1948.

Dupeux, G. *Le Front Populaire et les élections de 1936*. Paris, 1959.

Earle, E. M., ed. *Modern France: Problems of the Third and Fourth Republics*. New York: Russell and Russell, 1964.

Easton, David. *A Framework for Political Analysis*. Englewood Cliffs, N.J.: Prentice-Hall, 1965.

Eckstein, Harry. *Division and Cohesion in Democracy*. Princeton, N.J.: Princeton University Press, 1966.

Ehrmann, Henry W. *French Labour from Popular Front to Liberation*. New York: Oxford University Press, 1947.

———. *Organized Business in France*. Princeton, N.J.: Princeton University Press, 1957.

Fauvet, Jacques. *Histoire de Parti Communiste Français*. Paris: Fayard, 1964.

France. Chambre des Députés. *Journal Officiel de la République française, annales de la Chambre des Députés: Débats Parlementaires*. 16th Legislature, 1936–1938.

———. Rapport fait au nom de la commission chargée de réunir et de publier les programmes et engagements électoraux des candidats aux élections législatives des 26 avril et 3 mai 1936. Paris: Imprimerie de la Chambre des Députés, 1936.

Goguel, François. *La Politique des Partis sous la Troisième République*. Paris: Éditions du Seuil, 1946.

―――. *Les Institutions Politiques Françaises.* Paris: Université de Paris, 1967.

Greene, N. *Crisis and Decline: The French Socialist Party in the Popular Front Era.* Ithaca, N.Y.: Cornell University Press, 1969.

Guérard, A. *France, a Modern History.* Ann Arbor, Mich.: University of Michigan Press, 1959.

―――. *The France of Tomorrow.* Cambridge, Mass.: Harvard University Press, 1942.

Halevy, Daniel. *La République des comités: Essai d'histoire contemporaine (1895-1934).* Paris: Éditions Bernard Grasset, 1934.

―――. *Pour l'Étude de la Troisième République.* Paris: Éditions Bernard Grasset, 1937.

Harvey, D. J. *France Since the Revolution.* New York: The Free Press, 1968.

Joll, J., ed. *The Decline of the Third Republic.* London: Chatto and Windus, 1959.

Jolly, Jean. *Dictionnaire des Parlementaires Français.* 6 vols. Paris: Presses Universitaires de France, 1960–72.

Kindleberger, Charles P. *Economic Growth in France and Britain, 1851-1950.* New York: Simon and Schuster, 1964.

Larmour, Peter J. *The French Radical Party in the 1930's.* Stanford, Calif.: Stanford University Press, 1964.

Lefranc, Georges. *Histoire du Front Populaire.* Paris: Payot, 1965.

Lorwin, Val. *The French Labor Movement.* Cambridge, Mass.: Harvard University Press, 1954.

Luethy, Herbert. *France against Herself.* New York: Praeger, 1955.

MacRae, Duncan. *Issues and Parties in Legislative Voting: Methods of Statistical Analysis.* New York: Harper and Row, 1970.

Madaule, J. *Histoire de France.* Paris: Editions Gallimard, 1966.

Manevy, R. *La Presse de la Troisième République.* Paris: Foret, 1955.

Marcus, John T. *French Socialism in the Crisis Years, 1933-1936.* New York: Praeger, 1958.

Micaud, Charles A. *The French Right and Nazi Germany, 1933-1939.* Durham, N.C.: Duke University Press, 1943.

Montreuil, J. *Histoire du Mouvement Ouvrier en France.* Paris: Aubier, 1946.

Moore, B. *The Social Origins of Democracy and Dictatorship.* Boston: Beacon Press, 1966.

Nicolet, C. *Le Radicalisme.* Paris: Presses Universitaires de France, 1957.

Nolte, Ernst. *The Three Faces of Fascism.* Translated by L. Vennewitz. New York: Holt, Rinehart and Winston, 1965.

Oxgood, S. M., ed. *The Fall of France, 1940: Causes and Responsibilities.* Boston, Mass.: D. C. Heath, 1965.

Ollé-Laprune, J. *La Stabilité des Ministres sous la Troisième République, 1879–1940.* Paris: Plichon et Durand-Auzias, 1962.

Perrot, M. *La Monnaie et L'Opinion Publique en France et en Angleterre de 1924 à 1936.* Paris: Armand Colin, 1955.

Plumyère, J., and Lasierra, R. *Les Fascismes Français, 1923–1963.* Paris: Éditions du Seuil, 1963.

Priouret, R. *La République des Députés.* Paris: Éditions Bernard Grasset, 1959.

Rémond, Réné. *Les Catholiques, le Communisme, et les Crises, 1929–39.* Paris: Éditions Armand Colin, 1960.

———. *The Right Wing in France.* Translated by J. M. Maux. Philadelphia, Pa.: University of Pennsylvania Press, 1966.

———. *La Vie Politique en France de 1870 à 1940.* Paris: Université de Paris, 1959.

Reynaud, Paul. *In the Thick of the Fight.* New York: Simon and Schuster, 1951.

Sauvy, Alfred. *Histoire Économique de la France entre les Deux Guerres.* 2 vols. Paris: Fayard, 1965–67.

Sharp, W. R. *The Government of the French Republic.* New York: Van Nostrand, 1938.

Shirer, William L. *The Collapse of the Third Republic.* New York: Simon and Schuster, 1969.

Siegfried, André. *De la Troisième à la Quatrième République.* Paris: Éditions Bernard Grasset, 1956.

Simone, A. *J'Accuse.* New York: Kennikat Press, 1969.

Soulier, A. *L'Instabilité Ministerielle sous la Troisième République, (1871–1938).* Paris: Receuil Sirey, 1939.

Tarr, F. de. *The French Radical Party from Herriot to Mendès-France.* London: Oxford University Press, 1961.

Thomson, David. *Democracy in France since 1870.* London: Oxford University Press, 1964.

Tint, H. *The Decline of French Patriotism, 1870–1940.* London: Weidenfeld and Nicolson, 1964.

Werth, A. *The Twilight of France, 1933–1940.* London, 1942.

Wolfe, M. *The French Franc between the Wars, 1919–1939.* New York: Columbia University Press, 1951.

Wonnacott, Ronald J., and Wonnacott, Thomas H. *Econometrics.* New York: Wiley, 1970.

Wright, Gordon. *France in Modern Times: 1790 to the Present.* Chicago: Rand McNally, 1960.

————. *The Reshaping of French Democracy*. New York: Reynal and Hitchcock, 1948.

Articles

Asselin, J. C. "La Semaine de 40 Heures, le Chômage et l'Emploi." *Le Mouvement Social* 54 (January–March 1966): 184–204.

Colton, Joel. "Politics and Economics in the 1930's: The Balance Sheet of the 'Blum New Deal.'" In *From the Ancien Regime to the Popular Front*. Edited by C. K. Warner. New York: Columbia University Press, 1969.

Daalder, H. "The Consociational Democratic Theme." *World Politics* 26 (1974).

Dupeux, Georges. "L'Échec du premier gouvernement Léon Blum." *Revue d'Histoire Moderne et Contemporaine* 10 (1963): 35–44.

————. "Léon Blum et la Majorité Parlementaire." In *Léon Blum, Chef du Gouvernement, 1936–1937*. Cahiers de la Fondation nationale des Sciences politiques, no. 155, 1967.

Ehrmann, Henry W. "The Blum Experiment and the Fall of France." *Foreign Affairs* 20 (1941): 152–64.

Giradet, Raoul. "Notes sur l'Esprit d'un Fascisme Français, 1934–1939." *Revue française de Science politique* 5 (July–September 1955): 529–46.

Goguel, François. "The Historical Background of Contemporary French Politics." *Yale French Studies* 15 (Winter 1954–55): 30–37.

Gout, E.; Juvigny, P.; Mousel, M., "La Politique Sociale du Front Populaire." In *Léon Blum, Chef du Gouvernement, 1936–1937*. Cahiers de la Fondation nationale des Sciences politiques, no. 155, 1967.

Hoffmann, S. "Paradoxes of the French Political Community." In S. Hoffmann et al., *In Search of France*. New York: Harper and Row, 1963.

Jeanneney, J. M. "La Politique Économique de Léon Blum." In *Léon Blum, Chef du Gouvernement, 1936–1937*. Cahiers de la Fondation nationale des Sciences politiques, no. 155, 1967.

Kindleberger, C. P. "The Postwar Resurgence of the French Economy." In S. Hoffmann et al., *In Search of France*. New York: Harper and Row, 1963.

Kirchheimer, Otto. "Changes in the Structure of Political Compromise." *Studies in Philosophy and Social Science* 9 (1941): 264–89.

Lijphart, A. "Consociational Democracy." *World Politics* 21 (1969).

Nordlinger, E. "Democratic Stability and Instability: The French Case." *World Politics* 18(1965).

Pitts, J. "Continuity and Change in Bourgeois France." In S. Hoffmann et al., *In Search of France.* New York: Harper and Row, 1963.

Prost, A. "Les Grèves de Juin 1936: essai d'interpretation." In *Léon Blum, Chef du Gouvernement, 1936-1937.* Cahiers de la Fondation nationale des Sciences politiques, no. 155, 1967.

————, and Rosenzveig, Christien. "La Chambre des Députés (1881–1885). Analyse factorielle des scrutins." *Revue française de Science politique* 21 (February 1971): 5–50.

Rémond, R., and Bourdin, J. "Les Forces Adverses." In *Léon Blum, Chef du Gouvernement, 1936-1937.* Cahiers de la Fondation nationale des Sciences politiques, no. 155, 1967.

Rogers, Lindsay. "M. Blum and the French Senate." *Political Science Quarterly* 52 (1957): 321–27.

Sauvy, Alfred. "The Economic Crisis of the 1930's in France." *Journal of Contemporary History* 4 (1969).

Sawyer, John E. "The Entrepreneur and the Social Order." In *Men in Business.* Edited by William Miller. Cambridge, Mass.: Harvard University Press, 1952.

Touchard, J., and Bodin, L. "L'État de l'Opinion au Début de l'Année 1936." In *Léon Blum, Chef du Gouvernement, 1936-1937.* Cahiers de la Fondation nationale des Sciences politiques, no. 155, 1967.

Wahl, N., "The French Political System." In *Patterns of Government,* Edited by S. H. Beer and A. B. Ulam. New York: Random House, 1962.

Warner, G. "The Stavisky Affair and the Riots of February 6, 1934." *History Today* 8(June 1958): 377–85.

Warwick, P. "A Re-evaluation of Alternate Methodologies in Legislative Voting Analysis." *Social Science Research* 4(1975).

————. "The Definition and Measurement of Similarity Among Legislative Roll-Call Votes." *Social Science Research* 4(1975).

Wolfe, M. "French Interwar Stagnation Revisited." In *From the Ancien Regime to the Popular Front.* Edited by C. K. Warner. New York: Columbia University Press, 1969.

G. Ziebura. "Léon Blum à la Veille de l'Exercise du Pouvoir." In *Léon Blum, Chef du Gouvernement, 1936-1937.* Cahiers de la Fondation nationale des Sciences politiques, no. 155, 1967.

Index